S0-ATW-366

Who are the Russians?

Who are the Russians?

A History of the Russian People

WRIGHT MILLER

TAPLINGER PUBLISHING COMPANY
NEW YORK

First published in the United States in 1973 by
TAPLINGER PUBLISHING CO., INC.
New York, New York

Copyright © 1973 by Wright Miller
All rights reserved
Printed in Great Britain

No part of this publication may be reproduced or transmitted
in any form or by any means, electronic or mechanical,
including photocopy, recording, or any information storage
and retrieval system now known or to be invented, except by
a reviewer who wishes to quote brief passages in connection
with a review written for inclusion in a magazine, newspaper
or broadcast.

Library of Congress Catalog Card Number: 73-2554

ISBN 0-8008-8255-5

Contents

Illustrations

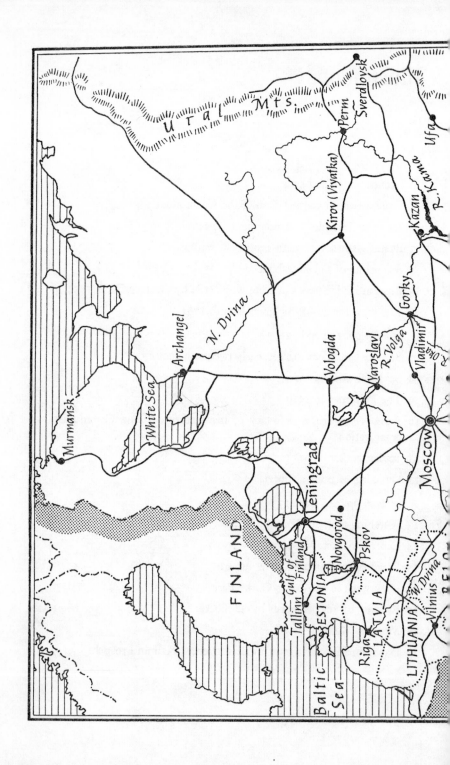

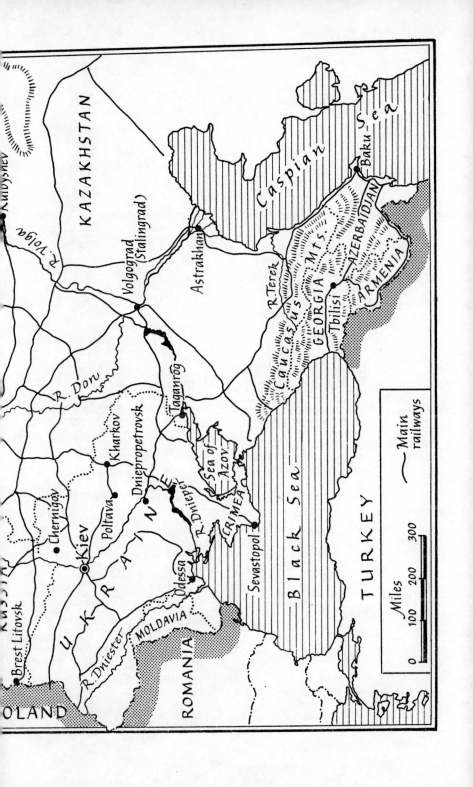

Introduction

This book is not written for specialists, but is an attempt to fill in some of the gaps between our school history which barely glances at Russia, and our later plunging into Tolstoy and Chekhov and Solzhenitsyn. I have tried to write about the events and influences and institutions which have made Russia and Russians what they are—which means that I have passed rather quickly over some of the best-known features, such as the glamorous empresses and the sad fate of the last Tsar, because they had comparatively little to do with what the Russian people were, or are today. I have also tried to fill in a little background for the events which get reported in our own press—something about the basic ways in which Soviet Russia works today: they are more complicated than would be expected if one thinks of 'Communism' simply as an all-embracing dictatorial principle without any history of its own.

If what we now see as Communism had been started first in some other country—in Germany, perhaps, as Marx expected—it would have been rather different from what has been set up in Russia. It is rather different even in the other Communist countries of Europe, although they owe their Communism to Soviet Russia: it is different in Poland, where most of the land is farmed by private enterprise and the Catholic Church flourishes; in East Germany, where there are several thousand privately-owned businesses; or in Hungary, where there are no portraits of leaders nor Party slogans in the streets, and they even have contested elections (between rival Communist candidates) in some constituencies.

Russia is unique indeed, and Russia was unique before 1917. Russia is a European country and has always been a European country, with Christian traditions—monotheistic and strongly man-centred traditions—and its cultural life has been formed, if rather late and rather haltingly, on normal European models. But it cannot be compared closely with any other country in Europe, because all of them are so small in comparison. Its problems have essentially been those of a very big country, open to invaders, and a country which, in spite of its size, has mostly been homogeneous in feeling and tradition, and which for

many centuries has had a strongly centralized government—unlike the
United States which, growing piecemeal, found it comparatively easy to
divide responsibilities between the states and the federal power. Communications have naturally been bad over the huge area of Russia, and
until quite recent times new ideas could only spread slowly: as late as the
1930s some peasants in the north-east of Siberia were said to be preserving portraits of Nicholas II in their huts—they did not know he was
dead. Inevitably any Russian government has been preoccupied largely
with the problems of maintaining its power over so vast a land, and one
may speculate whether the attitudes of British governments would have
been altogether dissimilar, if their territory had been equally large and
vulnerable.

It may be objected that I speak of 'Russia', and that the Soviet Union
is, as Tsarist Russia was, a country of many nationalities. Indeed,
according to the official figures no less than 110 *native* languages are
taught in Soviet schools, and of course one of the Soviet Government's
most laudable achievements has been to give an alphabet to tribes who
never had one, and education to those who had little more than an
alphabet. But most of these 110 languages are spoken by nationalities
which are very small—1,100 Eskimos and 400 Aleutians by the Bering
Straits, 93,000 Finns near the Finnish frontier, 59,000 Kurds, 1·4 million Tadjiks and 1·6 million Moldavians, the homelands of the last two
being dignified with the status of Federated Republics, of which there
are only fifteen in all.

But it is overwhelmingly, indeed exclusively, the Russian element
which has dominated in Sovietizing the country; when tribes give up
pagan customs, or Moslems give up veiling women and so forth, it is
Russian, or rather Russian-plus-Marxist, characteristics which take
over. The Russians are the largest nationality of all, and if one adds to
them their brother Slavs, the Little Russians or Ukrainians and the
White Russians or Belorussians, who differ comparatively little in language and tradition, one has accounted for more than three-quarters of
the population.* Where there has been any divergence between
Ukrainian and Russian tradition—the Ukrainians, for instance, were
much more often free peasants than the Russians were—then the

---

* The Russian language is gaining all the time on the languages of the
smaller minorities; at the last census 13 million people gave their language as
Russian but their nationality as something else. There naturally has to be a
common language, and people who want to rise only a little in the world find
that they are usually obliged to learn Russian. However, the languages of the
larger minorities with strong cultural traditions of their own—such peoples as
the Uzbeks, Georgians or Armenians—are likely to continue and prosper.

Russian-Marxist characteristic today outweighs the other. As for the Asiatic Republics, though they keep their own culture within their own borders, they have added about as much to the national 'Soviet' flavour as the Scottish Highlanders have added to the British national flavour. The markets of Samarkand or Bokhara and the mountaineers of Georgia add great picturesqueness to Soviet tourism, but nothing to the composite Soviet flavour. There is only one exception to the Russian dominance, and it is a minor one: the three Baltic peoples—the million Estonians, the 1·5 million Latvians, and the 2·7 million Lithuanians— had such high cultural standards, under Scandinavian or German influence, during their brief period of independence between the two wars, that they are sometimes cited by the Soviet authorities as examples which Russians and other Soviet citizens would do well, culturally speaking, to follow. This applies particularly to the Estonians, whose well-run little Republic is noted, and quoted, for the best industrial design, for good manners, for general convenience and efficient administration. One of my Moscow friends sent me an ecstatic postcard from his first visit to the Estonian capital, Tallin: 'Here all problems are solved!' Estonia is a favourite with visitors from Russia for these reasons, and also because one can there receive television from the outside world, that is, from Finland. Before the Revolution, too, when Balts and Baltic Germans were subjects of the Tsar, they were highly thought of for their reliability and often held important office, but their total contribution to the Russian 'image' was a minor one, then as now.

Russia is of course an Asiatic as well as a European power, but even today only a quarter of her population lives in the great Asiatic area of the country. All Siberia is governed as part of the Russian Federated Republic, and far eastern towns such as Vladivostok or Khabarovsk are almost indistinguishable in appearance from towns in western Russia. The influence of Asia itself has been minimal, and it is not helpful to think of Russians, in their distinction from peoples further west, as 'Asiatic'. It is true that in the later nineteenth century the intelligentsia, exasperated by the sluggishness and backwardness of their country, by the hopelessness, dirt and corruption in the little towns, took to using 'Asiatic' as a term of abuse. Chekhov wrote a famous letter to his brother Nikolai, begging him to 'sweat the Asiatic out of himself', and the ordinary Russian at the same period was using 'Asiatic' (*Aziatets*) as an equivalent for 'wretch' or 'dirty dog'—a fisherman used it of the fish that got away. But this use seems to have dropped out of the Russian vocabulary. The old intelligentsia were no doubt thinking of the squalor and idleness of the Asiatic provinces which had then not long been colonized by the Russians; but the Russians had not learned squalor and idleness from the inhabitants of Tashkent or Bokhara—they had been Russian characteristics all the time.

Geographically speaking, one naturally feels nearer to Asia in Moscow than one does in London: there are visiting Uzbeks in the streets in boldly-striped robes, and when one goes to a children's performance at the puppet theatre one realizes that the name which we pronounce as 'a-*lad*-in' is spoken more correctly, surely, by the Russians as 'Al-ad-Dîn'. But all this is only a mild shift of emphasis. And the great Russian yearning for travel, the insatiable curiosity about the outside world, is almost all directed towards the West.

And if Russia is not Asiatic, neither is she so exotic as might appear from the rebarbative exterior of her language. If Russia were a Latin country, for instance, Blagovestchensk and Rozhdestvensk would be called something like 'Anunciacion' and 'Natale', which is what the names mean. The Soviet Government got rid of all the place-names associated with the Tsars—Petersburg, Ekaterinburg, Tsaritsyn, and so forth, but it has changed very few of the thousands of Christian place-names which dot the map of Russia: the most impressive Kremlin gate, the Spassky Gate, for instance, is 'Salvation Gate'.

The Russian alphabet is derived from the Greek, and many people find they can learn it in half an hour. The language itself, of course, comes from the same Indo-European stock as Latin or German or Greek: it contains dozens of recognizable roots like *mat vidit sina brata* —'(the) mother sees (the) son (of her) brother.'

Russian is in some ways a clumsy language: you can have lumbering sentences as in German—'Makarenko devoted his strength not only to his immediate, demanding maximum energy, organized pedagogical work.' But you can also have the succinctness of phrases like 'Met lovely girl last night—*shto nado*!' (literally 'what needs', i.e. 'just what the doctor ordered'). Russian never had the corners rubbed off by having to assimilate the language of a conqueror, as Anglo-Saxon did with Norman-French; it went on as a 'folk' language, rich in proverbs, and did not become a literary language until late in the eighteenth century—one of the facts about which Russians can be rather sensitive—but it is a language of great subtleties and enormous vocabulary. It can express distinctions for which there are no simple words in English, such as the two words for 'to laugh'—*hihihat* and *hohohat*—to laugh tee-hee and to laugh ho-ho. The language has been a rich element in Russian national feeling: Turgenev wrote: 'If it were not for thee, o mighty, true and free Russian language, how would one not fall into despair at the sight of all that goes on at home?' And Pushkin: 'Our language is a world in itself, and nowhere can it be given that Russian spaciousness so well as in a tale.'

That Russian spaciousness—boundless, soul-expanding space, but also wearisome, endlessly-plodding space, space in the giant streets, in the straggling avenues, in the dribbling suburbs, in the stretches of parkland among the great forests, and space under the pitiless sun of the steppe—the Russians adore it and need it, and the warmest praise they give their national character is for its *shirota*, its breadth.

The sense of nationhood, of patriotism, in such a huge and open country, whatever its history, is bound to be different from what it can be in a land such as Holland or Denmark. Frontiers with other countries are not often uppermost in the minds of many Russians. As for a 'frontier' in the other, American sense, they can find that in most parts of the Soviet Union; they can find it only seventy miles west of Moscow, where the sandy soil is so thin and poor that sunflowers will only grow one foot high.

Soviet Russia is a country still wrestling with hundreds of elementary as well as sophisticated domestic problems; foreign policy, by contrast, occupies only a small part of the leaders' attention. I propose similarly to spend only a little time on Soviet international relations, but I hope to give some idea of home problems and the centuries of history behind them.

I. The First Russia

When I am in Moscow I sometimes turn with relief out of the Red Square into the Historical Museum—that fantastic Victorian-style building which we all recognize as the background to many pictures of Soviet processions. It is a good museum, but the first three or four rooms give me particular pleasure because they are devoted to the Stone Age and Bronze Age inhabitants of Russia. After the pervading Soviet atmosphere outside one feels curiously at home here, relieved to see the same kinds of stone axes and polished celts, bone needles and flint scrapers, as are dug up in England and in every other European country. There are even some of the same little steatopygous female figures as the 'Venus of Brassempouy', carved about 3500 B.C. in the region where Kiev now stands, and from the same excavation there are vases with bold swirling decorations like those of ancient Crete. Farther north, a thousand years earlier, in the basin of the river Oka, they had pottery decorated with nothing but holes, but in the North Urals, about 2500 B.C., they were already making dishes with the swan-neck or duck-neck handles which later became distinctively Russian.

There is no trace of the megalithic men, but there were several other well-developed Stone Age cultures in the territory which is now Russia, and they have all left some attractive handwork behind, whatever their social relations may have been. The Soviet authorities are not making them out to be superior to other Stone Age cultures, such as the Aurignacian or Magdalenian, nor are they trying to interpret them in terms of a class struggle, and this is a relief after the monotony and insistence of so many Soviet interpretations elsewhere. (Soviet archaeologists, in fact, usually have a high international reputation.)

As early as the Neolithic period, some time between 5000 and 3000 B.C., there began the natural differentiation between the peoples of the rich black southern steppes and the forest-dwellers of the north. In the south they turned from hunting livestock to taming and breeding them, and from gathering wild grass seeds to sowing them, and so to primitive agriculture, while in the forested and water-seamed north men still lived mainly by hunting and fishing, and their tools were still made of stone or wood. In the south they were learning to use metals, and as they grew more settled they also improved their pottery and domestic utensils. These more civilized habits eventually spread to the north too, but it was in the open south that the big changes came first.

The southern tribes probably did not make all this progress under their own steam; they were wide open to influences from the east across the steppe, and they may have learned agriculture, stockbreeding and metalworking from Mesopotamia or from the nearer parts of central Asia. It was the south, with its warm summers, rich soil, fairly reliable rainfall, inexhaustible pasture, game and fish which attracted wave after wave of invaders who usually became settlers and eventually traders, after which their prosperity attracted fresh invaders. About 700 B.C. the Scythians arrived, who spoke a Persian language, wove luxurious carpets, and worked in iron as well as copper. Because of their tough nomadic habits, and such customs as that of using the skulls of their enemies for drinking-cups, the Scythians remained a byword for barbarism among the later Russians, but they were no more barbaric than the many nomads who followed them and also settled for a while—the Sarmatians, Avars, Huns, Magyars, Khazars, Pechenegs, Polovtsy, and finally the Tatars and Mongols, who in the thirteenth century changed the whole course of Russian history.

The Scythians actually left more, and more artistic, evidences of civilization behind them than any of the later invaders. They traded with Greece, and Greek craftsmen made some of their richly decorated helmets and shields, but they brought Iranian traditions with them, and it was the east which bred the distinctive native Scythian style—that culture of highly stylized and elaborately interwoven animal forms, particularly the stag and the horse, which is so admired today. At the Hermitage Museum in Leningrad one now knocks at a special door and pays an extra fee to see the treasures of Scythian gold cups and harness mountings worked in these forms. Barbarians the Scythians might have been in their treatment of subject peoples, but their art was superb. Its influence was so strong—perhaps because of magical associations—that the complex interweaving and animal patterns spread northwards from South Russia and right across northern Europe. They became a principal element of the styles which we now think of as typical Old Celtic, typical Old Norse, and typical Anglo-Saxon. It seems extremely unlikely that the makers of the Book of Kells or of the brooches in the Sutton Hoo burial would have had any reason to recognize the Scythian origins of their work, but today the connection reminds us how much more mobile the peoples of Europe and the Near East were, in early times, than one would imagine from the primitive state of their communications. In the folk art of Russia itself the Scythian influence remains part of the national heritage right up to our own time, two thousand years after the Scythians disappeared from history.

While the southern steppes remained continuously and fatally open to the great migrations from Asia, the northern forests did not escape them altogether; they were thinly populated, but they received migrants from northern Asia, speaking languages of the Finnish, or Finno-Ugric family, and at first practising agriculture, if at all, only by the method of burning down a patch of forest, raising crops for a few years until the soil was exhausted, and then moving on to burn down another patch. (In the wilder parts of northern Russia people were still farming on these lines in the present century.)

But where, among all these wandering peoples, were the Slavs? There is much argument about the evidence for their first appearances, and where they came from is still more uncertain. However, since the Slav languages are a branch of the Indo-Germanic family, the proto-Slavs must have diverged somewhere along the way from the home of the original Indo-Germanic language in western or central Asia, in the same way as our own distant ancestors, the proto-Germanic and proto-Celtic wanderers, must at some earlier period have diverged. When the Slavs can first be identified—perhaps about 1000 B.C., but some would say not till 600 B.C.—they were already living in the regions of the Dnieper, the Vistula, and the Dniester rivers—what is now western Russia, the western Ukraine, Belorussia and eastern Poland. They mixed with the Scythians, they traded with the Greeks, Persians and Arabs, and from the remains they have left it is clear that they preferred settlement, agriculture and trading to the pastoral or plundering life of nomads. They moved about largely by water, of which there is only too much in the swampy west, and at some very early date they settled at the sites of the most ancient Russian towns, such as Kiev on its grand curving bluffs overlooking the Dnieper, Smolensk on a bunch of little hills, and far north, near the Baltic, what was to become the great trading city of Novgorod, so well placed and so well defended by water.

The earth in this western belt is mostly poor, swampy or sandy: one has a depressing view of it still, travelling by train from Warsaw to Moscow. In the clearings between the thin birch groves and bedraggled pine forests, and in the drier, raised places among the lakes and streams and marshes, the eastern Slavs had to live in small communities, and they had to clear the forest and till the soil communally, because an isolated family could rarely have scratched themselves a living. Here, probably, in the necessities of their austere beginnings, was the first origin of that most powerful and persistent of Russian characteristics— the natural preference and gift for doing things in common. Many peoples, and probably most peoples outside the modern West, show the same characteristic, but it has stayed peculiarly strong in the Russians in contrast to other Europeans. And this is particularly remarkable because it does not seem at first sight to fit a nation which has become so industrialized and modernized, and at such a pace, during the last forty-odd years.

Doing things in common, however, has never meant that Russians could not be adventurous. The early Russians advanced eastwards into the southern steppes, where they usually had to fight and were often defeated and sometimes enslaved. They advanced far into the central Russian forests, where they mixed peaceably with the Finnish settlers, in an assimilation which became over the centuries one of the most peaceful known to history. The rivers in the heart of modern Russia still usually bear Finnish names, as do some of the settlements, including Moskva (Moscow) itself, but most of the settlement names are Russian, just as in England the chief rivers usually have Celtic names, while the settlements (with a few exceptions, such as London) have Saxon ones.

This penetration must have been made mainly by water—a much easier and safer means of travelling than overland. Over their original western territory the Slavs made a system of portages which linked the rivers, from the Neva to the Dnieper, into a continuous route by which boats travelled from the Baltic to the Black Sea. The watershed between the rivers flowing north to the Gulf of Finland and those flowing south into the Black Sea is a very shallow one, and this route soon became one of the great trade routes of the early Middle Ages, leading as it did to the most important and wealthiest city in Europe—Byzantium, or Constantinople. The southern peoples wanted furs, tar for their ships, wild honey and beeswax from the forests, and amber from the Baltic shores; the northern peoples wanted grain, wine, fruit, spices, and luxuries such as gold, silver, jewellery, silks and carpets from the east. The north had less to offer, but the balance was made up by a lucrative trade in slaves, who were carried off and sold to Byzantium or elsewhere on the Black Sea, or even to the Arabs. (Hoards of early Arabic coins have been found in both Russia and Scandinavia.) The Slavs had established the route, and they had set up forts and indeed little cities at key points to exact tolls, but in spite of this it was mostly Slavs who got carried off into slavery, by raiders from the south, by raiders from the north, or by fellow-Slavs.

The most persistent and determined raiders were the Scandinavians —the 'Swedes' or 'Vikings' or 'Norsemen' or 'Danes', called by the Russians 'Varangians'. They were already harassing the northern regions of Russia a century before the first 'Danish' expedition landed in Saxon Britain. Just as in Britain, some of the Scandinavians settled alongside the natives; nationhood had little meaning at this stage of history, and soon there were Scando-Slav communities in the north, with an admixture of tall, fairhaired and blue-eyed stock whose descendants can be recognized among the very mixed Russian people of today. The Scandinavians were both raiders and traders; at one time they traded and plundered right down the Volga to the Caspian, but they met with too much Asiatic opposition, and by the end of the ninth century they had concentrated on organizing and dominating the whole of the Baltic–Black Sea route. They were better organizers than the Russians, and they were more enterprising, perhaps because they were far from their original base. They settled as a minority, and usually a ruling minority, but they intermarried with the natives, and in a comparatively short time they lost their language; their descendants became in fact 'Russians'.

I have put 'Russian' in inverted commas because, although it is convenient to speak of these Slavs as Russians before the Scandinavians came, they did not actually call themselves 'Rusi' until some time after the arrival of the Norsemen, and it was only in the tenth century that a state grew up called 'Rus' and based on Kiev. The 'Rusi' were at first the upper class of merchants and armed men, both Scandinavians and Slavs, who dominated and took tribute from the other Slavs, and 'Rus' first meant the district of Kiev alone. The name 'Rusi', however, spread before long to the whole people, and 'Rus' became recognized as the name for the western tract, more or less, which the Slavs had first occupied, along with the later Slav settlements in places such as Vladimir and Ryazan, in what is now central Russia. Many of the original Slav tribes had now migrated westwards, to become the ancestors of the Poles, Czechs and Jugoslavs, but 'the land of Rus' was united by a common language and traditions. Administratively it was scarcely a country in the modern sense of the term; it consisted of a large number of principalities such as Novgorod, Pskov and Vladimir in

the north, Smolensk and Minsk in the centre, and Kiev, Pereyaslavl and
Chernigov in the south. Their boundaries were often ill defined, and
the princes often at war with one another, not always joining forces even
when they had to face Oriental invaders such as the Polovtsy from across
the steppe. England at the same period was in a scarcely better state, of
course, with its princelings often failing to unite against the Danes.

In Rus, the Scandinavians under Rurik and Oleg were the first rulers
—in the late ninth century—to impose some kind of unity, though it
remained precarious. Rurik was a particularly tough Viking who, having been deprived of his lands, plundered the countries on the Baltic
and the North Sea, including England, before he seized Novgorod in
862. Later in the Middle Ages he came to be regarded as the founder of
the Russian royal house, which is one indication of the way in which the
Scandinavian flavour became absorbed into the Slav mass. Oleg, who
was related to Rurik, set himself up in Kiev in 882, and Kiev was the
place that mattered most.

'Mother of all Russian towns', as the old Russian Chronicle says,
Kiev does not have much of an ancient appearance today, since so much
of it was destroyed by the Nazis. But its wonderful position is still
unmistakable, high above the Dnieper, which is a quarter of a mile wide
here. Kiev has a warm and civilized air with its horse-chestnut blossom
and lime trees along comfortably rebuilt avenues, and it has preserved
St. Sophia, the oldest church in Russia, and a few other old churches. It
is a town that invites promenading, and from the green walks along the
three-hundred-foot cliffs above the river one looks over the meadows of
the further bank and the industrial suburbs to the steppe. It is no longer
the steppe of tall, waving feathergrass which fed the horses of the
Mongols and the Polovtsy: the road to the airport now takes you
through twenty miles of unbroken cornfield. But it is still the gently
undulating, limitless steppe which *expands* in all directions, like—to
quote almost any Russian classical author—the Russian soul!

The steppe brought food and tribute to ancient Kiev, as well as
periodic danger from the nomads. The wooded region, which gives way
to the steppe just above Kiev, supplied part of the furs, honey and so on
for traders, and more came down the river system from the north.
Manufactured goods came too, through Novgorod, from the German
Hansa towns—woollen cloth, glass, and metal products such as needles
—and some of these were conveyed onwards to Byzantium. Kiev had a
money economy, and the legal code included much regulation of money-
lending, and even provisions for bankruptcies. The city had an almost

impregnable position, commanding a good crossing of the Dnieper to firm ground on the lower bank instead of the usual marsh. And Kiev was near enough to the Black Sea to enable fleets of little vessels to sail or row to Byzantium and get back in a single summer, before the river froze. All these advantages made Kiev, in the eleventh century, one of the largest and most prosperous cities in Europe. The prince of Kiev became the senior of all the Russian princes. The very name of Kiev has been given, by later Russians, to this first great period of Russian history —the Kievan period—and its strength, character and importance were mainly founded on trade.

The princes of Kiev and other Russian cities were capitalists, taking part in all this foreign trade and in domestic trade as well. Their followers, the armed men, were not traders but were rewarded with land, and they did not receive this as a fief held from the prince, but as an outright freehold estate, which was often a very large one. It is the view of Jerome Blum in his massive study, *Lord and Peasant in Russia from the 9th to the 19th Century*, that these estates provided the root from which sprang Russia's greatest evil, serfdom, because it was eventually only through serfdom that they could be cultivated. However, during the Kievan period most of the land was still farmed in communal units by associations of kindred—the 'Great Family' basis found in so many other countries even today. There were in fact no serfs during the Kievan period, though there were slaves—mostly foreign prisoners, or sometimes men who had deliberately, but temporarily, sold themselves into slavery in order to discharge a debt. Serfdom is a later and, one could say, a more sophisticated institution than slavery.

The towns had their popular assembly, the *veche*, similar to the Anglo-Saxon moot, and when a prince died they had to approve his successor, who was selected, in theory, according to a table of genealogical precedence with complicated weightings. In vigorous Novgorod and Pskov this approval was much more than a matter of form: Novgorod even had charters limiting the powers of its princes, long before our Magna Carta of 1215. In Kiev the *veche* on one occasion got their own candidate elected—the outstanding statesman and popular hero Vladimir Monomach—instead of the prince who was technically the heir. Yet the *veche* cannot be considered an institution of representative government. It was a more primitive sort of assembly, a gathering of men who all felt united by a deep unconscious bond. The great characteristic of the *veche* was that it was understood that its decisions must be unanimous to be valid—an assumption which remained typical, and as it were sacrosanct, in Russian village assemblies right up to the twentieth century, and an assumption whose anachronistic echoes are to be felt in many Soviet institutions today.

The standard of living and the kind of life in Kievan Russia must have been very similar to those of Anglo-Saxon England, with the advantage in some respects on the side of the Russians, in others on that of the English. The peoples were not unlike each other in appearance and dress, the men wearing linen tunics and cross-gartered trousers, though in winter the Russians had to take to fur clothing in order to stay alive. Both nations made chased brooches and enamelwork, they both used a lot of honey, drank beer and mead, had a good deal of fish and game to eat as well as domestic livestock, found life hard in the spring gap, imported a certain amount of wine, silk, glass, and spices—and both exported slaves, though the English did this on a smaller scale. English merchants traded in many European ports, but England was not such a great trading nation as Rus, and she had no city of anything like the size and prestige of Kiev. The legal codes of Rus were not unlike those of the Anglo-Saxons, with a fixed scale of compensation for cutting off a man's arm, or beard, or finger; both countries used the ordeal by water or by iron as a test of good faith, and both divided inheritances among all the sons with little advantage to the eldest. But Rus was ahead of the English in having no capital punishment; fines were preferred. Capital punishment was first introduced in Russia after the Mongol conquest.

Our ancestors were already developing serfdom to a certain extent before the Norman Conquest, and in this respect historians may count them a more advanced society than Kievan Russia. They already had a better administration, which was perhaps easier to achieve than in Rus, owing to the smaller size and compactness of our country. There was more and better education in England, and neither Rus nor any other European country had a scholar of the rank of the great Northumbrian, Bede. Rus, like England, had a sophisticated, or one might almost say an aristocratic native literature, recited by bards, and preserved for the most part orally, so that it is rather an accident that in English we now have only *Beowulf* and a few other epic fragments, and in the language of Rus little but the *Lay of Igor*. (It was this which in the nineteenth century became the subject of Borodin's opera with its Polovtsian dances.) The bard of *Igor* draws on a stock of formal epic phrases, as does the bard of *Beowulf*: Igor's troops are 'like a flight of swans', and the menacing Polovtsy 'like a herd of cheetahs'. Igor's address to his *druzhina*, or band of warriors, recalls some of the speeches made by Saxons on an equally hopeless occasion, at the Battle of Maldon. Both Russia and England had written chronicles at an early date, but England developed a considerable Saxon literature, of religious poetry and prose, which has little parallel in Russia until much later.

There is nothing far-fetched about comparing early Russia with early Britain. There was trade between the two, and Anglo-Saxon coins have been dug up in excavations at Kiev. The connection must have been mainly by water, through the great crescent which was controlled by the Scandinavians, from Britain down to the Black Sea, by way of the Baltic. It was a powerful connection. After the last Saxon king, Harold, was killed at Hastings his family fled to Sweden, and a marriage was arranged between his daughter Gyda and Vladimir Monomach, who reigned in Kiev from 1113 to 1125. Harold Hardrada, King of Norway, whom the English Harold defeated and slew at the Battle of Stamford, had served in Novgorod as a young man, and married Elizabeth, daughter of Yaroslav, another great prince of Kiev. The sister of Vladimir Monomach married the Emperor Henry IV, the one who had to stand in the snow in penance before the Pope at Canossa in 1077. Henry I of France married Anna, daughter of Yaroslav I, and other marriages linked the princely house of Kiev with the royal houses of Sweden, Hungary and Poland. In fact Kiev, or Rus, counted as a greater power than Britain at this period, and it was the Scandinavians who had brought the country to this position of authority, though they contributed almost nothing else to the culture of Rus—less than they did in Britain.

If the steppe had not been so subject to invasion, or if the Russian princes could have combined effectively, so that Kiev was not destroyed by the Mongols, Kievan Russia might have grown during the Middle Ages into one of those large, loosely federated states such as Germany was before Bismarck. Moscow might never have been the capital, and St. Petersburg might never have been founded. But if the open east had been made safe from enemies, its openness would have encouraged Russian colonists the more, and Russia would probably have spread, in any case, into something as huge and unmanageable as she proved to be until Soviet times. It should never be forgotten, however, that Kievan Russia was a part of Europe, and an important part. Later Russians have looked back on it not only as a romantic-heroic period but also as a romantic-prosperous one; the great historian of early Russia, George Vernadsky, says Russians then were certainly 'better housed and fed than in later times'.

There were, however, some very great contrasts between Kievan Russia and early Britain, or indeed between Kievan Russia and the countries of Western Europe at the same period, and these have persisted and have had lasting results on the character of Russian society. If there had been no Mongol conquest, and if Russia could have stayed more closely in touch with the rest of Europe, these contrasts might in time have been modified.

In the first place, Russian agriculture was more primitive than the English: the open-field, three-crop rotation, strip system was not generally adopted in Russia until the seventeenth century, while England was already practising it before the Normans came. Also, England was mainly a land of independent farmers, often tied in various ways to their lords, but still individuals, not farming on the more ancient communal lines of the Russians. The land in England is better than in most parts of Russia—except, indeed, for the black-earth steppe which was open to so many perils—and it thus offered more encouragement for independent farming. When the Angles and Saxons arrived in Britain they seem to have established themselves in settlements of individual conquering farmers, while the Slavs had to expand as communities.

The Angles and Saxons and the Scandinavians and Slavs came from the northern and eastern world which had always been outside the Roman Empire. Roman ideas of administration and law, and Roman traditions of architecture, served as compelling models for most of Europe, but they filtered through very slowly and much later to these outer regions, if at all. Yet when the Angles and Saxons came to Britain they occupied a country which had been Roman for four hundred years, and though they neglected many of the Roman roads and used the Roman monuments for building stone, the Roman influence was very soon renewed for them because they were Christianized, by degrees, from 596 onwards, and naturally they were Christianized by Roman missionaries and received into the Roman Church. With this they acquired some Latin education, some Roman ideas of organization, and a few Latin models, for example, to absorb into their literature. The Russians, on the other hand, never occupied territory where the Romans had been, and they were Christianized later and from a different source.

For Rus took up the Christianity of Byzantium, which was not only nearer to Kiev but a more important city than Rome at the time. One needs to stress this point a little, because our elementary history books and our average stock of general knowledge in the West are still, even in the twentieth century, conditioned by the Western, that is the Roman Catholic, view of the great Schism which developed between the Western and Eastern Churches. This was not a matter of reformism or argument about new developments: the early Christian Church split apart by degrees, mainly for political but partly for doctrinal reasons, and each half came to regard the other as heretical and on several occasions excommunicated the other half, so that today the Roman Church and the Eastern or Orthodox Churches both claim to represent the only true and original faith of Christianity.

It was Constantine, the Emperor who made the Roman Empire Christian, who in 330 founded his city, Constantinople, on the site of the ancient Byzantium. It was to be a Christian city, free from the old taint of paganism which hung about Rome. And while Rome was repeatedly threatened and eventually sacked by Goths and other Germanic hordes, the Eastern capital remained comparatively safe and always prosperous. During the last century of the Roman Empire there were sometimes two Emperors—one in Rome and one in Constantinople —and sometimes only the one in Constantinople, but the Empire was still regarded as a unity. The 'Eastern Emperors' were still Roman Emperors; one of them was the great Justinian (527–565), whose codification of Roman laws is still the basis for students all over Europe. When, however, the Empire at last fell apart, and there were no longer any Emperors in Rome, the Popes managed to retain their see there, and now the real divergence began. For in the chaos left by the barbarians in the West, the Church was the only institution which seemed anything like an organizing and unifying power. Its priests and bishops were linked by their hierarchy and by their use of Latin, which set them apart from their primitive congregations, who spoke Germanic, Celtic, dog-Latin or other orally transmitted languages and dialects. In the East, however, there was not the same desperate need to establish order, and the language used in church was the language of the people, as it is to this day in the countries of the Orthodox faith—Russia, Greece, Romania, Serbia, etc. (In course of time the language used was no longer the language of everyday speech, so that in Russian churches, for instance, the archaic Church Slavonic still employed is distant from modern Russian, but no more distant than mediaeval English is from twentieth-century English.) In Western Europe the Roman Church achieved a position of overriding power and influence which enabled it, when political powers grew up again, to control and dictate to kings and princes and even to the new-style Emperor, the Holy Roman Emperor of German and Italian lands combined, who was set up with the help of the Pope in 962.

In the East, on the other hand, the Church was headed by a Patriarch who depended upon the Emperor at Byzantium for protection, which he was nearly always able to give, and from the time of Justinian the control of the Church here was in fact in the hands of the State. Such a subordination of the spiritual to the temporal power was bound to be regarded as fatally dangerous by the Popes of Rome, for whom the headship of the Christian world must naturally be centred there where the Church had been founded by St. Peter. This claim, however, is the rock upon which all attempts to reconcile the Western and Eastern Churches have foundered: the Orthodox would not and do not accept the supremacy of the Pope. For them he is the Bishop of Rome, first among peers but not above them. Their own national Churches are each governed by a Patriarch, but there is no senior authority over the Patriarchs, only a Council in which they meet from time to time.

The great political and social achievements of the Roman Church, and the tremendous intellectual energy which it has generated, and which ultimately fathered the Protestantism and humanism which have partly superseded it—these cannot be paralleled by anything in the influence exerted by the Orthodox Churches, civilizing, inspiring and solacing though their influence has been. It has been natural, therefore, for people in the West to pass lightly over the Byzantine world in all its aspects, following in this way, consciously or unconsciously, the lead given by Rome in turning its back on the Eastern heretics. The balance has been handsomely redressed by recent Western scholars, but it seems useful to repeat here that while Western Europe was struggling through the Dark Ages there were no Dark Ages in the Eastern world and civil authority did not break down. Byzantium was the one great city of the Christian world at this time; she was the greatest power in Europe for several centuries, a great political, diplomatic and trading power, rich enough to hire armies of mercenaries (including Vikings) while Western Europe was sunk in small-scale agriculture and local trade.* This was the centre from which Russia took her Christianity.

* 'Without the attraction exercised by Byzantium,' says the Belgian historian Henri Pirenne, 'without the necessity of fighting the Mussulmans, Europe would doubtless have continued for centuries in a state of purely agricultural civilization . . . Her commerce was not a spontaneous manifestation of the natural development of her economic life.' (*A History of Europe*, 1955.)

The people of Rus, or at any rate the people of Kiev for a start, were baptized *en masse*, by order of their ruler Vladimir, when he forsook paganism in 988. Christianity had in fact been reaching the upper class for some time before, beginning with Vladimir's grandmother Olga, and Olga and Vladimir both became saints in the Orthodox calendar. But it was Vladimir who cast down the pagan idols and created the foundations of Christian institutions in Kievan Russia. In recognition of this he was able to achieve marriage with the daughter of the Emperor at Constantinople—a jealously guarded honour.

Although superstitions and the practice of magic and sorcery remained rife among the Russian people, the pagan religion as a religion was overthrown, and the building of churches and monasteries and the spreading of the Christian faith went on so well that by the end of the thirteenth century Byzantium was speaking of the Russians as 'the most Christian nation'. The monasteries were not the home of monastic orders as in the West. Orthodox monks and nuns are simply Orthodox monks and nuns: the founding of orders such as the Benedictines or Dominicans is unknown. It would smack of dangerous and quite unnecessary divergence from the essential doctrine and ritual. Bishops are chosen from the monks, or 'black clergy', who of course are celibate, while parish priests in the Orthodox Church are married and are called the 'white' clergy.

The essence of Orthodoxy is to preserve the forms and beliefs long ago established, particularly the forms, such as the observance of frequent fasts, which are regarded as very important. As far as possible, the forms are to be preserved communally, in the congregation. Prayers are to be said in common rather than in private, and even confession is much more often a communal matter, in public, than the auricular confession of the Roman Church. The Russian word *sobor*, which means 'congregation, gathering, or meeting', equally means an important church or cathedral, whereas in the Latin languages a cathedral is named after the bishop's chair (*cathedra*). Most significant, perhaps, in showing the brotherliness and 'congregationality' (*sobornost* in Russian) of the Orthodox is the opening of their Creed with the words: 'Let us love one another, that with one mind we may confess Father, Son and Holy Spirit . . .' etc.

The individual alone, in the Orthodox belief, is not capable of controlling all his wrong impulses, particularly his violent impulses; this can only be done with the help of the community of which he is a member. This attitude, of course, has continued to the present day, even

among the mass of Russians who have forsaken their Church: it partly
helps to explain the 'confessions' at political trials, and among most
Russians it can still be seen at work in brotherly persuasions and even in
certain little institutions which the Soviet régime has created on the
basis of the old spirit. It is only in the last fifteen or twenty years, perhaps, that this ancient habit of mind has begun to give way a great deal
to attitudes of individual responsibility more like those which are
typical of the West.

'Congregationality' in religion came easily to the early Russians, who
were already used to a communal form of labour in the fields, and to the
'congregational' institution of the *veche*. The Russians also received
from Byzantium the concept of the 'symphony of State and Church', as
it was called by Byzantine writers. This was an idealization which
usually meant in practice that the Church was subject to the ruler—a
relationship which was to have a profound effect all through Russian
history; the Church never challenged the secular power in Russia as the
Western Churches did. What was most valued in Orthodoxy—what *is*
most valued—is not ecclesiastical power, nor convincing theology, but
the beauty of the services in the words of the liturgy, the singing, the
vestments, the holy ikons and the gilded interiors of the churches.
According to the perhaps legendary account in the 'Primary Chronicle',
it was the beauty of the Orthodox service in appealing to all the senses
at Constantinople—'we did not know whether we were on earth or in
heaven'—which overcame the emissaries whom Vladimir had sent to
sample the three religions—Rome, Moslem, and Orthodox—before he
decided to follow Byzantium. The Latins simplified the detailed early
Christian rituals many centuries since, but Orthodox services are still
long—in Russia they can last three and a half hours. And it is still the
beauty, even specifically the concrete beauty associated with the services, but most of all the feeling of being, through the ritual, in contact
with the essence, with the very state of mind of the earliest Christian
communities who created this ritual, which inspires and rivets the
Russian believer. Because they are meeting together, and because they
observe the ritual, they may be able to feel—*should* be able to feel—the
divine spirit amongst them. But to feel this they *must* be together.
Abstract ideas or intellectual systems of theology play little part in the
Eastern Church; the Orthodox have not usually gone in for scholastic
justification or debates with unbelievers or heretics. In fact a great deal
is left vague in doctrine, and the Orthodox Church has a comfortable
accommodation for variations in Christian belief about many matters,

such as Purgatory, or the Immaculate Conception of the Virgin. Enmity and hate are directed mainly against the Roman Church, and this principally, as in the early days, for political reasons. Catholic powers, particularly Poland and Lithuania, repeatedly attacked Russia from the West, while the other Orthodox countries in Europe usually sought Russian protection.

Byzantium contributed more to Russia than a beautifully ritualized religion. It was owing to the Byzantine connection that the Russians adopted, instead of the Latin script, the Cyrillic script developed by the early missionaries Cyril and Methodius. The Byzantine version of Roman law, civil and ecclesiastical, but particularly the latter, was welded into Russian customary law. And it was Byzantine art which gave rise to the great Russian schools of ikon painting, and Byzantine architecture which inspired the masterpieces of early Russian archi-tecture, beginning with the earliest of all, the Cathedral of St. Sophia which still stands in Kiev. Byzantine art was a blend of later Greek or Hellenistic art with Oriental influences, and during the early centuries of the Dark Ages it was the only flourishing, sophisticated art in Europe. After the Renaissance, and until quite recently in Western Europe, Byzantine art was regarded as second-rate because of its con-ventionalized though flowing lines, because of its exploitation of the possibilities of materials rather than aiming at 'purer', classical stan-dards, and especially because of its dependence on implied meanings rather than representation: the position and relative size of personages in Byzantine art, for instance, indicates their relative importance and has nothing to do with perspective. Yet after the fall of the Roman Empire, Byzantine art was the only channel by which the ancient plastic arts were preserved and transmitted to the West, and there it was to serve later as a basic influence in the work, for example, of Giotto, Cimabue and Duccio. Today when we are less exclusively attached to representa-tional art, and there is enthusiasm for such works as the great mosaics at Ravenna, Byzantine art is no longer under a cloud. And the tourist will find similar, though less imaginative mosaics, dating back to the eleventh century, in St. Sophia's at Kiev.

In the Byzantine world there was several times a strong puritanical reaction against the representation of divine personages at all. This was the movement known as Iconoclasm and it was one of the causes of the divergence from Rome, in whose churches sacred images were not only usual but were often worshipped by simple people. A compromise was eventually reached in the Orthodox Church which holds today: flat

3

representation is permissible, as in the many schools of ikon and fresco painting, but three-dimensional images are forbidden.

Kiev did not have long, unfortunately, to develop as a prosperous Christian power. Much of its trade was being lost to the Venetians, who had been energetically developing their sea route to Byzantium. In 1204 the great city itself was taken by the Crusaders, who set up a 'Latin Kingdom' of Constantinople which lasted only until 1261, but before that date Kiev had been sacked by the Mongols—in 1230—and its power dispersed. The Polovtsy, whom the Russians had had on their doorstep for so long, had by no means always been at war with them; some Russian princes had married daughters of Polovtsy chieftains, and the Polovtsy seemed ready to resist the Mongol invasion. Perhaps, if all the Russians and Polovtsy could have combined together, the Mongols might even have been repulsed, but the Russian princes could not overcome their ancient jealousies of one another, and the Polovtsy made common cause with the Mongols and became the chief element in their feared and famous 'Golden Horde'.

Kiev was reported 'a city of skulls' by a foreign visitor in 1246. The Mongols had no use for it; the 'capital' of the Golden Horde was Sarai, a city of tents eight hundred miles to the east, in the Volga delta. The Mongols even overran Poland, Hungary, Serbia and Bulgaria for a time, and when they retreated from these western areas it was the Catholic kings of Poland and Lithuania who moved into the old territory of Kiev. In fact Kiev and its whole province were not fully restored to Russian, i.e. Muscovite, power until the seventeenth century, and by that time the very language and customs of the people had come under Polish influence and diverged somewhat from Russian. The land became known as 'Little Russia' or 'the Marches', that is, the Ukraine. So that although Kiev is historically the 'mother of all Russian towns', it is today the capital city of the Ukraine, a country, or nation, which did not even exist in the Kievan period of history. To the north of the Ukraine another, smaller, border land, similarly under Polish influence, developed into 'White Russia', or Belorussia, as it is called today.

The focus of Russian history, after 1237, moves north, to the forest zone and 'Great Russia'. The Mongols subdued the northern cities such as Vladimir, Suzdal and Moscow (a junior among cities, first heard of in 1147), but what they wanted was a continuing, steady flow of tribute, once their savage onslaught had made clear that resistance would be useless. The primary duty of the northern princes was now to collect and hand over the tribute.

Some years before the Mongols arrived, in 1229, Pope Gregory IX had forbidden Catholics, that is to say all the peoples of Western and Central Europe, to have commerce with the Russian heretics. The Mongols, whose reputation put half Europe in fear, now completed the isolation of Russia from the West, and a long, austere, bitter period began, to last until the Mongols were finally repulsed in 1480. After this they retreated or were absorbed, but in the course of the two and a half centuries of their occupation the old Kievan Russia underwent profound internal changes which the departure of the Mongols did not alter. On the contrary, these changes dominated Russian life, increasingly to its harm, until very recent times. The reactions against them, and the secondary effects, are powerfully to be felt even in contemporary Soviet Russia.

2. The Mark of the Mongols

The 'Mongols' who took Russia captive and kept her out of Europe for two and a half centuries were not, most of them, of the same stock as the inhabitants of present-day Mongolia. Their terrifying leader, Batu Khan, and his troop were Mongols, but the bulk of the Horde were Tatars, and the whole occupying force were, and still are, indiscriminately called both 'Tatars' and 'Mongols' by the Russians. 'Horde' is itself a Tatar word, and these Tatars were ancestors of the same Tatars who remain in smallish national units in the Soviet Union—round about Kazan, for instance, in the Soviet Tatar Republic. Tatars in general are neither yellow-skinned nor slant-eyed but have European complexions. However, whatever their complexions, the Mongol–Tatar host who terrorized the Russians in the early thirteenth century were all the same sort—fierce and accurate archers, ruthless fighters who could outlast even the Russian powers of endurance, riding all the way from Asia with each a spare horse for meat, and refreshing themselves sometimes by tapping one of its veins and drinking the raw blood mixed with mare's milk.

The Mongols were led by generals of great ability, who planned whole campaigns as well as being skilled in ambush and feigned retreat. (Batu Khan was the grandson of Genghis Khan, the fabulous conqueror of China and Central Asia.) And the Mongols were also, particularly in comparison with the Russians, masters of organization. They were themselves organized in units of ten thousand, a thousand, a hundred, and ten, and when they occupied Russia they took a census in the western half, as a basis for tax-gathering and conscription, as early as 1245. They had their own system of communication by post-horses, they set up customs duties for the first time, and they had, at least in principle, a state monopoly of alcohol—an example followed by Tsarist governments later. When they were not fighting, most Mongols were herdsmen and hunters; they looked down on settled peoples as poor shackled creatures fit only to toil for their free-living masters, the nomads, yet they also encouraged and engaged in—quite remarkably for nomads—both domestic and long-distance trade.

36

They sucked Russia dry of handicraftsmen, whom they forced into their own employment, but the main weight of their yoke fell upon the unfortunate Russian peasants. Tribute meant not only money but levies of able-bodied men to fight in Mongol wars. Princes and the few well-to-do merchants were not taxed: they were the tax collectors. Important princes, however, had to journey to the capital of the Horde to make obeisance and hand over the tribute. Even the heroic Alexander Nevsky, who fought off the Swedes and Germans menacing Russia's north-west, was several times obliged to journey to the Horde. The Church, on the other hand, was treated with remarkable tolerance. It was exempt from tax, and it continued to enjoy this privileged position even after the Mongols became Moslems.

The Russians had now to live for the first time under an absolute system. The Mongols believed that they were divinely appointed to rule the world, and they themselves lived under an absolute Great Khan. Being numbered and accounted for, most of them, like the Russians, were liable for taxes and war service when required. The burden of the tribute meant that the Russian standard of living went down, and for many centuries it remained lower than it had been in Kievan Rus. It was not the warm and fertile south which was being squeezed by the Mongols, but the forested north, where agriculture was far less remunerative. Yet poor though the land mostly was, it was now the land, and not foreign or entrepôt trade, which had to be the principal source of such wealth as the nation could produce. The rich Dnieper lands were in other hands, and their trading importance had been filched away already. The northern principalities had been growing in strength, compared with Kiev, for some time before the Mongols came, and it was their princes who were now made the key agents for collecting the tribute. Only an autocratic and ruthless prince could be certain of extracting what the Mongols demanded; the Mongols had destroyed the institution of the *veche*, and the princes had apparently made no objection. If the subjects of a prince now rebelled against his exactions, the Mongols joined him in savage suppression of the revolt; if a prince tried to rebel—as some occasionally did—Mongol revenge was merciless. Everything was to the advantage of an autocratic prince.

The principalities were still small, and it seems partly accidental that it was the princes, or grand dukes, of Moscow who began to gain a lead over the others. Among all the old Russian towns on river bluffs, with ravines to defend them on the other sides, Vladimir, Yaroslavl, Ryazan, Serpukhov, Dmitrov, Zvenigorod and many more were important at various times. Moscow grew up on a steep granite cliff above the Moscow River, where the Kremlin and the Red Square stand today, but there is no outstanding physical reason why Moscow should have become the chief of all. What Moscow had was a sequence of twelve princes who all saw the advantage of keeping on good terms with the Mongols by prompt delivery of the tribute, and who channelled their own aggression into various ingenious, unscrupulous or bulldozing methods of adding to their own territory. One grand duke, Yury, won such favour that he married the sister of the Great Khan, who made him also Grand Duke of Vladimir. Eventually the Mongols recognized Moscow's prince as the senior among Russian rulers, and as the one who might be trusted to collect the whole of the tribute from others. The Moscow house broke away from the general Russian custom of equal shares in inheritance and started a tradition—probably for reasons of ambition and greed—of giving the eldest son the biggest share. So the Muscovite domain was preserved and grew, while in other principalities, if there happened to be too many sons, the patrimony might be fragmented into petty units which would be an easy prey for a stronger neighbour—very likely the Prince of Muscovy. Thus, in the leading princely house autocracy was doubly assured, while other noble families continued to divide their possessions equally among the sons, who all inherited their father's title—a practice which lasted until the Revolution. (The Russian equivalent of *Debrett*, a work still kept up among some émigrés, is not unnaturally an enormous compilation in many volumes.) In the early days princes with a poor inheritance often entered the service of the great ones, where they were given broader lands as a reward for service—a foretaste of the system of land tenure that was to spread all over Russia.

The unpleasant Prince Ivan (1325–1341) was known as 'Moneybags' (*Kalita*) because of his pitiless squeezing of the people for tax. He beat it out of them with cudgels, if we are to believe a little painting done in the next century. He collected a good deal on his own account as well as for the Mongols; he helped the Mongols to suppress revolts in other principalities; and he thus made the position of Muscovy safer than ever. In 1328 he moved the capital of his state to Moscow from Vladimir. The head of the Church, the Metropolitan, had already moved to Moscow two years before, so that the new Russia was henceforth Moscow-centred. Ivan was now known as a grand prince, and until 1598 all the monarchs in Moscow—Grand Princes at first and later Tsars—were direct descendants of Ivan 'Moneybags'.

There were of course no representative institutions to limit autocracy (except in Novgorod and Pskov, which managed to hold out until the later fifteenth century). Nor were there guilds of merchants such as became powerful in Western Europe. There was no institution of chivalry to furnish ideal standards and courtly models of behaviour: it would have been impossible to translate into contemporary Russian Chaucer's phrase 'He was a verray perfect gentle knight'. (As a good Catholic, Chaucer's knight had in fact ridden in expeditions against the heretical Russians.) All was already set for the pattern, familiar throughout later Russian history, of autocratic rule with a small and restricted upper class, a negligible middle class, and an oppressed mass upon whom almost all burdens were to be laid. Between Mongol autocracy and Muscovite autocracy there was very little but the Church; and the Church, with its Byzantine traditions, had always preached the duty of submission to princes, who were to be looked on as divinely appointed. As for the Mongol domination, it must be accepted as a visitation upon the Russian people for their sins.

All the same, it was mainly the Church which supported men's dignity and men's hopes during the Mongol period. The Church was never so strong as at this time; about two hundred fresh monasteries were founded, and most of these pushed settlement further north into the forests. For these were not monasteries in which to retire from the world and contemplate. Russian monks and nuns worked as hard as the peasants, built their own monasteries and churches, and extended the lands of the Church vastly; by the end of the Mongol domination the Church owned between a quarter and a third of all the cultivated area of Russia. There was work for thousands of peasants on these lands, and the Church was an easier master than the princes, since the Church did not have to furnish tribute. Church architecture flourished. There were charming wooden churches put up by pious builders, and the wooden churches which still survive (though they date from the seventeenth and eighteenth centuries) are among the glories of Russian architecture. Even the 'onion' domes were originally constructed in wood, as may be seen in the treasured northern churches at Kizhi. The loveliest and simplest masterpieces of Russian architecture, in uncomplicated white stone, were erected early in the Mongol period—some of them, such as the two cathedrals and the Golden Gate at Vladimir, even earlier. These are more to Western taste than the complex later churches such as St. Basil's in the Red Square. They derive from the same tradition as the Romanesque churches of Western Europe, and it seems rather scandalous that Russia was so long omitted from the standard Western histories of architecture.

The simple majesty of these buildings, or of the soaring 'tent'-style churches, their stylized but beautifully controlled ornament, and their small-windowed interiors covered with frescoes up to the springing of the roof—they must have lifted men's hearts and given them also a certain sense of security which the princes could not provide and had no intention of providing. The princes had their own body of men-at-arms whom they rewarded, but these men were building no castle strongholds; they could not afford to, and there were anyway not enough craftsmen. At most there was the strongly-guarded little Kremlin, or fortress, of the prince in some of the bigger cities. As one travels through the Russian countryside today, it is striking that the old strong points, with their high red walls, are nearly always monasteries—say at Zagorsk, Zvenigorod, Pskov, or several places right in the city of Moscow—and apart from the few Kremlins there are no old castles as elsewhere in Europe, nor anything equivalent to them, until the manor-houses of the more peaceful eighteenth and nineteenth centuries.

Within the walls of the monastery there was physical security for many, laymen and women as well as monks and nuns, in a particularly lawless age. Outwards from the monasteries the brethren tried to spread the Russian monastic spirit—the fostering of the early Christian sense of communal charity, and of the ideal of 'chastity, humility, patience, and love', to quote the words of a favourite Orthodox prayer. The monastic example of humility, patience and love must have spread a good deal among a people bowed down by the Mongols, and must have helped to produce, in some, that type of saintly, accepting character such as we know in later days from the works of Dostoevsky.

The Mongol period was also the period of great schools of ikon painting, and they sometimes depicted martial as well as holy subjects. The greatest ikon painter of all, Andrei Rublyov (*c.* 1360–1430), and his master Feofan the Greek are in a class by themselves; they expressed something more than a spirit of conventional acceptance. The Soviet film *Andrei Rublyov* deliberately shows the contrast between the ideals of hope and warmth, fellowship and compassion implied in the painter's work, and the prevailing brutality of the age, its murders, rapes, robberies and chicanery. There is a naturalness and serenity about the work of Rublyov and Feofan which is far removed from the severe Byzantine formalism of earlier ikon painters, and Rublyov's introduction of minute details drawn realistically from nature reminds one of some of the early painters of the Italian Renaissance. It has been suggested that this outward-looking upsurge of hope in Rublyov was partly inspired by the fact that Russia was beginning to be able to strike back at the Mongols, and in 1380 inflicted a famous defeat on them at the Battle of Kulikovo on the Don. The Church itself was bold enough, now that Russia could afford to be bold, to preach something of a crusade against the infidel Mongols, who since 1300 had been followers of Mohammed.

The Russians were still far from free. In 1382 the Tatars sacked Moscow in revenge for Kulikovo. But the Horde was at last beginning to split into several Hordes under several Khans, and it was itself threatened by a terrible new conqueror from Central Asia, Tamerlane. Although the fear inspired by his name reached even to the West, Tamerlane did not choose to conquer Russia, but he seriously weakened the Horde. He retired to his empire in the east where—rather ironically —his grave at Samarkand, and the exquisite mausoleum above it, the Gur Emir, were captured by the Russians four hundred years later, and they now lie within the Soviet Republic of Uzbekistan. Moscow fought off one more siege by the weakened Tatars and repulsed a last attack by the Horde in 1472, and then in 1480 the Mongol power came to an end with the peculiar unfought battle of the Ugra River. The troops of the canny Ivan the Great (Ivan III) faced the Tatar host across the water for four days without drawing a bow, after which both sides thought better of it and rode home.

So there was no more Mongol tribute. But what was Russia now? The autocratic power, which alone had been able to extort tribute and outface the Mongols, now became the enlarged autocratic tyranny of the independent Muscovite state. The rulers of Moscow extracted tribute as before, but for the benefit of their own treasury, and they were scarcely less brutal than the Mongols when they suppressed revolts of fellow-Christians, or conquered fresh lands. In 1471, Ivan the Great savagely subdued and annexed the free city of Novgorod which, if left alone, would probably have grown into a wealthy self-governing Hanseatic burgh like Bremen. (Novgorod had preserved its *veche* all through the Mongol period, but now it was destroyed.) Conquering Novgorod also meant acquiring a vast northern tract which had belonged to Novgorod, stretching to the White Sea, the Arctic and the Urals, and from which hunters brought in sables, ermine, beaver, squirrel, bear and fox. This acquisition more than doubled Ivan's territory (though not the number of his people), and it further swelled his treasury, since the state was getting almost a monopoly of the trade in furs, timber and grain. The key position of Moscow on the system of rivers which connects with the Baltic, with Archangel, with the Volga and the Caspian and the routes to Asia, was more significant than ever. Not that the geographical position was all that superior: Vladimir or several other towns would have done just as well, but it was Moscow whom greed, guile, aggression and naked autocracy had now made the undisputed master.

Autocracy was part of the price, in short, which the Russians had to pay for getting rid of the Mongols. They had to reckon with increased brutality all round, and most of them were probably themselves more brutalized. The first great Russian historian, Karamzin (1766–1826), speculated on this and wondered whether certain brutal features which he observed, in his own day, in the otherwise generous Russian character might not still be the result of the Mongol conquest, three hundred years after the retreat from the Ugra River. Capital punishment, unknown in Kiev, the use of torture, and the almost universal flogging, all seem to have been copied from the Mongols. There was no peaceful blossoming for the Russians after the Mongols left: in the centuries that followed they had to fight off Poles, Lithuanians, Swedes and Germans from the west, besides many attacks by bands of Tatars still from the east.

Yet in spite of the constant barbarities which the Russians suffered under the autocracy and its tax-farmers, the lack of a general system of justice, the power of the nobles which fed the growth of serfdom, and the quasi-impossibility of redress or defence or avoidance of injustice (other than by flight), the nation had, by the early sixteenth century, some cause for pride, and foreign visitors reported the Muscovites as indulging in a crude kind of exultation about the superiority of being Russian. They showed a strange pride in their absolute sovereign whether he was well-disposed towards them or not. It was Ivan the Great who began to call himself sometimes Tsar (i.e. Caesar, hence Emperor), and who scornfully rejected the offer of a crown from the Holy Roman Emperor, while Ivan the Terrible (1547–1584) and all the rulers after him adopted the title of Tsar for regular and official use. Politically speaking, Ivan the Great's position was immensely strengthened by his marriage to Sophia, daughter of the last Byzantine Emperor. Europe was learning that Russia was now a power of considerable if rather uncertain significance, and a symbol of this increased prestige, after Ivan's marriage, was that he took over from the defunct

Byzantine Empire its device of the double-headed eagle; this continued as the Russian national emblem until 1917.

The death of the Byzantine Empire was responsible for much more than an emblem and a title for the Russian Tsar; it was the cause of a new and more exalted status which the Russian Church took upon itself, and hence of a new and more exalted status for its protector the Tsar. In the early fifteenth century Byzantium was on the point of collapse, and the Eastern Emperor tried, through the Pope, to get Western help against the ever-threatening Turks. The Pope made clear that the price of help would have to be a reunion of the Catholic and Eastern Churches, and this was officially achieved at the Council of Florence in 1439, with an agreement to differ over some doctrinal matters, such as the use of unleavened bread at Communion. The reunion, however, was little more than an agreement among leaders; most of the Orthodox Churches reacted violently against the patching up of old differences, and the Russian Church furiously repudiated the union, so that in 1453, when the Turks captured Constantinople, the Russians considered this a fitting punishment for renegade Byzantium. The 'First Rome', i.e. the Catholic Church, had fallen away, they said, through heresy, the 'Second Rome' had likewise fallen away and was now in the hands of the infidel, so that Moscow was the 'Third Rome, and a fourth there will not be'.* Russia now became 'Holy Russia' or 'the Second Jerusalem', the only keeper and repository of the true faith. Clearly the Orthodox Tsar was in future to be not merely the protector and joint head of the Russian Church but the guardian of true Orthodoxy in general, i.e. of true Christianity. And although the Russian Church remained a national Church, it kept up the Byzantine tradition—one might almost say the myth—of the universal Church, the oecumenical Church. Typical of this tradition is the fact that while Byzantium accepted, just as the Catholics do, the conclusions reached at the first seven Councils of the early Christian Church, the Eastern Churches not only reject all conclusions arrived at by councils of the Catholic Church after the split: they have never called any Council of their own to clarify Christian doctrine further. Councils could only be called if the whole Church could be united once more; meanwhile the true Church in the East must wait for that happy day, piously conserving the truths and rituals which were agreed upon when the early Church was one and undivided.

* The world was expected to see the Second Coming of Christ in A.D. 1492, 7,000 years after the Orthodox date for the Creation. After 1492 arrived there were gloomy prophecies of the coming of Antichrist instead.

Henceforth, to be a Russian was, therefore, to be a member of a chosen race, ruled by the prime defender of the Christian faith, an all-powerful autocrat exercising his unlimited power by divine right, the joint head of the national Church, and the owner, also by divine right, of the whole land in which one lived. While the fall of Constantinople is the event which historians count as the beginning of 'modern history', with the flight of classical scholars to the West and so forth, for Russia on the other hand this would seem to be the time when the country launched upon a new and arrogant conservatism.

Actually Ivan the Terrible was only the first of many Russian rulers who have used a re-emphasized conservatism—of the autocracy, the Church, or the Party—as a bold and even aggressive cover for a certain reaching out towards the new. After the Mongols almost every Tsar was aware that Russia needed to 'return', in some sense, to Europe and to catch up, in some ways, with the rest of Europe, but they were never sure how this could be done effectively. There were inevitable misgivings—fears of contamination by the Catholic heretics and the peculiar customs of foreigners, while at the same time trading with them and profiting by their technology. One of the seventeenth-century Tsars used to wash his hands from a golden jug, kept specially for the purpose, every time he had received a foreign ambassador and had so risked contamination.

To assert a proud imperial power alongside the West it was first necessary to 'gather in the Russian lands', and this meant not only the southern and eastern steppes, where Ivan the Terrible had great success against the Tatars, but also the western borderlands which had now been in foreign hands for many centuries. In spite of repeated efforts in war, however, the Baltic remained obstinately closed to Russia by the Swedes, Poles and Germans; Russia could win no access to the Gulf of Finland until the victories of Peter the Great in the early eighteenth century. The West, in this respect, remained the foe, and at times an aggressive one.

Some foreign craftsmen were brought to Moscow: Ivan the Great had an Italian master of the mint, and he commissioned the Italian architect Fioravanti to build two of the palaces which still stand in the Kremlin, in a Russianized adaptation of Renaissance styles. But to open the country to the full influence of the Renaissance was not merely impossible; it was hardly a question that could arise. A few individuals were in contact with and affected by the intellectual searchings of the West; they were naturally regarded as subversive in Moscow. It was even impossible, apparently, to develop something from a promising native base: in some other country Rublyov would have become the initiator of a great, new humanist school of painting, yet after him there were no more ikon painters so original, and it is typical of the conservatism of the Church, and of the very limited support which the arts had in general, that ikon-painting fell back into conventionality, where it has ever since remained. (For a proper school of easel painting Russia had to wait until foreigners were imported in the eighteenth century.)

Ivan the Terrible* got Dutchmen to start up a steelworks and an arms factory, and he was able to attract dozens of craftsmen from abroad, including the English printers who helped to found the first Russian press. Then the enterprising Richard Chancellor, failing to find the North-East Passage, opened up trade between Britain and Muscovy by way of the White Sea and Archangel, and in 1581 the Muscovy Company was founded in London and did very well. Ivan the Terrible kept the power of the Russian state well in view during his dealings with foreigners; he corresponded with Queen Elizabeth as with an equal, and at one time he made overtures for a marriage with her relative, Lady Mary Hastings. In Muscovy itself there was always suspicion: the foreign craftsmen were made to live in a ghetto of their own outside the city walls, and foreign merchants found negotiation as slow and difficult—in spite of the apparent desire for an outcome—as their successors found four centuries later under Stalin.

An English merchant and diplomat, Giles Fletcher, was sent on a trade mission to Moscow by Queen Elizabeth in 1588. He had to endure the usual snubs and procrastinations and, like other English merchants, looked down on the Russians as barely to be accounted Christians, but his short account of the country, entitled *Of the Russe Commonwealth*, is still a valuable portrait, if an imperfect one, of Russia in the reign of Ivan the Terrible.

'The merchants and common people are very much discouraged by many heavy and intolerable exactions, that of late time have been imposed upon them: no man accounting that which he hath to be sure his own ... The late Emperor said his people were like to his beard, the oftener shaven, the thicker it would grow; or like sheep, that needs must be a shorn once a year at least, to keep them from being overladen with their wool ...

'They have no written law, save only a small book that containeth

---

* *Ivan Grozny*, as he is called in Russian, is more correctly rendered in English as 'Ivan the Dread' or 'Ivan the Stern'.

the time and manner of their sitting, order in proceeding, and such other judicial forms and circumstances, but nothing to direct them to give sentence upon right or wrong. Their only law is their Speaking Law, that is, the pleasure of their Prince, and of his magistrates and officers . . .'

(The Russians had lost most of their old folk law under the Tsars, and had to endure an autocratic, centralized legal system until the great reforms of 1864, while the English, at the time of Fletcher's visit, already had four centuries' experience of something like an independent system of justice.)

'For as themselves are very hardly and cruelly dealth withal by their chief Magistrates, and other superiors, so are they cruel one against another, specially over their inferiors, and such as are under them. So that the basest and wretchedest that stoopeth and croucheth like a dogge to the Gentleman, and licketh up the dust that lieth at his feete, is an intolerable tyrant, where he hath the advantage. By this means the whole Countrie is filled with rapine, and murder.'

Fletcher has no more to say, unfortunately, concerning the fundamental matter—the behaviour of the oppressed Russians among themselves as equals. As to the capacities of the people he says:

'Though there appeareth to be in them some aptness to receive any art (as appeareth by the natural wits in the men, and very children), yet they excel in no kind of common art [i.e. craft], much less in any learning, or literal kind of knowledge—which they are kept from of purpose, as they are also from military practice, that they may be the fitter for the servile condition, wherein they now are, and have neither reason nor valour to attempt innovation. For this purpose also they are kept from travelling . . . They might borrow of the Polonians, and other their neighbours, but that they refuse it of a very self pride, *as accounting their owne fashion to be far the best.*'

As a relief for the common people's miseries, Fletcher describes only the state liquor monopoly:

'In every great town of his realm he [i.e. the Tsar] hath a Kabak or drinking house, where is sold aqua vitae, mead, beer, etc. Out of these the Emperor receiveth rent that amounteth to a great sum of money. Some use to lay in twenty, 30, 40 roubles or more into the Kabak and vow themselves to the pot until all be spent. You shall have many there that have drunk all away to the very skin, and so walk naked. While they are in the Kabak none may call them forth whatsoever cause there be, because he hindereth the Emperor's revenue.'

However, though Fletcher seems to have been reliable so far as his observations extended, it does not appear to have occurred to him to wonder why the better-off Russians thought their own ways the best, or to examine the possibility that the battered common people might find some satisfaction or even some pride in being Russian.

In his earlier years on the throne Ivan the Terrible was a responsible Tsar who conquered all the Tatar lands down to the Sea of Azov and the Caspian Sea, and when in 1552, after a great siege assisted by German military engineers, he destroyed the Tatar city of Kazan, there was nation-wide rejoicing. Ivan in thanksgiving ordered the building of St. Basil's Cathedral which still stands in the Red Square. (The Red Square, incidentally, received its name hundreds of years before Communism had been thought of.) There was now no longer any Tatar stronghold within seven hundred miles of Moscow, and the Volga–Caspian route was completely open to trade with the East; a few Russians soon visited India that way. There were new ways for adventurous Russians to escape the growing threat of complete serfdom, and Fletcher describes how. 'You shall have many villages and towns of half a mile and a mile long stand all unhabited, the people being fled all into other places by reason of the extreme usage and exactions done upon them. So that in the way towards Moscow, between Vologda and Yaroslavl, which is little more than an hundred miles English, there are in sight 50 villages at the least that stand vacant and desolate.'

Peasants could often flee as free men to the south, where they formed the first bands of Cossacks in the new lands. They borrowed the Tatar word for a free warrior—*kazak*—as their name, they lived in strongly masculine fraternities under a sort of Robin Hood code, sometimes fighting the Tatars, and sometimes recruiting individual Tatars into their number, rather like American frontiersmen against the Indians. Beginning in 1582, some of the boldest Russians made expeditions into Siberia and colonized it. Surprisingly few in numbers and enduring the severest hardships, they fought their way forward against the scattered population of native Siberians with remarkable speed, faster than the Americans did across their continent. Tobolsk, Omsk, Tomsk, Irkutsk, and even Yakutsk in the far north-east were all founded before 1638, and in that year the first Russians reached the Pacific Ocean. These towns, whose names have become symbols of outlandishness for the West, all retain some little remnant, in their centre, of seventeenth- or eighteenth-century Russian architecture.

For the majority who could not flee, there was still the pride of knowing that the Mongols and Tatars had been cast out—a victory whose glory is not forgotten by Russians today, when they sometimes jealously remind Western peoples that it was they, the 'backward' Russians, and no one else, who saved Europe from the Mongols. But in the sixteenth century, was it any better to be beaten by a Russian cudgel than a Tatar cudgel? The Russian cudgel must often have been wielded, at first, by someone who had helped to put the Tatars to flight. And there was a sort of stoical pride in serving a Tsar who could be so fierce to his enemies—though also, secondarily, to his own people. One of the English merchants in Moscow thought no prince was more feared than Ivan the Terrible, 'yet none better beloved'. Ivan was a sado-masochistic character, murdering his own son in a rage, then kneeling in paroxysms of remorse, contributing to monasteries as well as plundering them, and ordering masses to be sung for the souls of those he had murdered. The Church would have seen to it that the masochistic side was known to Ivan's subjects as well as its opposite.

Even—or perhaps rather especially—in the blackest years, when half the country suffered the excesses of Ivan's murdering, black-hooded Oprichniki, or again in the chaotic years after Ivan's death, the sense of being a member of the true, the chosen, Church supported Russians in their miseries as it did for centuries afterwards. The Church did not always and only preach acceptance; the powerful monastery of St. Sergius (now Zagorsk), the richest in Russia, was the first leader of resistance against the Polish occupation in the shameful year of 1612. And if at other times the Russian Church has been too much inclined to preach the acceptance of suffering, so that one may follow in the footsteps of Jesus Himself, at least it has never much tortured its children with a sense of original sin. In later Russian literature there are some well-known self-torturing characters obsessed with their sins, but what is much more typical of the Russian people as one learns of them through Russian literature in general, and of the Russian people so far as some excellent foreign observers reported on them during the Tsarist period, and of the Russian people so far as I, for one, know them in the Soviet period, is a sense of inner security and rightness which can endure through all misfortunes.

One would like to know a great deal more—but the direct records are too slender—about the sources of Russian peasant optimism, or if optimism be too rosy a word, about the peasant's refusal, throughout history, to be permanently cast down. It is this which has carried the Russian people through tragic sufferings such as only a few other

European nations have endured. It comes partly from the confidence bred by a warm, unpuritanical upbringing as a child, but partly also—socially, one might say—from a sense of personal rightness (rightness rather than righteousness) which was bred by the Russian Church for so long that it has lasted over into the comparatively godless Soviet period, just as the Puritan spirit of self-examination and self-doubt has lasted over, in Britain, from early Protestant times to the comparatively godless period of today.

In the case of the Russians one may also take into account—though this must be more speculative—the sources of their pre-Christian beliefs and attitudes. For the remarkable thing about Russian folklore compared with Germanic folklore is that the gods of the Russian heathens were less anthropomorphic than the Germanic ones, and further, that there is nothing in Russian legend resembling a *Götterdämmerung*—nothing to impose a sense of a fatal hurtling towards doom. There are some figures of horror in Russian folklore, such as the witch Baba-Yaga, deep in the forest, in her hut on cock's feet; if you so much as caught a sight of it, you were doomed to die. But there is not much of a cruel strain. In nature worship there is always an expression of fear, as there was in the old Slavonic Perun, the god of thunder, but nature worship is by no means only the expression of a relationship of fear. Some of the most powerful Slavonic gods were life-givers, such as Mokosh the moist earth-mother, Stribog who sent the winds, and Dazhbog, the sun in his life-giving aspect. (The warriors of Prince Igor were addressed as 'descendants of Dazhbog'.) The old Slavonic religion came from a warmer climate than the old Germanic religion, and if it was not actually introduced by peoples from further east, it was certainly influenced by them. The steppe was benign for most of the year, and it was much more than just a featureless ocean of tall grass. 'So soon as the Snows are departed, which lie but two or three months with them, the Tulips, Roses, Lilies-of-the-Valley, Pinks, Sweet Williams, and several other Flowers and Herbs spring up like A Garden. Asparagus, the best I ever eat, grows so thick that you may in some places mow it down.' (So wrote an English traveller to the virgin steppe in the time of Peter the Great.)

It does not seem altogether fantastic to suggest that some of the residual benignity and hope which the Russians preserved in the northern, colder stage of their history may have filtered through from the old religion. It may be that the warmth of a nature-worship, and of their own communal organization, made it more natural for the Kievan

4

Russians to accept the warmth of the concepts of Christian charity and brotherhood when they were converted—or more likely, perhaps, that it led them to blend the old with the new. Russian peasants kept up many pagan practices well into the twentieth century: the old gods had been overthrown, but the innumerable lesser spirits and sprites of trees and waters were still respected, ancestors were thought of as inhabiting birch trees instead of (or perhaps as well as!) ascending to heaven, and many old pagan rituals less offensive to the Church lived on, in wedding and funeral ceremonies, in superstitions and folksong, till well after the Revolution, and may well survive in out-of-the-way villages today.

One needs to stress this partly Christian, partly animistic basis among the peasants, and the goodness that might arise from it, because there were so many crushing circumstances and so many bad examples tending to brutalize them, and naturally it has much more often been peasant murders, burnings, rapes and rebellions rather than examples of peasant goodness which were reported—at least until literary men began to take an interest in their lives, in the nineteenth century.

I have tried to suggest what kind of people the Russians probably were, after the Mongol occupation, during the century and a half when they were being chained down more and more to the land, until their bondage was made complete in 1649. The savage internal policies of Ivan the Terrible were largely responsible for bringing about an eventually complete serfdom, and the whole situation is so crucial for Russian history that it must be allowed a new chapter.

The Tatars did not all go back to Asia after their big defeats. Some joined other Tatar communities on the fringe of Russia, for example in the Crimea, from which they raided northwards, sometimes as far as Moscow. The Crimea was not conquered by Russia until 1783. And when Tolstoy was a young soldier he was still fighting against other Tatars, as he describes in *The Cossacks*, on the banks of the Terek, which flows into the Caspian Sea.

But still more Tatars joined the Russians and were assimilated rather quickly, some of them being granted land in return for service. The Tsar Boris Godunov, who reigned from 1598 to 1605, was half Tatar, and according to Vernadsky, by the seventeenth century about one-sixth of the noble families of Russia were of Tatar or Oriental origin. The family of the historian Karamzin were of Tatar stock, and the same is true of anyone whose name begins with *Kara*, the Tatar or

Turkish word for 'black' or 'dark'. Today Russians are often rather proud of having a Tatar streak, as many Americans are of having Indian blood. The total percentage of Tatar blood among the Russians is probably small, but it has left a mark in a great many facial types, with flattish features and snub noses, which one would hardly call Asiatic but which are rarely seen in Western Europe. (One pure Tatar is constantly seen in public in Western Europe and America—the dancer Nureyev.) The average Russian today, one could say, is likely to be a Finno-Tataro-Slav, with perhaps a dash of something swarthy from the south, just as the average Englishman is likely to be a Celto-Dano-Saxon or Anglian, with perhaps a dash of French or of something olive-skinned from the pre-Celts.

I have met a good many pure-blooded Tatars in Russia—for there are still large communities of them—and they were all remarkably proud of being Tatar. They had a stocky dignity and quiet independence which are not very Russian, although in features they were usually indistinguishable from Russians. Tatars also have the reputation of being particularly clean in their personal habits. 'When I was a child before the Revolution, on the Volga', an émigré told me, 'my mother would always prefer to buy food at the door from a Tatar rather than a Russian.' But perhaps these characteristics may be a hangover from the time when all Tatars were strict Moslems, rather than anything specifically Tatar.

Collectively the Mongols and Tatars left singularly little mark on Russian cultural habits, apart from the brutalizing effects already mentioned. Only a few Tatar words—but these very significant ones— were adopted into Russian: they include the word for 'toll', the word for 'money' itself, and 'label', from the Tatar word meaning an officially-recognized mark of rank or station.

The word 'horde' has never descended into such generalized use in Russian as it has in English; it still implies a fearsome enemy host. The main street leading south from the Kremlin is still 'Great Horde Street' (*Bolshaya Ordynka*), recalling the days when it was the track for fearful messengers bearing tribute to the Tatars in their tents not far south of the city. The Nazi armies were 'the accursed horde' (*proklyataya orda*) in one of the popular songs of the last war, and when Yevtushenko or some other Soviet poet writes an anti-Chinese poem today he is sure to make some reference back to Mongol hordes. 'But now there are enough of us', writes Yevtushenko, 'to win any number of Kulikovos.'

3. Serfdom, Service and Tyranny

If there is one fact that everybody knows about Russian history, it is that serfdom lasted until well on into the nineteenth century—actually till 1861, when it was abolished by Alexander II, 'the Liberator'. When Turgenev and Gogol, Pushkin and Lermontov were writing, when Glinka was composing, when Russia already had railways and the electric telegraph, and there were grand pianos and all the fripperies of Western Europe for the few well-to-do, and while in Britain popular education and Reform Bills were struggling into life, Russia was still weighed down by the dismally belated, mediaeval institution of serfdom. The effects, or some of the effects, are familiar to every reader of Russian novels. And the hopelessness and despair, the brutality and laziness and petty cheating and thievery, and the all-pervading material backwardness—naturally they did not cease of a sudden, did not undergo some magical metamorphosis, when the church bells rang out to proclaim the Emancipation in 1861. A large number of elderly Russians today—men and women of all ranks in Soviet society—must have had grandparents who were born serfs, and many of them must have had fathers and mothers whose view of the world had scarcely, in some respects, advanced beyond what was characteristic of serf agriculture. To root out the vestiges of such a view of the world, and to haul the nation at top speed out of its backwardness, was of course a major intention of those who made the November Revolution.

One of the reasons why serfdom ended so late in Russia was that it also began so late. Not until the fifteenth and sixteenth centuries did Russia go through the kind of development which in Western Europe had brought about serfdom three or four hundred years earlier.

The basic condition in Russia, as in many other places, was that there were never enough hands to till the land. In the earliest days of Muscovy, say in the fourteenth century, peasants were free to transfer from one lord to another, a richer one for preference, or perhaps to the easier service of a monastery. There were also many free peasants, paying taxes direct to the state. Small landowners found it difficult to get their land cultivated; a powerful princeling would raid the lands of a weaker one and carry off, or more probably entice, his labourers. Men who had been shanghaied might take off again, as they had a right to do, but they could be decoyed, and once decoyed they were in danger of being permanently ensnared. For the peasants were nearly always in debt to that primitive capitalist, their landlord—for the price of their cattle, their plough or other tools, or simply for food to carry them over till the harvest. Contracts could be twisted, the laws concerning debt were extremely severe, there were no courts which were any help to the peasant, and he had no right to seek another master until his debts were paid. Money was hard to earn, and debts could be interpreted in labour days as well as, or instead of, in cash or kind. It was a situation familiar to many peasant countries, but was particularly severe in the hard agricultural conditions of Central Russia with the added burden of the Mongol tribute. A large number of peasants thus drifted into the condition of serfs before serfdom in general was spoken of. As the population increased, there were in some districts more and more landless labourers: some remained bound to the same landlord as their fathers; some went elsewhere and bound themselves as share-croppers; some bound themselves completely to another lord, so destitute were they of any resources but their two hands.

When the lands of the princelings were all merged into Muscovy under a Tsar, and when, after the Mongols departed, Russia was doubled and trebled in size by conquest, the problem of cultivating and defending all this territory became a national affair—that is, it was the affair of the Tsar. The need to provide men for defence, as in other countries, was one of the prime causes of serfdom. The usual solution was for big landowners to supply able-bodied men—that is to say, peasants—and there were already plenty of big landowners in Russia: *boyars*, or nobles. But no Tsar was going to allow his nobles to become so powerful as to menace his own position—which was what happened in France, for instance. Ivan the Great began to create a new class of small landowners, the *pomeshchiki*, by rewarding men who had served him in war with grants of land, including the peasants who lived on it. Ivan the Terrible carried the process a great deal further. He created many more *pomeshchiki*, promoting common soldiers, foreign mercenaries, Tatars, and even slaves (a category who still existed at this period) if they were experienced in war. The *boyars*, with their great manorial estates where they were self-supporting, were becoming an economic as well as a political anachronism because of the nation-wide growth of trade, and Ivan removed them from the responsible official positions which they had held under earlier Tsars. He prevented them from disposing of their own lands and later, in his savage period, he killed off great numbers of them, confiscated their lands, and divided them among the new class; a whole noble house would be destroyed if one of its members was suspected of disloyalty. Ivan the Terrible thus brought about something of the same drastic change in the upper ranks of society as William the Conqueror or Henry VII did in England, but though he was more brutal than the Conqueror, he did not impose serfdom on the peasants as a 'system'. No Russian ruler imposed it as such. Ivan's hand lay as heavy on the peasants as on other classes, and it was partly his oppression which drove whole villages to flight, leaving the strings of uninhabited huts which Giles Fletcher saw. But it was not, in essence, the state's oppression which constituted serfdom.

There were punishments for those who fled, if they could be found and brought back, and for the majority who stayed there was the landlord, progressively encroaching on what liberties remained. The accumulation of the landlords' seizures, privileges, exactions, powers, floggings and fines, as they became the fetters of custom—that was largely what made 'serfdom'.

After Ivan's death, Boris Godunov continued his restrictions of the great nobles, but there was then civil chaos for many years—'The Time of the Troubles'. The most powerful of the remaining *boyars* fought among themselves, and there was even a *boyar* Tsar for a short time. Then followed the disgrace of a Polish invasion and for three years a Pole was Tsar. However, the new Romanov dynasty became established with absolute power after some shaky beginnings, and the class which upheld it, and which drove out the Polish occupiers, was the *pomeshchiki*. They provided the bulk of the armed forces, and the final result, later in the seventeenth century, was exactly what Ivan the Terrible would have wished. Private land, it came to be understood, was held by virtue of service to the Tsar, as a reward for supplying men for defence—against the Poles, the Swedes, the Germans, the Crimean Tatars. No land could be held without an obligation of service; and most service—that is, for the upper classes—was recognized by a grant of land.

But lands were useless without men to till them, and the Tsars wanted to prevent the stealing of labour by one landowner from another. Successive decrees limited the peasant's right to change his landlord even after his debts had been paid, until finally it was made legal for a runaway peasant to be reclaimable by his original lord, not merely one year, or ten years, but for an unlimited period after his departure. At the same time it was of course made illegal for any lord to retain a peasant who had left another master. This was enacted in the Code of 1649, and complete serfdom may be reckoned from that year—the same year, incidentally, that the English executed Charles I for his too rigid attachment to the divine right of monarchy.

Peasant families were now bound to hereditary labour on the land-lord's estate; no peasant could marry without his landlord's permission; serfs might be taken off the land and made into house serfs; the landlord was confirmed by the Code as the absolute master of his serfs. He had the right of judging them for all offences, though not of killing them; however, flogging with the knout often amounted to the same thing. These burdens were not imposed by the Code of 1649: they had grown up during a century or two of usage and were now merely codified. Some of them were not even mentioned in the Code; there was in fact never any complete statement in law of the rights and duties of serfs and their masters.

The distinction between the serf state and a state of slavery was that every serf family, other than the house serfs, had a patch of their own where they could labour when the lord's needs had been satisfied; they could trade, with his permission, in any surplus which they managed to extract from their own land, and they all still shared in the common rights of pasture, wood-cutting, etc., which were allotted by their own commune.

The 'service' landlords or *pomeshchiki* were now the rule; they were responsible to the state for taxes which they had to wring from their land, and they could pass on their land to their heirs, but only on the understanding that it carried with it the same obligation of service. Thus in Russia there was no feudal system as practised in the West, with lesser lords as dependants of great ones. There were no 'vassals of a vassal'; all land was held direct from the Tsar, or one might say from the State, on conditions of service alone.

Some of the land was still worked by small peasants without a master —in Siberia, and in the north of European Russia, because landlords had never been much attracted to these harder regions. Serfdom was also patchy in the Ukraine, when that province returned at last to Russian rule in the 1780s. Catherine the Great rewarded her favourites with huge tracts of land in the south, which meant reducing their inhabitants to serfs, but the Odessa district and its great hinterland, which she conquered from the Turks, was colonized by free men. However, all these 'State peasants' were often spoken of as 'State serfs' because their lot was only marginally easier than that of the manorial serfs or bondmen. They could not change their condition, they were oppressed, like everyone else, by massive State taxes, and their able-bodied young men were liable, just like the able-bodied bondmen, to be dragged off for military service—usually for twenty-five years.

In Central Russia, however, the old Russia, the typical Russia, in all the regions within hundreds of miles of Moscow and over much of the land adjacent to St. Petersburg, serfdom under individual proprietors was the rule, and this is what one reads of in the Russian classics.

The position of the serfs, in so far as it was due to official action, was made worse as time went on. Peter the Great, in his raging search for revenue to sustain his wars and build St. Petersburg, imposed the poll tax in 1718—a head tax on all males, whether in town or country, except for the nobility, the gentry and the clergy. This became the principal direct tax in Russia for the next 170 years, instead of a tax on tilled land. Since most males were serfs, and the serf-owners were made responsible for collection of the poll tax, there was an overwhelming tendency to regard serfs as creatures attached to the lord, as his property, in fact, and not as labourers assigned to the land, which had been the original principle at the base of serfdom. Serfs were now freely bought and sold without land, though at various later times this was supposed to be against the law. They might be sold at an auction, a family being torn apart with its members scattered among various buyers. Sometimes serfs were exchanged for animals, and got their names from the exchange—Sobachy or Sobakin because he was swapped for a dog (*sobaka*), or Svinukhin who was swapped for a pig (*svinya*). Serfs were spoken of as 'souls', and a landlord's wealth was reckoned by the number of 'souls' he possessed rather than the extent of his lands. Chichikov, the chief character of Gogol's great comic novel, *Dead Souls* (1837), tried to make himself a reputation as a rich serf-owner by buying up, from a large number of landlords, their lists of serfs who had died but on whom they were still obliged to pay poll tax until the next census, which was many years ahead.

Peter swept the whole nation, except for the clergy, into his scheme of service—the peasants were tied to the land, the merchants and traders to their trading, and the nobles and gentry, although they escaped the poll tax, to their obligation to enter the state service, either civil or military, with its fourteen grades established by Peter. Everyone

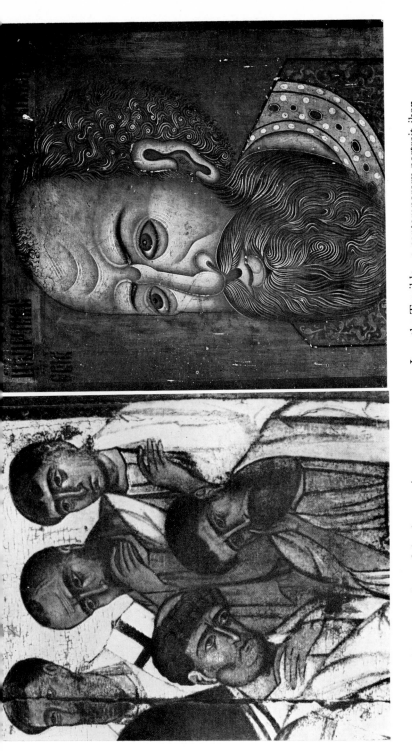

1. From a twelfth-century ikon of the Assumption

2. Ivan the Terrible—a contemporary portrait-ikon (National Museum, Copenhagen)

3. Rostov—the seventeenth-century Kremlin (Novosti)

4. A meeting of the *mir*, about 1800 (John Freeman)

Arrivés bientôt à comprendre toute la justesse de la devise de *Robert-le-Diable*, les seigneurs russes changent leur enjeu et jouent leurs biens en terre, et par suite leurs biens en chair.

5. Russian landowners gambling with serfs, by Gustave Doré, 1854 (John Freeman)

6. The punishment of the 'great knout', 1761 (John Freeman)

was to have his place, and right up to the Revolution all Russians were compulsorily recognized, and entered in their identity papers, as members of one class of society or the other. Not that it was impossible to advance from one class to another, or to be degraded to a lower class. Degradation was a frequent punishment, but on the other hand any educated person could apply to enter the state service, and when he had been promoted to the eighth grade—equivalent to the rank of colonel in the army—he was automatically ennobled, and privileged to own serfs. The length of one's pedigree meant very little. Nobles might find themselves forced by Peter, under severe penalties, into unpleasant tasks such as starting up a new mineral enterprise in some inhospitable part of the Urals, while army officers were supposed to pass an examination or be condemned to serve in the ranks. But after Peter's death, though the fourteen grades remained, the serf-owners found the general obligation of service too irksome by far, and they began to default. In 1762 they took advantage of the feeble Peter III and forced him to rescind it by decree. Peter III reigned only a few months before he was murdered (with the connivance of his long-suffering wife, who became the Empress Catherine the Great), but compulsory service for nobles and gentry was never restored. They had slipped out of the national plan. The serfs knew only too well that their position was at the bottom of the pile, but it was at least a recognized position, and when they heard that nobles were no longer bound to serve, they at first rejoiced, thinking that the decree must be but a prelude to the abolition of their own obligations. Rumours of emancipation went round, and after his death, Peter III was for a long time more honoured than 'the German woman' who succeeded him; she had only been on the throne three years when she added to the serfs' burdens by empowering the masters to send them, by way of punishment, to forced labour in Siberia.

From the Code of 1649 to the Emancipation of 1861 was only 212 years, and long before 1861 enlightened Russians were agitating for the abolition of serfdom; even Catherine the Great, inspired by liberal ideas from France, considered abolition, but the outbreak of the French Revolution frightened her into a completely reactionary attitude. When in 1790 one of her civil servants, Alexander Radishchev, wrote an exposure of the worst abuses of serfdom, calling for its abolition, and implicitly attacking her authority, she wrote ten pages of acid annotations on his book, *A Journey from St. Petersburg to Moscow*, and had him sentenced to death, though this was later commuted to exile in Siberia.

In 1812, under Alexander I, there was a public competition for essays about serfdom, and though the prizewinners all favoured abolition, no one got into trouble. But Alexander fell away from his early liberal ideas, ignored the proposals of his best minister, and did nothing to forward emancipation. In 1825 there was the first Russian conspiracy ever to aim at political reform—the 'Decembrist' conspiracy of officers and noblemen influenced by Western ideas, who sought not only the abolition of serfdom but also a liberal constitution. They had little support and were easily suppressed by Nicholas I, the 'Tsar Gendarme' who made Russia into a police state. Yet even he sometimes discussed the possibility of emancipation, though he did not see how it could be done without endangering the government. It was finally left to his enlightened son, Alexander II, to use his autocratic power to force liberation on the landlords.

But meanwhile what of the miserable peasants themselves? Their reactions to serfdom are clearly crucial to the whole ancestry of the Russian people, for to say 'peasants' is as good as to say 'Russian people'; at the census of 1783, for example, they constituted 94·5 per cent of the population. They had had to become accustomed to serfdom by degrees, and as something inevitable, but they never lost the feeling that the land ought to belong to those who tilled it. 'We are yours', they said to the masters on several historic occasions, 'but the land is ours.' It was the brutality of individual masters, rather than the general principle of mastership, which generated hate. There must have been thousands of acts of revenge similar to the killing of Dostoevsky's father, who was found tipped out of his carriage by the roadside, with his skull smashed in and his testicles crushed by a stone. During the nineteenth century, in many years, several hundred manor-houses were burnt and their masters murdered—outbreaks of wild resentment by men at the end of their endurance. There were also, during the period of serfdom, four peasant revolts amounting to minor civil wars. They all arose in the south-east frontier region and were led by Cossacks, sometimes joined by Tatars and other non-Russians in revenge at their oppression by the Russians. These were the rebellions of Bolotnikov (1606–7), of Stenka Razin (1670–71) (still celebrated in song), of Bulavin (1707–8), and most threatening of all, in 1773–5, of Pugachev, whom it took one of Catherine's best generals with large forces to subdue. The aim of the rebellions was always the same—'to kill the landowners and take the land', but they all stopped short of rebellion against the Tsar. Pugachev, in fact, gave out that he was the Tsar Peter III, whose death, he said, had been falsely reported; he was now returning to depose Catherine the Great.

Yet all these revolts were comparatively unorganized, they had no political programme, and they were unable to get much support from serfs in the heart of Russia. The typical Russian serf lived far from the 'frontier', there seemed little advantage for him in escape, and his Church had always preached submission, quoting in support St. Paul in *Romans* xiii: 'Let every soul be subject unto the highest powers. For there is no power but of God. The powers that be, are ordained of God. Whosoever resisteth the power, resisteth the ordinance of God, and they that resist shall receive to themselves damnation.' The 'higher powers' with whom the serf had to reckon were, of course, powers whose position was maintained by superior physical force—the police and the armies of the Tsar. Also, the Russian family, in all classes of society, was a strongly paternalistic one, and this, combined with the centuries of inescapable submission under serfdom, must have a good deal to do with that typical Russian character-pattern, described by Russian and foreign observers alike, at all periods—the pattern shown in very long spells of uncomplaining endurance and acquiescence, breaking out only at long intervals, and in extreme circumstances, into brief orgies of uncontrollable violence and rage.

However, it would be inadequate to describe serfdom entirely in stark terms of submissive masses and dominant masters. When one thinks of serfdom nowadays one is bound to think first of the inhumanity of the condition—the brutalities and the degradation involved in serf status, and the perverting of the masters as human beings, through the absolute power that in theory they enjoyed. Brutalities indeed there were, and naturally enough it was these which were remembered and reported—the frequent floggings, which visitors were sometimes invited to witness as an entertainment, or the seduction of serf maidens, or forced marriages between serfs, or such amusements as the putting of serfs into leather collars, coupled together on all fours like dogs, for a drunken lark. Yet such incidents were not so usual nor typical. The master was certain now of the services of his serfs, and he needed good service from them. It was common sense to treat them tolerably, and in any case, Russian good nature and easygoing slatternliness were just about as likely to be found among masters, at least at intervals, as among peasants. The gulf of status was shameful but it was not an apartheid: masters and serfs all attended the same church on Sundays; they all sat on the same outdoor benches, if there were any benches;

and even if he usually gave the master more attention, they all used the services of the same priest.

There were monsters and misers among the masters, who worked their serfs six or even seven days a week, instead of two or three, but there is also plenty of evidence of the warm and intimate relationships which could grow up between members of the two classes in the lopsided world of serf-owning Russia. Robert Pinkerton, who worked for the British and Foreign Bible Society in the early nineteenth century, described what happened when Prince Volkhonsky died in Moscow in 1803. A delegation of no less than two hundred serfs came from his village, which was near Moscow, saying: 'We have come to take farewell of our father and to carry his body to the grave.' When it was pointed out to them that the Prince was to be buried at his other estate at Barovsk, ninety versts away on the far side of Moscow, they made no difficulty; they insisted on carrying the coffin to Barovsk in relays of two versts (a mile and a quarter) at a time, as though it would not have been proper for his funeral to have been served in any other way. And the Prince was not even an old man; he was only forty-six when he died. This kind of relationship can hardly be ascribed solely to the softening of general manners among many members of the upper classes throughout the eighteenth century: it is obviously rooted in something primitive and ancient.

Prince Volkhonsky was probably a man of good will, but we do not need to imagine that he was an exceptionally liberal-minded landlord, who never, for instance, had his serfs flogged. The fact was, as foreign visitors pointed out, that while under serfdom house servants could not give in their notice, they also could not be dismissed, so that for male serfs flogging seemed to be the only ordinary sanction that could be applied. Both masters and men were caught in the degradation imposed by the system, and flogging, of course, had been regarded as a normal punishment since the Mongol conquest. It was better, at least, than being sent for a soldier.

William Tooke, an economist who was both a Fellow of the Royal Society and a member of the Russian Imperial Academy of Sciences, published his large and solid *View of the Russian Empire* in 1799. Some lords, he acknowledged, oppressed their vassals, but a great part of the ordinary population, it seemed to him, 'live happily, grow rich, and would hardly be persuaded to change their condition for what passes under the name of freedom'. About the same time the lively Irish sisters, Martha and Catherine Wilmot, were guests of Princess Dashkov for five years at Troitskoye near Moscow. In their voluminous letters home they described 'the peasants outside the window in white trousers and shirt with scarlet embroidery', and said that 'those who imagine the Russian peasantry sunk in sloth and misery imagine a strange falsehood'. The sisters wished, in fact, that the peasants in their native Ireland were 'half as well fed and clothed'. In general they thought it was in the master's interest to treat his peasants or house serfs well. As to the government of Russia, on the other hand, they came to look on 'every Noble as an iron link in the massy chain that manacles this Realm'.

Troitskoye was a prosperous estate, and there were many like it; since public entertainment was out of reach in the country districts, some proprietors even had their own theatres and orchestras and trained promising serfs as actors or musicians. On the whole the life of the house serfs seems in many, or perhaps in most, households to have been little worse than that of domestic servants in Victorian England; in respect of human relations it may often have been warmer, in spite of kicks when the master was out of temper and prostrations when he came home. In the untidy Russian way, there were always too many house serfs rather than too few, few Russian houses were obsessively tidy, some serf maids were taught fine stitching or hairdressing, while others did the heavy work, and almost every well-born Russian who has written about his childhood during the period of serfdom has spoken with affection of the serf nannies who brought up the children and spoiled them. Pushkin's old nurse, a freed serf, was the only affectionate figure in his childhood, and the folk tales she told him are immortalized in his narrative poem, *Ruslan and Ludmila*.

In a district with good land some of the farming serfs did so well that they could offer to buy their freedom—an offer which proprietors, often in debt, did not always refuse. Another way of achieving freedom was to get oneself somehow recruited for the growing industrial enterprises—the mines and ironworks, for instance, which made Russia at the end of the eighteenth century the greatest producer of pig-iron in Europe. A few landowners, such as the Stroganovs, ran their own industrial enterprises, but far more of these were organized by the State. The courts, of course, were supposed to reclaim runaway serfs, but one wonders what use they may have been to a poor or middle-rank proprietor, when one of his strong young serfs turned up 500 miles away and offered himself to a mine or factory which was always looking for more hands.

Most proprietors were not enterprising, and few of them learned much about agriculture. They were too easy-going or too idle, and in any case they did not have the capital to develop their land. They could rarely dispose of any part of their lands, which were more than likely to be mortgaged already. It was only in the most favourable natural conditions—growing wheat, for instance, on the giant farms in the newly-opened south—that the land could be made to yield more than a modest living when taxes had been paid.

The methodical German landowner, August von Haxthausen, who visited Russia in 1843-4 and wrote a classic account of the country, calculated that in the province of Yaroslavl he would need seven men and seven horses to work an area of land which, in the valley of the Main in Germany, or in France near Orleans, could be worked with four men and four horses. And the Russian estate would bring him in only 2,600 thalers, against the 5,000 which he would expect from German or French soil. The harvest yield in this central Russian province, he said, was only three times the amount of grain sown, whereas on the Main he could raise six or seven times as much.

The Russian proprietors suffered, too, just as the peasants did, from 'the population problem'. They had no custom of primogeniture, so that younger sons, instead of ambitiously going out to seek their fortune in the world, like English younger sons, received a fraction of an ever-diminishing estate. In Catherine's time about a third of the land-owners had less than ten serfs apiece, and by the mid-nineteenth century many were little better off than their serfs. Some of them turned into misers, hoarding mouldy grain, starving their servants, and entertaining the rare guest with a piece of hard, ancient cake, kept in a locked cupboard in case any of the house serfs should be tempted by such a delicacy. (*The Golovlyov Family*, Saltykov's novel which describes such an estate, is perhaps the most terrible picture of human avarice ever written.) But more of the impoverished landlords, probably, sank into listlessness, letting the serfs manage as best they could, getting drunk occasionally with the house serfs for want of other company, and living in villages where one has the impression of a civilization whose prevailing colour was that of dishwater—the pale weathered brown of unpainted log huts and the unpainted manor-house, the watery-brown soup, the coarse buckwheat porridge, and the mud that got into everything for half the year.

As the eighteenth century wore on, more and more of the serfs were able to commute their forced labour obligations into money payments (*obrok*)—a form of serfdom which some had always enjoyed, though rarely in the rich lands of the south, where the proprietors needed all the hands they could get and worked them to the limit. Those who paid *obrok* were still legally bound as serfs, but what this might mean depended upon the individual proprietor. Some peasants earned money by handicrafts, and some kinds of goods became almost a monopoly of certain groups of villages; for example, cutlery and samovars in the Tula district. This craft production was an important element in the as yet very limited industry of Russia. A few serfs even became employers of labour, but it was much more usual—and more Russian —for craftsmen to work as a co-operative.

By Turgenev's time, a good deal of Russian serfdom was beginning to drift, rather as French serfdom did before the French Revolution, into something more petty bourgeois. Comparatively few serfs actually became independent proprietors, which was what happened in France, but Turgenev's first published work, *A Sportsman's Sketches* (1847–52), gives us a great variety of pictures of serf life: an estate in the hands of its serf bailiff, who cheated all the neighbouring proprietors as well as his own master; Fedosya, the serf who made a good living as a dress-maker in Moscow, paying her mistress in the country 'a quitrent of $182\frac{1}{2}$ roubles a year'; Ovsyanikov, the peasant proprietor who 'did not attempt to pass for a nobleman, did not affect to be a landowner . . . did not take a seat at the first invitation to do so', etc.; the young gentleman, Karatayev, who tried in vain to buy the pretty serf Matryona and even-tually eloped with her, because he loved her; and Arina, a serf girl trained as a lady's maid, who was twice refused permission to marry the footman and then, when she became pregnant—'I gave orders, of course,' said her master, 'that her hair should be cut off, she should be dressed in sackcloth, and sent into the country . . . the ingratitude of this girl!' But in the country, even with her hair cut off, and pregnant, Arina attracted the local miller, and he, being comparatively well off, bought her freedom and married her.

Socially, one might say, the Russians managed to make of serfdom a viable way of life on the whole, although a poor one. At least it did not turn the masters into a perfumed, nose-in-the-air, aristocratic class. There never was such a class in Russia except for a limited circle round the court; the other landowners simply did not have the money. Radishchev, writing in the 1780s, said that 'boasting of one's ancient lineage' was 'an evil eradicated from Russia', eradicated, he meant, through the rise of so many new men and through Peter the Great's

Table of Service Ranks. Early in the twentieth century that excellent observer, Maurice Baring, wrote that he could find no feeling of aristocratic class-consciousness among the Russian nobility, as compared with the landed families in Britain. But this also meant there was less of a tradition of 'noblesse oblige'; the better landowners, apart from a few who were very Westernized, would act more from general good nature and the brotherliness of true believers, rather than from a sense of individual responsibility—that quality which Russians have so typically found difficult to cultivate.

And if, humanly speaking, the Russian character was able so often to bridge the gap between the classes, it could do very little about the cultural gulf—in the widest and most primitive meanings of the word —between the privileged few and the majority who had to get a living from the soil; a gulf which yawned all the wider after the Westernizations of Peter the Great and the Empress Elizabeth and the frenchifying of Catherine the Great, for these affected the peasants not at all. Haxthausen, in 1843, admired the peasants' winter work—the carving of wooden objects, the making of sandals, the extracting of turpentine and pitch—and thought them 'fit for any kind of craft or industry'. But he commented sadly that there was 'a great gulf between the upper class and the people'. It was resentment at the cultural division of the nation, as well as resentment at the division between a rich minority and the masses of the poor, which in the end provided most of the driving force towards revolution. There were many among the educated class who foresaw that result more than a century before 1917.

Serfdom was a pitifully inefficient and unproductive basis for agriculture, which was Russia's major occupation; it absorbed—or rather it sapped—the energies and talents of more than 95 per cent of the population. The inefficiency, and the inequity, were obvious if anyone thought about them, but the impossibility of doing anything about them seemed equally obvious to all (apart from a few very exceptional men), so that serfdom encouraged, in both classes, in landowners and in peasants, the greatest of Russian vices—the slackness, idleness, lack of initiative, hopelessness, and all that is included under the name of *accidie*—all that foreigners have come to condemn in the Russian character under the catchword *nichevo*. The first native writer on agricultural reform, Pososhkov (1652–1726), took it for granted that the peasants were idle, and sixty years later Radishchev wrote: 'The field is not their own, the fruit thereof does not belong to them. Hence they cultivate the land lazily and do not care whether it goes to waste because of their poor work.' Oblomov, in Goncharov's novel, the man who never did anything, but lay on his bed in Petersburg and vaguely hoped for a remittance from his estate where the peasants were behind with their rent, and some of them were running away, and the police were too lazy to fetch them back—Oblomov is only the most extreme case, or one might say the most wholehearted case, of this typical Russian disease.

After the Emancipation a great many peasants had to continue working for a landlord and, as might be expected, they did not change their attitude to work very much, as Tolstoy found when he tried to improve his own estate. Speaking in the character of Levin, who closely represents himself, Tolstoy in *Anna Karenina* says: 'What the labourer wanted was to take it as easy as possible, with rests, and, especially, not to have the trouble of worrying and thinking.' The peasants spoiled Levin's new machines with clumsy, lazy handling, they carelessly mowed clover for hay when the field was wanted for seed, they let the horses stray into the wheat, and so on. And all this slackness floated on a sea of general good nature; it was 'not because anyone wished ill to Levin or his farm; on the contrary, he knew that they liked him and considered him a homely gentleman (the highest praise they could bestow)'.

In the nineteenth century, both before and after the Emancipation, and all through the twentieth century, foreign visitors have repeatedly been charmed, captivated, even spellbound by Russian good nature and the Russian capacity for warm human relations which has always helped to make life more bearable within the meshes of the crude governmental machine. The German, J. G. Kohl, travelling in the 1830s, wrote: 'At the first glance there is certainly something extremely repulsive in the Russian muzhik. His hair is long and shaggy, and so is his beard; his person is dirty; he is always noisy; and when wrapped up in his sheepskin, he certainly presents a figure more suitable for a bandit or murderer than for a man devoted to peaceable occupations. This apparent rudeness, however, is less a part of the man himself, than of his hair and beard, of his shaggy sheepskin, and the loud tone of his voice. The stranger who is able to address him with kindness in his native language soon discovers in the muzhik a good-humoured, friendly, harmless and serviceable creature—"Zdravstvuitye, brat! Good day, brother, how goes it?"—"Zdravstvuitye, batyushka! Good day, father; thank God, it goes well with me. What is your pleasure? How can I serve you?" '

'Englishmen', says Kohl, 'are too apt to attribute the courtesy of the

5

Russian to a slavish disposition, but the courteous manner in which two Russian peasants are sure to salute each other when they meet cannot be the result of fear engendered by social tyranny. On the contrary, a spirit of genuine politeness pervades all classes, the highest as well as the lowest.'

Kohl's fellow-countryman Haxthausen, in the 1840s, spoke of 'the absence of all warlike tendencies among the Russian people', and a British Member of Parliament, H. D. Seymour, wrote of them in 1855 as 'the most pacific people on the face of the earth; upon this point I believe no difference of opinion exists among all observers ... Even in their quarrels among themselves, which are rare, they hardly ever fight, and the duel is a custom imported ... They take no pleasure in the fighting of beasts or birds ... When the Russian is drunk, which often happens, he is never quarrelsome, but on the contrary caressing and given to tears. But on being aroused, he exhibits a degree of patient endurance which is astonishing, and a steady enthusiasm which shows great power of feeling, and which is very deeply rooted in the national character.'

Maurice Baring, in 1911, found the Russians the same when in drink, and also wrote: 'In my experience of the Russian peasantry I have never witnessed on their part any single example of brutality; whereas I have come across hundreds of instances of their good nature and their kindness ... The peasant learns to suffer, and therefore to sympathise with suffering; he learns to bear suffering with stoicism, and therefore to inflict it with insensibility when the occasion arises.' (*The Russian People.*)

Finally, in the present period, when two-thirds of the Russian people are no longer peasants, the Russian character has continued to enchant many long-term visitors in spite of the difficulties, monotonies and intermittent barbarities of Soviet life. 'As anyone who has lived among Russians can testify, probably their most charming quality as a people is the wonderful simplicity and sincerity of their relationships with one another. The young élite is no exception in this respect.' (An American student at Moscow University, Peter Taylor, in the magazine *Survey*, 1964.)

In a later chapter I want to discuss the Russian character more fully; I have gathered these quotations here in order to emphasize the deep-lying pacific and co-operative strain in Russians, and to stress that this is not, I am convinced, primarily due to the effects of serfdom. The earliest accounts by foreigners such as Giles Fletcher, in the sixteenth and seventeenth centuries, stress the barbarity of the Russian people, but it seems to me that these travellers may only have seen the shaggy exterior. The earlier Russians who mingled peaceably with the Finnish peoples, who accepted so easily the dominance of small bands of Scandinavians and then assimilated them, and who among themselves had the institution of the *veche* with its primitive unanimity—these seem to be the recognizable ancestors of the peaceable Russians whom many nineteenth-century visitors found so sympathetic.

These were the typical Russians who developed, no one quite knows when, though it must have been early in their history, the remarkable institution of the *mir*, or village commune. The early Russians did not farm in common, with the fruits shared among all members as in a kibbutz. The Russians have never had that sort of communism, but at an early date they had communal arrangements for pasture, water, the use of woodland, fishing, bee-keeping, and so on. When the villagers became tied by serfdom to a fixed area of agricultural land for their own use, they seem to have assumed, over most of Russia, that this land was owned by the commune. (They may have taken this view of the land, in some parts, before they became serfs, but the early records are too scanty to provide evidence of this.) The crucial point is that, in order to make sure that every household had a fair share, the commune distributed the land in strips—one for each male in the household—so that one family's share might consist, for instance, of one-quarter fertile land, one-quarter sandy, one-quarter middling land at an inconvenient distance from the village, and one-quarter middling land near the village. As the family grew or decreased in numbers of males there would be a redistribution of strips, but also, after a minimum of three years—since the land was farmed on a three-year rotation of crops and fallow—there might be a general redistribution for the whole village, to re-ensure fair shares all round. The frequent change of ownership did not make for the best agriculture, but the peasants were more concerned about justice among themselves. They practised redistribution, with minor variations, whether they were state serfs or manorial serfs. At first a local custom, redistribution became universal soon after 1718; it was the peasants' answer to Peter the Great's poll tax. If the households were to be taxed according to the number of males, the *mir* saw that they had equitable shares of land, by tilling which they could make enough to pay the tax.

All the strips were open, unfenced land, so that times for ploughing, sowing, harvesting and so forth had to be agreed by the commune.

Decisions about these were taken by the village meeting, also often called the *mir*. And it was this meeting which fixed the distributions of land, settled disputes, and decided on the communal use of pasture, woodland, etc. The peasants gathered in the open air, there being nowhere else for them to meet, the proceedings were extremely informal, and unanimity was the rule just as it had been in the *veche*. If, occasionally, a vote had to be taken, the minority always accepted the verdict of the majority. An elder, or *starosta*, led the meeting when it needed a leader, but no one, it is said, was anxious to be elder, though once he had been chosen he was obeyed by all. Usually he proceeded by 'getting the feel of the meeting' rather than by imposing himself. The commune became universally recognized as the proper channel for dealing with the peasants, and the government later made it responsible for collecting the taxes, and even gave it power to send an erring member to Siberia.

The unconscious or semi-conscious feeling of unity in the *mir* impressed the nineteenth-century intelligentsia deeply when they began to study the peasants: some of them expressed a mystical admiration for it as a God-given contrast to the individualism and competitiveness of Western Europe, while Herzen and many other reformers saw it as an institution which might lead Russia straight to socialism without having to pass through the reprehensible bourgeois stage. (Lenin, incidentally, had other views.)

The *mir* continued after the Emancipation right up to 1917, in most places, and in many places until the collectivization of 1930. After they had been freed, the peasants were left to run the villages themselves, and in fact, no one but a peasant was able to take a share in governing a village, since membership of the *mir* was hereditary. This did not help to advance agriculture much; it also sometimes meant that the government of a village might be divided among three different *mirs*, where the land had originally been the property of three different serf-owners.

Few institutions illustrate better than the *mir* the gulf between West European tradition and Russian tradition. In the West, it has been a universal maxim that no one can be kept in co-proprietorship against his will, or to quote Maine's *Ancient Law*: '*Nemo in communione potest invitus deteneri.*' But in Russia co-proprietorship was what everyone wanted—at least until the late nineteenth century, when a minority began to break away. 'The Russian cannot imagine life outside his society, outside the *mir*,' wrote the progressive L. A. Tikhomirov in

1886. The *mir* is the ancestral Russian form of democracy, and Tikhomirov goes on: 'To a Russian, the profound respect of the English working-man for the gentleman is an almost incomprehensible sentiment. Even serfdom could not destroy the sentiment of democratic equality among the people. Of course, it could not be without influence on the peasant's character. But despite all this, he has not turned slave. Our serfdom to its very end was rather a colossal abuse by the nobility and the Government than a well-established social order. The peasants were always convinced that serfdom was a transitory institution, and obstinately went on believing that the lands of the nobility belong to those who work on them. In a word, the spirit of the people was not cowed. The sentiment of liberty became dulled; the feeling of human dignity less acute, but on the other hand the very yoke of their common slavery gave the peasants new reasons for closing up their ranks, and attached them to their *mir* by a closer tie. For the *mir* was the only institution in which they found they were men. The history of serfdom reveals to us miracles of self-abnegation on the part of the peasants for the sake of the *mir*.' (*Russia, Political and Social.*)

I have skipped from end to end of a period of three hundred years or so in this chapter, because the material condition of the masses of the Russian people under serfdom was very little different in the nineteenth century from what it had been in the sixteenth. The old rhyme—*Shchi i kasha—pishcha nasha* ('Cabbage soup and buckwheat porridge are our food') was as true in the early twentieth century, in fact, as in the sixteenth. Black bread was eaten, of course, in quantities, and the occasional onion, and honey, wild berries and mushrooms in season. Foreign observers thought this diet seemed to make a strong and healthy people, if only they would lay off the vodka. But the monotony of the diet was typical of the general monotony of peasant lives—in one-room log huts widely spaced along the very broad dirt road of the village (as they still are today), and inside the huts some of the animals sleeping with the peasants, who often had only benches instead of beds, and for other possessions only a few pots and wooden bowls and spoons and an ikon. When I first saw Soviet Russia there were still plenty of huts like these, except that the animals had been kicked out or no longer existed, the clothes and bowls were no longer home-made, and a few books and an alarm clock might have been added to the household goods.

Let there be no doubt that the peasants resented serfdom. It has sometimes been said by outsiders that serfdom and Tsardom were the inevitable price which had to be paid for liberation from the Mongols. Tsardom was almost certainly inevitable, but serfdom would surely have arrived without any Mongol conquest, just as it would have arrived in England if there had been no Norman conquest. Russia would have been a quite extraordinary exception among European countries if she had not endured serfdom. Even in Denmark the serfs were not freed until 1788, and further east, Prussia and Austria consolidated their serf system as late as Russia did, and got rid of it not very much earlier. But the difference in Prussia and Austria was that, in spite of autocracy, there was some circulation of liberal ideas, the landlords were not so all-powerful as in Russia, and there was a sizeable middle class which began to make these countries rich, as well as better managed, while Russia remained overwhelmingly poor. If Kievan Russia could have continued, there would have been a prosperous and surely talented middle class, who would have made Russia a very different place, but actually there was so little capital in Tsarist Russia to finance trade and industry that the State became the chief entrepreneur. As late as the 1840s, Haxthausen found that if a landowner wanted a private loan to develop his estate, the prevailing rate of interest was between $1\frac{1}{4}$ per cent and 2 per cent *per month*.

Although the Tsars did not create serfdom in Russia, the country was so huge, and the landowners so many, that the Tsars had to reinforce serfdom as an institution in order to maintain the pyramid of centralized power. Russia was a land power, the upper class were either in State service or tied to the land—very often both—and the major source of revenue could only come, ultimately, from the labour of the peasants, that is, from the serfs.

Some advances indeed were made under eighteenth-century serfdom: to pick a few examples, the production of pig-iron increased ten times; the British Navy came to depend heavily upon Russian hemp, tar and ropes; petroleum was got from Baku for the first time; merino sheep and some foreign bloodstock were introduced; the Academy of Sciences was founded; a serf called Polzunov built a steam engine in 1763; and the self-taught genius Lomonosov, son of a poor northern fisherman, made important discoveries in physics and chemistry (as well as tidying up the Russian language). But nothing was made of the inventions and discoveries, and although foreign trade grew, there was not an urban population of any great size. In the first half of the nineteenth century the towns contained no more than between 5 per cent and 9 per cent of the population, as to whether one counted the serf labourers who went home to their villages every year, or only those who were permanently employed in town.

And yet, if serfdom was never accepted, Tsardom, from the fifteenth century onwards, was. The peasants rebelled repeatedly against the landlords but never against their 'little father' (*batyushka*) the Tsar. Except for that tiny group, the intelligentsia, which began to appear for the first time towards the end of the eighteenth century, there was a steadfast loyalty to the Tsar's person among all classes, which only began to wear thin at the very end of the nineteenth century. The Tsar was the nation's landlord and the personification of the nation, he was the leader of the true faith, he was *samoderzhets*—'the man ruling by himself', a tyrant, at times a benevolent one, at times a monster, but always accepted unless he interfered too much with old customs as Peter the Great did—and then the rumour went round that the man on the throne must be an impostor and not the true Tsar.

So there was the comfortable matiness of the *mir* at one end of the scale, and the absolutism of the Tsar at the other. There was not a great deal in between, and therein lies the sad and halting story of government in Russia.

4. How Can an Autocrat Govern?

'Rule, in the name of God, for me!' said Peter the Great to his Senate. He asked nothing better than that they should take responsibility. They were not, of course, elected Senators; they were all nominated by Peter—nine of them at first—and they were to be the highest authority under the Tsar, to control the whole administration. During his repeated absences with his armies, they were to govern with almost plenipotentiary powers—'and if you do not do this conscientiously, you will answer to God, and will not escape justice here below'.

The Senators, like other officials, were indeed made answerable by Peter; if a member of the Senate failed to turn up, or was responsible for a stupid decision, Peter might fine him or beat him with his own hands. (He even laid about his great favourite, Menshikov, with a cudgel, on occasion.) But Peter could not stand over his Senate continuously, and he appointed first an Inspector-General, and then a Procurator-General, to keep them hard at work, chair their meetings, and punish them on his behalf when required.

Yet even if this arrangement worked satisfactorily—and who could be certain that a Procurator-General should be all-wise?—the administration below the senatorial level was infinitely less reliable. Everyone expected it to be corrupt, because salaries were so low, and most officials were also lazy, or when they did undertake anything they were finicky and procrastinating. Peter, for all his colossal energy, was trapped by the insoluble problems of the autocrat—how is he to be certain that orders are being carried out? How is he to be sure that necessary matters are brought to his attention? How is he to avoid being burdened with trivial decisions? Peter's admiring (and admirable) contemporary Pososhkov wrote in 1724: 'Nowhere has the Tsar got an honest counsellor . . . The Tsar pulls uphill alone with the strength of ten, but millions pull downhill.' If Peter could have had a few thousand more of the right men, his administration might have worked honestly; there were honest men, apparently, to be had, but who could be trusted to choose them? So corruption and laziness and timidity clogged the works and made many of Peter's reforms a deadletter. After eleven years of existence the Senate had a backlog of '16,000 unresolved problems'.

Universal loyalty to the Tsar did not mean loyalty to his officers, nor even loyalty to all his decrees. Noblemen who were mobilized for the army would quietly disappear for a while, taxable possessions would be mysteriously concealed, and as for the tax-collectors themselves, according to a German diplomat stationed in St. Petersburg they looked on their duties as 'merely opportunities to suck the marrow from the peasants' bones'.

Peter was aware of all these kinds of abuses; he appointed a sort of Ombudsman to receive complaints, and he rewarded informers handsomely, sometimes promising them the whole estate of the person informed against. But how safe was it to inform? An English civil engineer, John Perry (the man who ate the wild asparagus in the steppe), wrote after serving Peter for fourteen years that 'The common Boors or Peasants who have been sent upon the Works under my Command have complained to me with Tears of Wrongs and Injuries that have been done them by the Governors of Towns, and the officers in the Districts under the Governors. And when I have offered to represent the Injustice done them to the present Admiral Apraxin (who had then the Command of that Province) and have promised them that I would do my utmost and engage to obtain Right for them, they have thereupon earnestly begged me by no means to mention the things which they have complained of, alleging this for their Reason, that even tho' they should obtain Right at that Time, yet that they were sure afterwards to suffer, and to be ruined for complaining of those in Power over them, who would mark them out as informers.'

Running the administration of a huge country was nothing like so easy as building St. Petersburg in the Baltic marshes. The building of the city, it is true, was very badly organized, and thousands died of dysentery or cold, but Peter himself was on the spot a great deal of the time, making his own drawings, probably hewing and heaving stone sometimes, urging men on, and all from no grander headquarters than a modest wooden hut (still preserved in modern Leningrad). This was the towering six-feet-seven Peter, proud of his calloused hands and his huge appetite for food and strong drink, who fought the Swedes for twenty-one years, cleared them off the whole Gulf of Finland, defeated the Turks, gave Russia a standing army and navy, started up ironworks, and got rid of the Patriarch so that the Church was for ever after subordinate to the State; this was the Peter who was always striding at a great pace, dressed as a soldier, a workman, or a sailor, the Peter who cut off his courtiers' old-fashioned beards and shortened their sloppy gowns with his shears, who learned shipbuilding in Holland and in England, through the offices of William III, at Deptford Dockyard, who made furniture, pulled teeth, practised engraving, collected pictures, recruited thousands of foreign craftsmen, reformed the Russian alphabet and calendar, who wrestled, played the fool or got drunk with his own soldiers.

During his own lifetime he became a legend, admired and adored by thousands who worked or served with him, but balefully regarded by many of the faithful as Antichrist, not least on account of his impious habit of smoking tobacco. Today in Soviet Russia he is still a legend—historically speaking, for having dragged Russia into so many Western ways, and personally as a sort of Paul Bunyan among Tsars: my sleeping-car conductor, the last time I travelled to Moscow, insisted that the broad Russian railway gauge is due to Peter the Great (who died, incidentally, 126 years before the first railway was built in Russia!). Of course the Russian gauge must be wider than the European—wider, runs the story, by the length of Peter's redoubtable sex organ!

For all this universal energy, however, Peter was better at dealing with individual practical problems—of military tactics, carpentry, industry—than he was at comprehensive or general schemes; his instructions to subordinates were so simply expressed that they were often difficult to interpret. But towards the end of his reign, when the country was groaning under hydra-headed taxation, when the armed forces were costing five times what they had when he came to the throne, and when he had had some success in encouraging basic industries to support them, he realized that new administrative institutions and new men were needed. He studied the Swedish and German systems (he never ceased from studying foreign practice), and on the Swedish model he set up ten 'Colleges' or ministerial departments, to deal with Foreign Relations, Revenue, Justice, Financial Control, the Army, the Navy, Commerce, Mining, Manufactures and Estates. Each College was run by a board of eleven members, with a Russian president, *and a foreign vice-president.* Peter had a great respect for the self-discipline of the Protestant peoples, and he was constantly trying to inject it into the easy-going Russians. The civil service of some German states already had a reputation for probity and conscientiousness, and Peter now persuaded hundreds of Germans and a number of Swedes to serve in his administration.* This

* A lot of them came from the shores of the Baltic, conquered by Peter, but largely developed, both then and later, by German colonists, who helped to make the more advanced and orderly character of the republics of Latvia, Estonia and Lithuania, which continues to this day.

was the beginning of the love-hate relationship with German *Ordnung* and with austere, stiff-necked Germans, which lasted all through the Tsarist period. (In fact Lenin's plans for the first Bolshevik administration were drawn up on the model of the Imperial German administration during the First World War.) Thousands of Germans settled in Russia during the eighteenth and nineteenth centuries and prospered, despised by the Russians for their bureaucratic obsessiveness, but secretly admired for their efficiency, which they usually preserved in later generations even though they lost their language and became thoroughly Russianized in other ways. Tusenbach, the worthy, pedantic young baron who is killed in the duel at the end of *The Three Sisters*, is a typical Russian-German character.

Peter was not fundamentally inhuman in personal relations, though he could be brutal in punishment, or in order to get things hurried up, but he had a tendency to regard human beings in the mass rather as he regarded the world of objects, to be shaped with axe, plane and chisel, all of which he so well knew how to use. It seemed to him that the giving of an order should in itself be sufficient to achieve a result—as when he fantastically commanded that the peasants were to reap their corn with scythes and rakes, 'as they do abroad', instead of with time-consuming, old-fashioned sickles. But where were millions of penniless peasants to get scythes from? They stuck to the sickle because they had no other tool—otherwise, two hundred years later, the Soviet symbol might have become 'the hammer and scythe'.

So although St. Petersburg and the Ural iron industry remained and flourished, and the reformed alphabet and calendar were not changed back by Peter's successors, his decree on compulsory primary education for the privileged classes came to very little: schools were not popular, and very few were started. It was the same with Peter's attempt to strengthen the responsibility of landowners by introducing the English custom of bequeathing estates to eldest sons alone. The landowners stuck to their old ways, and after Peter's death his decree was rescinded.

Peter's Senate was reformed by later Tsars and lasted until 1917, the Colleges became Ministries and continued to do some useful work, and Peter's Table of Fourteen Ranks, and the general prestige of state service, were preserved although the compulsion to serve was abolished in 1762. The machinery of government was at least a great deal better than it had been before Peter, when there had been, in the middle of the seventeenth century, thirty-six unco-ordinated departments created at various times, mostly *ad hoc*.

But all this, to our modern minds, is merely a story of administration, not of government as we understand it—because the autocracy always remained. And if such a titanic personality as Peter the Great was unable to enforce his will throughout his huge realm, what hope had other Tsars of doing so? They became inevitably dependent on sub-ordinate bodies—the private secretariat, the police, the secret police, the ministries, various advisory councils, so that 'even at the end of the nineteenth century it could be said without much exaggeration that autocracy or tsarism was an irresponsible federation of independent departments, whose relations with each other were not always friendly, or even neutral, and sometimes partaking of the character of almost open hostility'.* But to relieve the Tsar of any of his burden or to impose order on the departments by responsible representative institu-tions, to subject any of the machinery to popular control, would pre-sumably have implied subjecting the omnipotence of the Tsar himself to popular control. A typical governing motto was that of Catherine the Great (1762–1796): 'Everything *for* the people, nothing *by* the people.'

Yet the surprising thing is that, in the troubled century before Peter's reign, Russia had seen some small stirring of representative government —that is, among the minority of the population who were not serfs—in the shape of an advisory body, the Assembly of the Land, which for a time looked like developing into something bolder. And although it all came to nothing, it needs to be described, because it contrasts so sharply with the history of England and several other Western countries, and because to us it may cause the sequence of Russian history to look simply upside down.

It began, anomalously enough, with Ivan the Terrible, who in 1566 first summoned an 'Assembly of the Land' (Zemsky Sobor), with repre-sentatives of the new small-scale landowners whom he had created, and of townspeople, which meant merchants and craftsmen. The Assembly was no doubt meant as a counterweight to the Tsar's traditional council of *boyar* advisors, since these were the heavyweight nobles whose power Ivan wished to reduce.

Not a great deal is known about the way in which members were elected, or selected, to represent the greater and lesser nobility, gentry, urban dwellers, and even sometimes a few free peasants, in the Zemsky Sobor, though in connection with one Assembly it is recorded that town governors were to call meetings of 'the best men who were good,

* B. H. Sumner, *Survey of Russian History.*

intelligent, and steadfast'; they would be men of substance but they were not, apparently, required to be literate. 'Election' was probably only a matter of consultation between local leaders of the appropriate rank; it was certainly not an affair of balloting, though one feels that there might have been at least a show of hands in Novgorod and its associated cities, Perm and Vyatka, where something of the old tradition of control by the *veche* remained.

The Assembly submitted their views to the Tsar, concerning taxes or the code of laws, for instance, and they were at times consulted by him, occasionally even over a decision whether to make war or not. But they held no debates and they had, of course, no kind of power over the Tsar. It was quite likely due to pressure from the small gentry in the Assembly that the Code of 1649 was drawn up, but this would not have happened if it had not suited the Tsar to have the terms of serfdom defined more clearly. The Code was drawn up by a committee of no more than five men, who neither reported to the Assembly nor submitted anything for its discussion. The Assembly did not normally meet except at the Tsar's summons, which was by no means an annual event.

Yet the impressive thing is that the Assembly acquired enough status to act as an interim, representative body when there was no Tsar on the throne. In 1598 there was no obvious hereditary candidate for Tsar, the Assembly was called together by the Patriarch, and they elected Boris Godunov—that is, they chose the candidate of one group of powerful nobles rather than the candidate of another group. Again, after the Time of the Troubles the Assembly met, in 1613, to elect Michael Romanov, who was proposed by the nobles because he was only sixteen and pliable. But when, after him, the Assembly confirmed his son Alexis on the throne, the hereditary principle was restored, to everyone's relief, and the election of Tsars died out even as a formal principle.

Next door to them the Russians had the warning example of Poland's elective monarchy: every time a king of Poland died, the nobles chose one of their number to succeed him, and imposed their own limitations on his power. This seemed to the Russians to be not liberty but rather stupid licence: 'If the Tsar acts unjustly, that is his will: it is easier to suffer injury from the Tsar than from one's own brother.'

According to Western ideas, the Zemsky Sobor ought to have gone on, to have developed into a truly representative assembly of at least the privileged classes, and grown strong enough to be able to put some pressure on the Tsar. But the power of the state was already too great in Russia when Ivan the Terrible called the first Assembly: they did not

gather of their own accord—he summoned them. It was the reverse of
the English barons putting pressure on King John, three hundred and
fifty years earlier. Actually, when the Zemsky Sobor elected Boris
Godunov they wanted him to accept a charter which would define his
powers, but he refused, and no more was heard of it. The Assembly
never discussed fundamental rights, and such a Roman conception was
foreign to Russian communal ideas. The Zemsky Sobor was at best, and
then only for a short time, about as significant as the Estates-General of
France, the occasional and ineffective body sometimes summoned by
the French king. After 1653 the Zemsky Sobor was never convened in
full meeting again. But why not, since it was possible for the Assembly to
flourish at least for an interim period and for limited purposes? Russia,
it is true, had been going through an unstable and humiliating period,
and the Romanov dynasty—which lasted, of course, until 1917—was
welcomed somewhat as the English welcomed the Tudors after the
Wars of the Roses. But why did the people acquiesce in the disappear-
ance of their only representative body? Why were they, with very few
exceptions, apparently so supine?

The answer depends upon who 'they' were. First, the townspeople:
nine years after the last Zemsky Sobor, when there were riots in the
towns over the introduction of a copper currency instead of the familiar
silver, it was some of the townspeople, not the nobles, who asked for
the summoning of a Zemsky Sobor to discuss the matter. They had no
response at all from the Tsar (Alexis, who was by no means one of the
worst Tsars). But probably if the merchants and craftsmen had been
more numerous, and richer, on the West European scale, so that the
Tsar needed their wealth, they would, as in other countries, have
pressed for some share in government and perhaps even won it. They
might even have built a bourgeois foundation for some sort of parliament, which is the way that most other parliaments grew up. But they
were too few and too weak: the country's wealth came mainly from the
land, and the landowners, scattered as they were across the great
expanses of Russia, were difficult for the Tsar to reach effectively, and
were concerned almost entirely with the interests of their own class. The
Tsar personified the State, and it was his job to run it: all they wanted—
apart from an enlightened minority of them—was to be left to run their
own estates and keep their privileged position. The State meant
primarily defence, which could mean conscription of one's sons or even,
if one was not clever enough, of oneself; and it meant ruinous taxation.
But at least, after Peter, Russia had a standing army which took care of

defence. The merchants and craftsmen, on the other hand, were concentrated in comparatively few cities, they were much more vulnerable to a foreign enemy, and they were of course much more accessible to the Tsar's tax-gatherers. They were in a poor position to make themselves felt.

The nobility and gentry went on to have their special status and rights confirmed by Catherine the Great in her Charter of 1785: they were exempt from poll tax and corporal punishment, they would be tried by their peers if anyone tried to dislodge one of them from his special status, and they had the right to travel abroad. In every province there was to be an 'assembly' or 'corporation' of local nobles, with powers beyond the affairs of their own class, but few nobles showed much interest in exercising such powers. (Levin in *Anna Karenina* attended one meeting of his local assembly, wonderingly, and thought it a waste of time.) Nothing was said in the Charter about the participation by nobles and gentry as such in the central government, nor did any great number of them seem to want it.

Finally as to the peasants, the 95 per cent or so of the population who had practically no political status at all. They could no more have conceived of an elected Tsar, says the greatest of Russian historians, than of an elected father or mother. The *mir* was not an institution of representative government; it was in fact rather anti-representative. It took the burden of decision off the individual, through communal decisions which outsiders sometimes called 'mystical', but which were surely no more than a reflection of the great identity of interest among the members, and of their simple egalitarian passion for justice.

The Tsar, like heaven, was far off, to quote an old folk proverb. In the earlier days, fighting the Tatars, he was a martyr-saint. And later, though somewhat less of a martyr, he was still heroic, and he was not only the country's champion, he was still taking up the burden of exercising power over others, and of being *responsible for them*—that burden which Russians in general have always been so unwilling to take up. *He* would keep *boyars* and landlords and rapacious merchants in check—and tax-gatherers too, if he but knew of their perversions of his *ukazes*. *He* could murder and savagely imprison, and bear all the sin on his conscience—'for the grandiose sin of a few promises total salvation to all'. (I quote from Erik Erikson's brilliant analysis of the Russian character in *Childhood and Society*.) In earlier days, at least, it was not merely peasants who could conceive of the Tsar in this way: it was mainly for this reason that seventeenth-century nobles felt it to be 'easier to suffer injury from the Tsar', who was so exalted above every-one, both in his powers and his suffering, rather than from 'one's own brother', who would be just a jumped-up human being like oneself.

It would seem as if the Orthodox of all classes—which is as good as to say all Russians—were united in pressing absolutism upon the Tsar. When Peter the Great's daughter, Elizabeth, took the throne in 1741 she even placed the imperial crown upon her own head at the coronation ceremony, and all her successors crowned themselves in the same way.

But it would be too simple, too artificially logical, to assume that all these pressures, apparently so irresistibly building up an impregnable foundation for Tsarist autocracy, were in every way inevitable.

Russia was huge, and Russia was poor; her poverty at home was inevitable after all those wars. Granting all this, and considering where it was, geographically, that the Russians had to live, I think it is a mis-take to look on them as a completely different sort of human animal from ourselves. In so far as their ideology was Christian it was different from our own, but it was still Christian; also, the great majority of Russians found they could survive best, in their poverty and misery, by preserving many of the ways of a society more primitive than any which is actually recorded in the history of England, but this kind of society is familiar enough in other countries and may have existed in England in earlier times.

It was not inevitable that the Russian landowning class, who might have taken a key part in affairs, should have opted out of taking a share in central government; it was simply a lot easier for them to do so, it accorded more with ordinary human inertia and self-interest, which we share with the Russians, that they should stick to their own affairs, in such an unwieldy country with very bad communications. It was not inevitable, either, that they should have insisted on clinging to a primi-tive egalitarianism in their attitude to inheritance: a few of them did take up the custom of primogeniture, and if they had all done so the land would have been improved, the individual landowners would have become more powerful, and as a class they would probably have wanted, and got, more of a part in government.

It was not inevitable that all the Tsars should have rejected any kind of representative government. In fact they did not all completely do so; if they had asked for it they could have had it, weak and ramshackle though it would probably have been at first. Alexander I did consider, and *might* have accepted, the proposals of his excellent minister

Speransky, in 1809, for a State Council to be elected by owners of property. If this had come about there might have been no Decembrist revolt, and less repression under the next Tsar, Nicholas I. Nicholas's son, Alexander II, after liberating the serfs and introducing other revolutionary reforms, did actually take steps towards a constitution, just before he was assassinated in 1881. His son, Alexander III, reacted with a reign of severe repression, but a wiser man might have continued, in spite of the assassination, with his father's reforms. Finally Alexander's son, the luckless and ungifted Nicholas II, need not have obstinately tried to preserve the ancient inertia until there was no alternative, in the circumstances of the First World War, but the sudden collapse of the whole worn-out edifice. It was not inevitable that the last Tsar should have been such an unimaginative and fumbling little man.

It needs to be stressed, incidentally, that almost all the men and women who sat on the Russian throne were conscientious rulers, in the sense that they worked hard at their job; there was not one who used his position for gross personal indulgence, like the late King Farouk of Egypt. They slaved at their desks over thousands of individual cases, which under a more rational system of government would have been decided at a lower level. They spent a great deal of time over police control, but they nearly all also thought about, and consulted about, the major domestic problems of their country. Nicholas I (1825–1855), who made Russia a police state, who was known in his lifetime as 'the Tsar Gendarme', and whose ideal was a monolithic model of government, with an incorruptible and absolutely trustworthy corps of gendarmes in sky-blue tunics and white kid gloves, to convey the people's grievances to their paternalistic Tsar—even Nicholas thought about the injustice of serfdom, introduced some small reliefs for the serfs, and in St. Petersburg, at least, went about with few attendants and was understood to be approachable by any of his subjects at set times.

The autocrats in their heyday certainly 'made Russia great', to use the conveniently vague phrase of statesmen and historians, and in our enthusiasm for liberal institutions and civil freedom, we ought not to underrate what the Tsars achieved. They made Russia, in the first place, physically huge, by extending their territory till it reached the Arctic Ocean, the Baltic and the Black Sea, so that Russia covered four or five times the area of the original Muscovy, without reckoning Siberia. Apart from the rather large part of Poland which Catherine gobbled up, and a few other border areas, all this expanse was predominantly inhabited by Russians or had been inhabited by Russians at an earlier date.

6

On the whole, Tsarist Russia did not grow by despoiling other nations.*

The old Muscovy had been about the same size as the kingdom of Poland, and like Poland, it could have fitted into the contemporary idea of Europe if that had been wished. For reasons of religion this was unlikely, but it might have happened if the Russians had not been cut off for so long by the Mongols and if, when they had fought themselves free, they had not shown such a primitive pride in their backward ways, as was noted by Giles Fletcher. The chance of a *rapprochement* was missed, and once the Empire of Peter and Catherine became so huge, relations with Western Europe clearly had to be on a different basis. After Peter had defeated the otherwise invincible Charles XII of Sweden in 1709, Russia became recognized not only as a huge country but as a power to be treated with respect and possibly feared. When the troops of the Empress Elizabeth struck terror into the Prussians of Frederick the Great in the Seven Years' War, when Catherine's armies rolled back the Turks, and when Alexander I became the hero of Europe because his people repulsed Napoleon, respect for the Russian giant inevitably increased, however much dirt, backwardness, injustice and misery might be discovered inside the country by visiting foreigners. Russia might be the enemy of Austria or Prussia or Sweden at various times, but she was indubitably a European power as well as they; towards the end of the Napoleonic Wars she was one of the four great powers of the Grand Alliance.

Some idea of Russia's 'greatness' filtered down to the mass of serfs through proclamations and through returned soldiers, and even through popular ballad sheets and crude caricatures sold by pedlars. Garbled though the news must often have been, it did all give the suffering peasant some further reason, beside his Church, for pride in being Russian. Soviet Russians are still proud of this expansion, even though it was brought about by autocratic Tsars: without it Russia would not be Russia. And this pride has been on the whole an unaggressive pride, because Russians in general were not, and are not, a military-minded people; they have not been avid for '*la gloire*', nor predators among the nations, as the Tatars and Turks have so often been.

But though Russia was accepted as a European power, there remained an awkwardness about this backward newcomer among the nations. It was the two Empresses, Elizabeth and Catherine, who brought the

* Turkestan indeed was acquired by military conquest during the mid-nineteenth century, but the Christian nations of Armenia and Georgia joined the Empire voluntarily because they sought protection against the Moslem Turks and Persians.

Russian upper class into European society. They Westernized, they Frenchified the court entirely, and by their prestige, their personal charms, their civilized taste, and their indefatigable encouragement of French, German, Italian and English literature, architecture, drama, music, manners and dress—but above all French manners and the French language—they created a glamorous and inspiring fashion which spread right through the landowning class and which affected part of the middle class (such as it was) as well. Where Peter's blunt, Westernizing commands had often aroused hostility, the tremendous style of the Empresses, the excellent taste of their lavish spending, and the judicious intelligence of Catherine succeeded. Education began at last to spread, and the habit of speaking French, even to the exclusion of speaking Russian, became the mark of the upper class, as it continued to be, right up to the Revolution. In Russian plays and novels, throughout the nineteenth century, a familiar character is the merchant's daughter whose clothes and jewels are lavishly expensive but who is pink with shame because she can only stammer a few sentences of French. In 1805 one of the Wilmot sisters wrote: 'They can't educate their children without unprincipled adventurers from Paris to act as tutors and governesses.' Even as late as the 1960s I used occasionally to meet elderly people, still playing a part in Soviet life, who spoke a rather artificial French which they had learned as children, from a mademoiselle who had been part of the family.

Under both Elizabeth and Catherine, Italian architects—Rastrelli and Quarenghi and Rossi—and the Russians who learned from them built the palaces which make Leningrad enchanting to this day, and which were imitated in the Palladian manor-houses and in the provincial capitals. The noble proportions and the great spaces—the frequently rather too great spaces—made the new pattern for Russian cities, turning away from the crammed mediaeval Kremlins and the bobbly-styled churches, and this grandiosity has been the model ever since. As you pick your way across a huge square in a Soviet city today, hastily asphalted and full of puddles, and you feel dwarfed by the distances and by the size of the buildings when you come to them, whether they are of Catherine's stucco or Soviet concrete, you may thank Catherine the Great, ultimately, for the whole principle of these disproportionate, uncomfortable spaces, as well as for such triumphs as the imposing promenade high above the Volga at Yaroslavl, or the golden needle of the old Admiralty building, glittering at the end of the Nevsky Prospect in Leningrad.

Under Catherine it was not only the enjoyment of the arts that was liberated; there was also the encouragement of famous mathematicians, and the eager reading of foreign philosophers—of Voltaire and the French Encyclopedists, of Adam Smith and Jeremy Bentham, of Blackstone's *Commentaries*, and above all of her favourite Montesquieu. Catherine's ambition was nothing less than to lead (as a despot, of course) a nation whose culture (meaning the culture of a privileged class) should surpass that of any European country.

The cultured class continued after her and grew, but her reading of liberal ideas, of the ideas of the Encyclopedists who helped bring about the French Revolution, came to nothing as soon as she was faced with the actual shock of that event. She smashed her bust of Voltaire, banned the Encyclopedia, and imposed a general censorship. Politically, in fact, very little was achieved under Catherine the Great, and she justified the prophecy of her admired Montesquieu, according to whom despotism was inevitable in Russia on account of the great size and backwardness of the country.

As to the mass of Russians who could have only occasional perceptions of what it meant for 'Russia' to be 'great', the principal result of Westernization for them was to widen still further the gap which separated them from the privileged class.

The upper class still crossed themselves as the peasants did, before the corner ikon with its little red lamp, and on Easter Day they exchanged the heartfelt kiss of thanksgiving with all and sundry, but for nearly all the well-to-do, the part which religion had previously played in their lives was greatly reduced by the new entertainments and the general worldliness, not to mention the philosophy, the spirit of inquiry, and even the political speculation. The Church had become more and more subordinate to the government after Peter abolished the office of Patriarch, and as for the old daily pattern of Orthodox life, Catherine completed its dissolution, which Peter had begun. She offered the privileged classes something brighter, more exhilarating, more elegant, luxurious and entertaining—the normal life of aristocratic Europe, in fact. The old Muscovite dressing-gown life had been austere in its standards and almost Judaic in its regulation of detail: your whole day was guaranteed by rituals drawn from the traditional monastic guides to household life, starting with your prayers on rising, and going on till you retired to bed with your wife, scrupulously remembering to draw a little curtain in front of the ikon if you intended to make love to her. Not that all such rituals were abandoned, by all the privileged classes, even in the twentieth century, but the totality of them ceased to be the framework of life, except for a pious minority.

The peasants, for their part, kept the rituals—such as they had time and opportunity for—and indeed they asked for nothing better than such comforting familiarity. They had, as before, the unaccompanied church singing, the church buildings, the innumerable ikons (often dripping with hearty Orthodox kisses), and the dazzling robes of the priests (if the priests were rich enough), as their share of civilized beauty. Otherwise they had their own folk culture—choral dances and round dances, and a thousand superstitions about house goblins, forest goblins, water sprites, witches, water maidens, 'wise women' and magic remedies, and they had the old folk patterns which they embroidered into linen or carved into wooden gables, wooden tools, wooden spoons . . . After the Westernization of architecture there was little work for woodcarvers on the great stucco houses, and they used their talents in the villages and little towns instead, carving such things as the distaff, a century and a half old, which hangs above the desk where I write: it shows, incised in outline of an Egyptian simplicity, two peasant women in huge skirts gossiping across the samovar with its little teapot. The practice of peasant carving has now all but died out; it could not survive the long starvation of the early period of collectivization, but in many country places, to judge by complaints in the Soviet press, the peasants cling to traditional medicines, charms and superstitions, just as they cling to the numerous saints' days which still provide an excuse for easing off work.

There was one little bridge between the ways of the two classes, after Westernization, and that was in the life of the house serfs. Most of them benefited a good deal from the new fashions of their masters and mistresses—in food, in reading, in music, and in dress; some of them even picked up French. Some of these house serfs, especially if they were careful with money, were able to leave domestic service and join the ranks of the middle classes, after the Liberation. And one Western habit somehow spread through the whole nation—the habit of tobacco, introduced by Peter the Great. The peasants learned to grow their green *makhorka* leaf, whose choking smoke is part of the traditional smell of Russia, though nowadays it is less in evidence than it used to be.

But the deepest and most lasting result of Westernizing was one which in the end was to help powerfully in bringing down the autocracy: it was the creation, for the first time in Russian history, of an intelligentsia.

There had been a few outstandingly well-read and thinking noblemen about the court in the seventeenth century, and one or two of them engaged in such controversy that they had to take refuge in Poland or Sweden. But there simply were not many books of any kind in Russia at that time, and it was not until Catherine's reign that one could speak of a class which was interested in ideas. Inevitably, they became interested not only in political ideas but in the realities of life in their own country, in the systems of other countries, and in the necessities and possibilities of reform. Radishchev has always been regarded as the father of the Russian intelligentsia, and today in Soviet Russia he is honoured with statues, but though he was the one who suffered most under Catherine, he was not the only one of his kind during her reign. A little later it was the officers of Alexander I, triumphantly entering France after the defeat of Napoleon, who gathered more foreign ideas at first hand, saw a little of their working in practice, and admired the constitution of the young United States. When Alexander withdrew from political reform into mystical contemplation, these officers organized themselves in secret societies and eventually formed the conspiracy of the Decembrists in 1825. Very poorly organized, with some of its members republicans and others aiming at constitutional monarchy, it was easily put down by Nicholas I. Its leaders were executed or exiled to Siberia, but the British Minister in St. Petersburg wrote: 'I think seeds are sown which one day will produce important consequences.' The Decembrists remained a symbol and a rallying-point for the intelligentsia under the repressive régime of Nicholas and his Third Section, and indeed for ever after.

The word *intelligentsia*, from meaning at first simply 'intelligence', soon acquired its special and honourable Russian meaning, indicating not just intellectuals, but the class who used their intelligence and education to make themselves responsible for criticizing their own society unsparingly and for taking on, so far as was possible in Tsarist Russia, the burden of reform and revolution. Rather strangely, it was the introduction of certain orders of freemasonry from abroad which helped to develop a social conscience among many of the aristocracy; the Russian Church was never at any time on the side of reform, but supported the established order. (In *War and Peace* Tolstoy has a somewhat satirical treatment of a masonic gathering at this early period.)

Catherine had wanted Russia to have not only the most cultured régime but the most 'rational' régime in Europe—one where the citizen should understand that it was in his interest, as well as his duty, that he should observe the law. This was dangerous doctrine, as any of her successors (except perhaps Alexander II), let alone her predecessors, would have told her. For if the citizens are to be allowed to contemplate their own interest, how can the autocrat be sure that their interests and his own will coincide? A politically reformist despotism was a contradiction in terms. When Alexander II tried, with excellent intentions, to resolve the contradiction during his reign, which lasted from 1855 to 1881, he achieved some real reforms, but this partial releasing of the brakes also released such a mood, such chaotic and ill-informed expectations and ideas among the already rumbling revolutionaries, that the result was his assassination.

So the autocracy, armed with military power, was able to expand and preserve the huge state of Russia; the autocracy, armed with wealth and prestige, was able to bring culture to a privileged class, but in other respects it remained necessarily the wielder of repression always, be it noted, against widespread passive resistance and sporadic active resistance—a typical pattern, probably, for a country of such an unfortunate size and unfortunate history, and a pattern often to a certain extent repeated under Soviet government in the twentieth century.

Could the enlightened Catherine, or some other enlightened imperial ruler, possibly have 'Westernized' the mass of the Russian people, whatever 'Westernization' might have meant for a poverty-stricken population of forty or fifty million? The task was too great, and if education had in fact been offered them the peasants might well have turned against it as an invention of the devil. (It was to be different when the system started breaking up, but that was only in the last decades before the Revolution.)

For the peasants, life had to go on marking time; they got no reward for helping to defeat Napoleon. For the privileged classes, the energy which in other countries might have gone into government was diverted a great deal into philosophies and speculations but also, most grandly, into the creative arts, into the golden age of Russian literature and music, from Pushkin and Glinka at the beginning of the nineteenth century to Tolstoy and Scriabin at its end. Not one single Russian writer whose name is remembered was a supporter of the Tsarist state of things. Westernization rose to a peak of critical bitterness in the famous *Philosophic Letter* of Chaadayev, for publishing which, in 1836, he was officially declared insane. Speaking of Russia's past, he wrote: 'While the whole world was building, we created nothing; we remained crouched in our hovels of log and thatch. In a word, we had no part in the destinies of mankind.'

5. The Rise of the People

Looking back from the 1970s at the antecedents of modern Russia, at the kind of forces and the kind of people who helped to form its nature and attitudes and habits, one now sees that the most significant characteristic of the period before 1917 is what may be called the rise of the people. In saying this one is not putting a halo round the concept of 'the people'; one is making a simple statement about the changing status and growing social strength of the great majority. Their strength was not usually well organized, and by the time the First World War broke out their standard of living had not greatly improved, nor had they achieved much of a share in government, but they had reached such a pitch of independence that an English journalist reported that 'there seems to be not an organized but a tacit conspiracy against all forms of authority'. From the mid-nineteenth century onwards, the old order was being so threatened and undermined, and was coming to appear so inadequate, in spite of its repeated attempts at repression, that even before the twentieth century began, people of every class were anticipating a revolution of some kind or other. The threat came partly from the political activity of the intelligentsia, with their underground movements and agitations, not to mention their bombs and assassinations, but it came much more from the 'tacit conspiracy'.

The impulse which began to change the lives of the people came, of course, from industrialization, which meant the gathering together of large miscellaneous groups of men and women for the first time in Russian civil history. Industrialization, however, was not possible on any great scale until the serfs had been freed by Alexander II, and the beginning of the pre-revolutionary period may be dated from the Emancipation of 1861.

Alexander, 'the Great Reformer', was the son of Nicholas I, who had been known all over Europe as 'the Policeman' for his 'Third Section', his grinding censorship of literature and the press, his severe restrictions on travelling abroad, and his disciplinary interventions, such as the degrading of officers for smoking in the street: the ordeal of the reprieve at the gallows-foot, suffered by Dostoevsky and his comrades, was per-

sonally stage-managed by Nicholas—roll of drums, last rites, and all—
'to teach the young men a lesson'. In spite of all this, some Russians
admired Nicholas's attempt at monolithic government, but like many
another martinet, he simply fumbled when he had to face big issues. He
died in the middle of the Crimean War, and Russia's defeat in that war
turned the balance of opinion overwhelmingly in a liberal direction.
Alexander, fortunately, had been given an excellent liberal education by
his wise mother and his tutor, the poet Zhukovsky; he had taken care to
find out something about the kind of life the serfs had to lead and he was,
incidentally, an attentive reader of Turgenev's *Sportsman's Sketches*.

When he came to the throne he told the landowning classes that 'It
is better to abolish serfdom from above than to wait for the time when it
will begin to abolish itself from below.' But when the scheme of emancipation was announced, the serfs' reaction was 'We have been cheated!'
They got their liberty—to move about, take up other work, engage in
trade, marry as they pleased and so on, like other citizens, but what they
expected was the land, as a free and natural gift to those who worked it.
They got, indeed, a share of the land, but rather less, in all, than the
patches which they had been accustomed to till on their own account,
and for this they had to pay on crippling terms, and terms which as the
price of their freedom they could not escape. The landlords kept the
rest of the land, and for what they gave up they were compensated, not
at the market value of the land, but at the capitalized value of the serf
labour on it. The freed serfs were compelled to pay this value, by way
of redemption, in annual payments at $6\frac{1}{2}$ per cent interest for 49 years,
that is until 1910. The State advanced 80 per cent of the redemption
payments to the landlords, but many of their estates—two-thirds of the
land of Russia, altogether—were mortgaged already, so that the windfall
from the State went to paying off their debts, and they had then only the
remaining 20 per cent of annual payments to look forward to. The
peasant share of the land was handed over to the commune, the *mir*,
which was made responsible for the instalments, though if any peasant
could somehow make enough money to pay off the whole of his part of
the redemption at once, then his share of the land became his own
property. In many places the peasants rioted when they heard the terms
of emancipation, and a strong rumour went round, which Alexander had
to deny in person, that there would soon be another decree freeing the
land from this burden of debt. Actually the payments proved so heavy
that after the great disturbances of 1905 they had to be abolished.

Alexander also gave Russia a system of independent, irremovable judges, and open trials, with a jury, for the first time. The administration of justice was thus at last separated from the arbitrary, bureaucratic state administration, which had hitherto acted as prosecutor and judge in its own cases, with no chance of appeal unless, possibly, to the Tsar in person or the Senate, if they could be reached. The peasants were excluded from the new system, however; they had to go before Justices of the Peace elected by the new local councils, the *zemstva* (*zemstvo* in the singular). These councils were another innovation of Alexander's, and although the landowners were given much more power than the peasants in electing them, they attracted a lot of members with a social conscience and did some excellent work: the country doctors, teachers, nurses, agronomists and civil engineers whom we read of in Russian novels were usually employed by the *zemstva*. These officials were generally liberal-minded and, on the whole, the *zemstva* themselves became a great liberal force in Russia. Many of the towns were now also given elected councils for the first time—elected by the bourgeoisie and upper classes indeed, but they usually set up primary schools. Censorship was of course much relaxed, the universities were allowed more freedom, and military service was put on a basis of conscription for all classes.

As the result of these reforms one could say that Russia was at last ceasing to be mediaeval; but as Alexander himself well knew, the change had come painfully late, and its tardiness had brought other serious problems which could not easily be disposed of. Political life, or rather political discussion, was still confined to private groups of intelligentsia harassed by the police, and it was still impossible for people who were interested, or who thought they were interested in politics, to get any practical experience in representative government, except at the local level through the *zemstva*. So they theorized, and the theorizers, like so many Russians both then and now, scorned ideas of compromise or give-and-take; they lacked, typically, what one of their soberer politicians later called 'the cement of hypocrisy'. Their passionate whole-heartedness and frightening devotion expressed itself in the endless discussion and exaggeration of ideas gathered from other countries (and often already discarded by them), and also contrariwise, in the school of the Slavophils. Far from believing, as Chaadayev had done, that Russia had fallen contemptibly behind among the nations, the Slavophils believed that Russia was a land nurturing peculiar gifts, with a special destiny which must be developed. The old sense of a sort of sacred mission for the Russian people was resurrected in the ideology of the

'Populists', in spite of the fact that, like most Russian reformers, they rejected their traditional Church.

'We have no traditions: therefore, so far from being inferior on that account to countries who possess them, we are superior to them.' So wrote Herzen, a cultured nobleman and first-class writer who had to flee to England to carry on his political work. He expected Socialism to become the great regenerating force of the modern world, just as Christianity had been the inspiration of the world up to that time, but he understood Socialism in an ideal rather than an economic sense of the word; it was to be based, he thought, on the pure human relations of the peasant commune.

The Nihilists were concerned only to question everything that had previously existed; the more extreme of them were active terrorists, concerned mainly to destroy in order to hurry on a glorious future. Bazarov, the hero of Turgenev's *Fathers and Sons*, is the classical Nihilist; in fact it was Turgenev who invented the word, though he was no Nihilist himself. The Populists 'went to the people', in a famous phrase which described a whole enthusiastic movement, but they became very disillusioned when they found that the peasants had no wish to listen to them and often denounced these townsmen to the police. Bakunin, the philosopher of Anarchism, believed quite mistakenly that the peasants were ready to rise against both the landlords and the State, and both Populists and Anarchists had to discover that they had little conception of what the Russian people were really like.

There was one great writer at this time who through his own bitter experience knew and understood the Russian people, and that was Dostoevsky. His account of life in his Siberian prison, *The House of the Dead*, is scarcely out of date at all in the light it throws on comradeship among rank-and-file Russians. Speaking of their attitude to prison officers, he says: 'The convicts are ready to prefer the sternest men to the most merciful, if the former has a smack of their own homespun flavour.' In later years Dostoevsky turned his back upon all reforming ideologies, and his novel *The Possessed* (also known as *The Devils*) has become famous for its classic if horrifying picture of extremist discussion and conspiracy; its characters are closely founded upon real persons. Dostoevsky idealized the simple Russian, and Orthodox Christianity, so that many of the intelligentsia regarded him as a renegade and a reactionary; for the same reason his works were mostly kept out of circulation for many years of the Soviet régime, though the ban was lifted after the death of Stalin.

Among the more original revolutionaries a lesser figure, Tkachov, is remembered because he advocated the seizure of power by a disciplined minority, and some years later this idea influenced the young Lenin. Among the major figures, Herzen is revered in the Soviet Union —next after Lenin, Marx and Engels, to judge by the frequency with which his portrait is displayed. But he is revered as an inspiring forerunner who opened the minds of those who were willing to listen; he was too exclusively an idealist, too little concerned with economic factors, to be recognized as one of the direct ancestors of Bolshevism like the Marxists. They come into the picture a little later in the century.

When it became possible to found real political parties in Russia, the ideas of Populists, Anarchists and early idealistic Socialists all contributed something, but during the time of Alexander II these factions are remembered more for another reason, unfortunately crucial for Russian history: one or two small sections decided on assassination as the best way of toppling the old order. These were high-minded assassinations, which were expected to inspire popular enthusiasm and kindle the flame of revolution (though they never succeeded in doing so), and they were as likely to be organized and carried out by women as by men. Vera Zasulich shot at Trepov, the Governor of Petersburg, because he had flogged a political prisoner, and political prisoners were privileged persons, not supposed to be flogged. She failed to kill him, was brought to trial, was acquitted, against all the evidence, by a sympathetic jury, and was whisked away to Switzerland by her friends. As a result the new independent courts, after only fifteen years of existence, were deprived of all power to try any cases which might be considered 'political'; these were left to the arbitrary action of the police, in whose hands they stayed to the end of the Tsarist régime and, of course, through most of the years of Soviet rule as well.

Alexander II allowed police controls to be stiffened after some attempts on his own life—there were seven in all—but he kept his enlightened Armenian police chief, Loris-Melikov, who believed that the best way to fight terrorism was to get the people to take part in reforms, which he saw as inevitable, and he was able, mainly by velvet-glove methods, to calm the country down. It had been expected that, after a few years' experience of representative government in the *zemstva*, the Russian people, or at any rate some of them, would be entrusted with a share in electing a central government for the first time, under this reforming Tsar. At the suggestion of his police chief, Alexander now signed a document which should have been a landmark in Russian history, calling an assembly of representatives from the *zemstva* and from the councils of the chief cities, to draw up a constitutional reform. A few hours later, however, Alexander was dead from a terrorist's grenade.

His son, the huge and bear-like Alexander III, asked his Privy Council for their opinion on the plan for an assembly, and they voted seven to four in favour of continuing with it, in spite of the assassination. But the new Tsar decided to overrule them, and publicly announced his determination to preserve the autocracy. Loris-Melikov was dismissed, repression and censorship returned, and the extremists saw that even the assassination of a Tsar apparently had no beneficial result. The courts were already weakened, and the *zemstva* and the universities now found themselves heavily supervised and interfered with: all Alexander II's reforms were either undone or watered down—except for the Emancipation. That had gone too far already.

Nicholas II succeeded Alexander III in 1894 and announced that he would keep to the same policies and attitudes as his father; ideas of national representative government were 'absurd'. At this some of the *zemstvo* liberals wrote him an 'Open Letter', saying: 'Your speech has provoked a feeling of offence and depression, but the living social forces will soon recover from that feeling ... You first began the struggle; and the struggle will come.' In extenuation of Nicholas's miserable record it can at least be said that in his upbringing as a boy and a future Tsar he hardly had a chance. He was small, shy, and not good at his lessons, and his giant of a father treated him with good-natured contempt. When his grandfather had been struck by the grenade, Nicholas was taken in to see him as he lay dying, with one leg and one arm blown off, and one eye forcibly closed in his bloodstained head. Nicholas had then reached the impressionable age of thirteen. He must have been completely confirmed in a boyish mixture of fear and resolution, already probably almost ineradicable, which would decide that the only possibility for him, when he succeeded to the terrible throne of Russia, would be to follow as closely as possible in the footsteps of his awesome father. Nicholas's wife does not seem to have made any attempt to discover the real causes of his timidity and rigidity—people did not then usually look into early circumstances for the roots of someone's character in the modern way; she only urged him constantly, up to the eve of his abdication, to 'be great', to 'be like Peter the Great', which did not help very much.

Was Russia just unlucky in the assassination of 1881, or were all the reforms in her history always too late? If either Alexander II or Alexander III had brought in some kind of representative constitution it would probably have been only a partial reform and would not have silenced the terrorists, but it would have started something which could have grown, if all other circumstances had continued favourable. In this huge country a reforming Tsar would still have had to employ most of the old personnel and much of the old bureaucratic machine. (He would have faced the same sort of dilemma that plagues reformers at the top of the Communist Party in Russia today.) The educated minority would have continued to fulminate from their theoretical bases, the conscientious work of practical men under the new constitution would not have been recognized for some time, and peasant unrest would certainly have continued. But there might just have been a chance of breeding a generation of practical politicians and statesmen, and an even slenderer chance that they would have been allowed and been able to push through the political reforms which the new industrializing Russia needed, and so to get some closer understanding between government and people. Anyhow the chance was missed—and it was the last chance for gradual reform.

The terms of the Emancipation had emphasized that Russia was a poor country; the only way to increase her wealth was to industrialize fast; and the Tsarist Government now gave massive aid and encouragement to railways, mines and manufactures. In doing so they used the same policy as the Bolsheviks used later: they squeezed agriculture to finance the expansion of industry. There was little else that could be squeezed other than agriculture, and there were few people to bear the burden of taxation other than the peasants. The well-off, however, were lightly taxed in comparison with the peasants who, in addition to their redemption payments, had to find the kopecks for taxes on necessities such as matches, paraffin and sugar—not to mention vodka. Most of them still worked for a landlord as well as on their own account, but on his land they also used their own poor equipment and animals, so that agriculture improved very little, except in Siberia and on the big estates in the south, where there were some enterprising owners. In order to pay for foreign machinery for industry, Russia became a great exporter of wheat and barley and eggs and butter as well as timber. (Siberian butter was being sold in my suburb when I was a boy.) But much of this food was wrung from the peasants' own needs. In 1885 the Society of Russian Surgeons, concerned about the peasant death rate of 36 per thousand, reported that 'the primary cause of this frightful mortality is deficiency of food—mostly bread. It is thus obvious that the reduction of one-seventh in the peasant's consumption of bread during the last twenty years, as is shown by the computation of corn exports and corn production, has not come out of the people's superfluities but is literally wrung from their necessities.'

A few men made fortunes out of wheat, but the peasants' chief enemies, thirty years after the Emancipation, were not so much the landlords as, firstly, the Government, who taxed them and flogged them when they did not pay, and secondly, in every village, their own hard and grasping fellows who lent money, hired out horses and so forth at exorbitant rates, in short the *kulaks*. (The term *kulak*, meaning originally 'fist', is not a Soviet invention; the word was used before the end of the eighteenth century to describe a grasping peasant.) Stepniak* wrote in *The Russian Peasantry*, published in 1890:

'Every village commune has always three or four regular *kulaks*, as also some half-dozen smaller fry of the same kidney. The *kulaks* are peasants who, by good luck or individual ability, have saved money and raised themselves above the common herd. They turn to their profit the needs, the sorrows, the sufferings and the misfortunes of others. They are members, generally very influential members, of the village commune. This often enables them to use for their private ends the great political power which the *mir* exercises over each individual member. The distinctive characteristics of this class are very unpleasant. It is the hard, unflinching cruelty of a thoroughly uneducated man who has made his way from poverty to wealth, and has come to consider money-making, by whatever means, as the only pursuit to which a rational being should devote himself'.

Lopakhin, who bought the cherry orchard in Chekhov's play, may be counted a well-to-do *kulak*. Between the Emancipation and the First World War the landowners sold out half of all their land to the new class of Lopakhins.

But there were eight million landless peasants even at the time of the Emancipation, and in spite of a heavy death rate the population grew so fast that by 1905 the average peasant family who owned land had only about two acres per head. Some of the surplus millions worked on the big estates at low wages, some became tramps or hauliers on the Volga like the characters in Gorky's stories, but great numbers endured the

---

* Stepniak (the man of the steppes) was the name taken in exile by Kravchinsky, a nobleman who stabbed the chief of the hated 'Third Section' in the street and killed him. He fled to England and wrote books about the Russian peasant which are still classic reference works.

slum conditions of the new industries or helped to build the railways.

Fired by great stacks of wood, chugging slowly because the tract was laid across thousands of miles of Russian marsh, the railways grew from a mileage of 2,000 at the Emancipation to 50,000 just before the Revolution. No wonder that the stations, and the honking long-distance trains, and the telegraphs that went along with them, are so often the centres of drama in Russian literature; they brought a fresh dimension into Russian life. Especially, they changed life for the peasants: moving up to the cities for work, moving back, the migrants carried new ideas and new possibilities everywhere in spite of all the poverty. Peasants squatted patiently in the station dust all day—as they often still do—until at last a train arrived; some would travel out of nothing but curiosity, and they had their own devices—as some of them still do—for travelling without a ticket—arguing, cajoling, or tricking their way past the inspector. The third-class lavatories were large in those days and had no seat: the peasants arranged that one man, in obvious distress, should open the door a chink and show his ticket to the inspector, while a dozen others huddled silently and ticketless behind him. As for first-class travel, it was usually luxurious; the Trans-Siberian line, when it opened, even had a grand piano for passengers' use. The railways also brought more education, and more desire for education, to the villages. At the census of 1897 it was found that half the peasants under twenty were able to read and write. But the *raison d'être* of the railways was that they were the lifelines for exporting wheat and timber and butter and eggs, for importing new machines, for getting the new manufactures to those who could afford them, and for hauling the coal and iron which the manufacturers needed.

Capitalist Russia grew fast, but it was the State which had to take the initiative and which played the major part in stimulating industry and financing the railways, eventually owning a considerable part of them. Russian landowners needed a lot of encouraging before they would risk investing the redemption payments from their land to start up other people's factories, and the great growth of industry was due at first to the many-sided energy of the statesman Witte, a practical man trained in railway administration, and one of the most able ministers any Tsar ever had. The squeezing of agriculture was his policy, but he did not succeed, as he had hoped, in reaping such advantages from industry as would restore the balance in the standard of living after a decade or so. Eventually Nicholas II, with typical stupidity, dismissed Witte because he disliked him personally. All the same, between 1870 and 1900 the total annual production of all manufactures in Russia increased four and a half times, and by 1914 Russia was the fifth industrial power in the world, first among oil-producers, fourth for cotton goods, fifth for steel. The new capitalists had more freedom than any other class of Russian, they certainly exploited the labour of their wretched workers, and yet they were not free like capitalists in other countries to exploit the market freely: that would have seemed too dangerous to the autocracy. So the State not only protected industry from foreign competition by its tariffs, and from workers' revolt by its Cossacks and police; the State was not only the chief customer for heavy industry; it was also the State which controlled credit, the State which exploited some of the market through State enterprises, and it was even the State which appointed its own chairmen to all the associations of industrialists—the oilmen, the ironfounders, the flourmillers, and so forth.

In other ways, too, Russian capitalism was different from the capitalism of countries to the west. It attracted a good deal of foreign enterprise, from famous firms such as Siemens of Germany and Ericsson or Nobel of Sweden, besides a lot of foreign capital, particularly from France, Germany, Britain and Belgium: the state of Russia's industry was sometimes spoken of as 'semi-colonial'. Huge combines, using up-to-date methods, drove out lesser ones, and soon there were more plants employing over 1,000 workers apiece than there were in the United States at that time. But these workers were almost all unskilled; the skilled men stayed for the most part in the tiny craft enterprises which still flourished, or in the workmen's co-operatives, the *artels*, which turned out samovars, cutlery, leatherwork, silverware, and a thousand other articles. These craftsmen remained mainly in the country or the small towns, but the big new factories made the urban population grow at last, so that it trebled in size between the Emancipation and the Revolution. Yet even in 1917, 85 per cent of Russians still lived in the country. (Nowadays the figure is much less than half.) And of the urban 15 per cent how many were to be thought of as industrial working class in the sense in which we understand the term? They went back to their villages to get in the harvest, or just for a change of life or a change of food, and a large proportion of them were still on their village roll and paid their share of the village taxes—40 per cent of them in Moscow, for instance, as late as 1918. Only in St. Petersburg was there anything like a large worker population of the second or third generation.

There was scarcely time before the Revolution for a sophisticated

7

working class to grow up, a class with its own culture, like the culture of the Cockney, the Berliner, or the inhabitant of the Bronx. But there was time enough for these worker-peasants, or peasant-workers, to develop a political sense of their position as a class. Their wages were hopelessly low, too low for a man to be able to support a wife, and it was the policy of the Government, as well as the employers, which kept them low, since it was thought that low wages would help in the overriding aim—a faster growth of industry. The workers lived in miserable, over-crowded barracks, and for descriptions of these we need not turn to accounts by Soviet writers; we have the reports of the Tsar's horrified factory inspectors, or the article in the Tsarist Encyclopaedia (passed, of course, by the censor), under the heading *Factory Workers*:

'. . . huge, many-storeyed barracks with central corridors, and deal partitions not reaching to the ceiling. Nowhere, in all the factories in the Moscow province, is there any norm for the accommodation of workers in their barracks; they are simply packed to capacity, with less than two cubic yards of air space per man, and sometimes less than one cubic yard. Shelves are provided to sleep on, very rarely anything in the way of a table or stool. Often the accommodation is in two tiers, the top tier being little more than two feet from the roof.'

They lived, in short, like battery hens, except that they were not so well fed. They had as a rule to buy most of their food from the factory shop, and the same Encyclopaedia article estimates that Moscow indus-trial workers were worse off, in respect of food, than the average peasant in the Moscow province. (We have already seen how limited a standard that was.) There were a few better factories, clean and well-provided, run on paternalistic lines, and there were others, equally paternalistic, where the proprietor walked around with a fierce dog to encourage discipline. Trade unions, of course, were forbidden (until after 1905), and strikes were also illegal, but they did take place, though usually only for short periods.

This tale of misery for factory worker and peasant does not at first sight seem to justify the title 'the rise of the people' as a label for the period. The peasants had a reputation for passive, fatalistic acceptance, which naturally made them welcome in the new factories. But the deracinated men in the barracks, mostly young, mostly enjoying no skill, accompanied by few women, began to think of themselves dif-ferently from what they would have done if they had been family men on their own plots, safe in the brotherhood of the *mir*. Their common interest lay in their condition, not in something local or hereditary like the *mir*; the men in a single barracks might come from villages all over Russia. Even back in the reign of Catherine the Great, the workmen who were extending the Winter Palace and facing the great embankments with pink granite made organized protests—not riots but organized protests—against having to live in dugouts and work long hours. And now some of the more established workmen were actually beginning to form societies of their own. Some of them had been approached, had in fact been pestered, by the intelligentsia, and as early as 1879 a workmen's society was formed 'to study political problems *without any intelligentsia*'. This was in St. Petersburg, where progressive movements so often began, and where, before long, pretty well all the manual workers somehow learned to read and write. Illegal or not, strikes broke out on an ever-increasing scale. At the coronation of Nicholas II many workers found they had lost pay for the official holiday, and 30,000 men and women left work for a week, with properly concerted action between one factory and another. Later another great strike obliged the Government to grant an $11\frac{1}{2}$-hour day—though in practice longer hours than this continued to be worked. The army had frequently to be called in to suppress workers' demonstrations—as many as five hundred times in the year 1902.

All these efforts failed to raise the workers' wages, because they had the Government as well as the employers against them in that matter, but they won themselves some other small alleviations. More important is the fact that they took their revolutionary ideas and their new-found sense of strength back to their villages, and so the peasants at last began to realize that it was no use hanging on passively waiting, forty years after the Emancipation, for a benevolent Tsar to order a free distribution of land—an event to which they had childishly pinned their faith for so long. There was so much unrest in the countryside that the Government twice reduced the redemption payments due from the peasants, but this did not much relieve their lives, since their numbers continued to grow and agriculture continued to stagnate: there were five famine years between 1891 and 1901. The peasants burnt down manor-houses and murdered unpopular landlords, as they had always done, but in many places they now grew bolder. They took possession of land and burnt the land registers, killed some of the detested local officials (the 'land captains'), seized forests and cut the timber, and robbed some of the more miserly landlords of grain stored for trade. Usually they met with brutal punishment in the end, but the local forces of law were small, and the military could not be brought in everywhere at once, nor could they be brought in quickly; two or three days' march from the nearest rail-head, over a quagmire of a road with slatternly wooden bridges, was typical of journeys in rural Russia—and still often is. Yet the villages were not quite so isolated as they had been: through the railways, and the telegraph, and the increasing literacy, they got to know much more quickly about other people's rebellions and were encouraged by them.

At the same time there were strikes of industrial workers without number besides, within one short period, a big railway strike, a strike of 70,000 textile workers who stayed out for two and a half months at Ivanovo, and a strike of oil workers at Baku which extracted from the employers a collective agreement on wages and hours for the first time in Russian history. One can only admire the courage and self-discipline of these desperately hard-pressed men and women who had no strike pay since they had no trade unions, still less, of course, any kind of charitable or government support for their families. And these were the same sort of people, and often the same individuals, who a decade or so earlier would have been part of the passive peasant mass. Crude though strikes are as a means of political action, the industrial workers had no other possibility open to them, and as events showed later, by holding up industry they were aiming a blow not only for their immediate needs but also for democracy in Russia.

Some real political parties, though much harassed by the police, were now in existence, the chief ones being the Social Revolutionaries, the Social Democrats and the Constitutional Democrats or 'Cadets'.* The Social Revolutionaries had by far the widest support, chiefly among peasants, since they were in favour of expropriating the landowners; their ideas were a mixture of socialism and 'back to the land' idealism; they believed in terrorism, and assassinated a sizeable number of police chiefs and provincial governors. The Social Democrats, who saw no point in assassinations, were a truly socialist party, based on Marx. Their support as yet was small, and confined to the industrial workers, but Lenin, Trotsky and Stalin were already at work among them, and they gave rise, of course, to the Bolshevik Party, which must be de-scribed more fully in the next chapter. The Constitutional Democrats were a middle-class liberal party, small because middle-class, but for the same reason influential, and much supported by people experienced in the local *zemstva*. They wanted a representative government for

---

* Constitution is spelled with a *k* in Russian, so the party were known as the 'K.D.s', which is pronounced *kah-day* in Russian, and since most of the members spoke French, they turned this into the French spelling (though not the French meaning), writing it as *Cadets*.

Russia but had little to say about the conditions of the mass of the population. They were presumably thought of as respectable by the authorities, but the other two parties, and almost all the little workers' societies which sprang up, were penetrated by police spies in the time-honoured way.

The Tsarist police practised this art to such a pitch that they were not always sure on which side their double agents were working. The incredible Azev was a trusted inner member of the Social Revolutionary Party, and so was able to tip off the police when an assassination was planned, but to avoid suspicion some of his tips were deliberately ignored, and one or two police chiefs and at least one Minister had to pay with their lives so that Azev's cover should not be blown. Azev eventually escaped to live on the Riviera. The double agent Bogrov, on the other hand, repented after betraying many of his former political comrades, and taking advantage of his protected position and his dress suit, he walked up to the hated Prime Minister Stolypin in the Kiev Opera House in 1907 and shot him dead. Another police device was to start up 'unions' where workmen could be 'educated in the right sort of ideas', and these Zubatov unions (so named after their inventor) actually had some success in persuading workers that their problems were being understood; naturally, however, the workers became inclined to take over these unions themselves, and so they were later dissolved.

Such was the state of political life in the middle years of Nicholas II's reign. The Government were frightened; they had revolts among the minority nationalities—the Poles, the Finns, the Georgians and other peoples south of the Caucasus—as well as demonstrations and protests in the universities. They turned to the old expedient of autocracies—a little war to divert the nation's energies and interests. The stupid Russo-Japanese War of 1904–5 was undertaken against the advice of Witte, who knew how ill-prepared Russia was, but he was overruled by the Tsar's more authoritarian advisers, who were convinced that a successful little war would stave off what they, and many others, were already speaking of as 'revolution'.

They could not have been more mistaken. Their navy was destroyed at Tsushima, and on land the Japanese easily defeated the Russians, supplied as they were at the end of the Trans-Siberian Railway (which was not even completed until after the war began). It was only the intervention of America and other powers, alarmed by the rise of Japan, which made the peace terms less humiliating than they might have been.

At home, unrest boiled up in 1905 into a whole year of strikes, demonstrations and mutinies in the army and navy which, collectively, almost everyone at the time and for long afterwards called a revolution, although there was no concerted plan for taking over power. It began in January, with the infamous 'Bloody Sunday'. One of the Zubatov union leaders, a priest called Father Gapon, had his hand forced by the mass strikes in St. Petersburg, and he organized a peaceful procession of 150,000 people, some of them carrying ikons and portraits of the Tsar, to the Winter Palace to present a petition calling for basic human rights and reforms and an end to the war, but opening with a humble preamble: 'We are poverty-stricken, we are oppressed, we are burdened with unendurable toil; we suffer humiliation and are not treated like human beings . . . We are being strangled by despotism and tyranny. The dreaded moment has arrived when we would rather die than bear these intolerable sufferings any longer.'

Gapon had given due notice of the procession, with the result that the Tsar stayed away from the Palace, and an armed reception was prepared for the totally unarmed demonstrators. Without warning the guards opened fire on the crowd; they fired again and again, while Cossack horsemen cut down men, women and children with their sabres. Over a thousand were killed and thousands were wounded. The press of the whole world broke out in shocked headlines, while inside Russia such a torrent of feeling arose as was never to be reversed. Foreigners who were there at the time confirmed Lenin's judgment: 'The revolutionary education of the proletariat made more progress in one day than it could have made in months and years of drab, humdrum, wretched existence.' Within a few days 440,000 workers were on strike all over Russia; later there was the famous mutiny on board the battleship *Potemkin* and other mutinies at Kronstadt and Sevastopol, while the countryside was alive with acts of peasant violence. In August the Tsar was obliged to promise a parliament, or Duma (based on a very limited franchise), and in October, when more than a million men were on strike, from Warsaw to Vladivostok, he was forced by Witte to take 'the terrible decision', as he called it, of watering down the 'sacred trust' he had received from his father, by promising (or rather, appearing to promise) a constitution. He issued a Manifesto which proclaimed a certain amount of civil liberty, and which promised that all new laws should be subject to the Duma.

The workers thought very little of either the Duma or the Manifesto; an old Bolshevik once told me how they improvised new words to one of the rude old concertina tunes:

Old Tsar Nick, he saw the Manifesto,
Gave the nobles liberty, and us—the arrest-oh.

The great advance for the workers in 1905 was that they set up their own organs of government for the first time—the first Soviets—in St. Petersburg, Moscow and many other towns, and also among soldiers and sailors and in some places among peasants. There is nothing fundamentally Bolshevik about the word 'soviet'; it merely means council. The Tsars always had a Privy Council called a Soviet, and there was no reason why the local councils established by Alexander II should not have been called soviets instead of *zemstva*. The Soviets of 1905 were elected on the basis of the places where people worked, so that they had every chance of knowing their delegates personally; at the same time they showed their contempt for the allegedly 'representative' character of the promised Duma. The Moscow Soviet, led by Bolsheviks, started an armed uprising which was soon suppressed; the St. Petersburg Soviet (where Trotsky was co-chairman) and most other Soviets called on people not to pay their taxes, and warned them about the Duma.

The Government regained the upper hand entirely within two years, and the Soviets and the whole revolutionary movement were suppressed, by shootings down, punitive expeditions, and drastic executions and sentences of imprisonment. But the Soviets were not forgotten. They sprang up again spontaneously during the March Revolution of 1917, and since the Bolsheviks were eventually able to use them as organs for seizing power, the word 'Soviet' has acquired an honoured historical significance in modern Russia. 'Soviet citizen', for instance, is intended to indicate a citizen of the country where the people won freedom from autocracy through their Soviets. At the same time the word still means 'Council', and it is applied, under Communist dictatorship, to governing bodies from town councils up to the Supreme Soviet although, as everyone is aware, there is no choice of candidate or of policy in the elections to these bodies, and when 'elected' they have only very small possibilities of influencing policy.

The 1905 Revolution was suppressed, yet Tsarist Russia was never the same again. It was changed because of the Duma (limited though that body was); because trade unions were now permitted (though sharply watched and regulated by the police); because the peasants' redemption dues were abolished; because Stolypin's agricultural policy encouraged a tough independent peasantry outside the *mir*; because universal primary education was enacted in 1912 (and would have reached the whole country by 1922); because there was an increase in the (still small) proportion of worker and peasant students at the universities; because there was rather more liberty for the press; and finally and most important, because the peasants and workers—that is to say, 90 per cent or more of the Russian population—almost unanimously came to realize the nature of the tyranny under which they lived, and their own potential strength against it. This was the period when foreign journalists found 'a tacit conspiracy against authority' everywhere, and when peasants for the first time were openly reviling the Tsar. The American journalist W. E. Walling visited Sorotchintsa in the Ukraine, where there had been floggings and indiscriminate shootings because the peasants had taken the Tsar's promise of liberty literally, and had started on some genuine local self-government. They now told Walling that 'they knew the Tsar did not care how they lived, but that he cared precious well for the landlords ... He did away with the liberty he granted us ... What a crook!' 'What is interesting in these expressions', said Walling, 'is not only that they were new, but that they were said openly before strangers.'

The new measures showed that the autocracy was badly shaken. It had introduced some 'Westernizing' reforms, but it dared not make any radical change in the most crucial and fundamental matter—in the structure of government itself. To have done so—to have given direct representation to the hungry 150 million Russians—would of course have been suicidal. At this late stage there was no salvation for the autocracy either way, whether through suppression or through reform. In the elections to the Duma the traditional registry of social classes was used, and it was arranged that the votes of 2,000 landowners, or 7,000 townspeople, should have an equal weight with the votes of 30,000 peasants or 90,000 workers. Even on this basis, the First Duma included a few Social Democrats, and it produced such radical demands and such inflammatory speeches from almost all sides that the Tsar hurriedly closed it down. The same thing happened with the Second Duma; consequently the electoral law was changed so as to weigh still more heavily in favour of property, and the Third and Fourth Dumas consisted mainly of conservatives, reactionaries and 'Cadets'. The Government, that is to say, the Tsar's ministers, were responsible to him alone, not to the Duma, and while the Duma served as something of a useful mouthpiece for grievances, and had some powers in discussion of finance, it played a feeble part when the March Revolution broke in 1917.

Stolypin's policy, while putting down rebellion with an iron hand, was to forestall revolution by trying to 'give the peasants a stake in the country', to use the phrase of English conservatives—turning them into independent proprietors, and encouraging, as he said, 'not the feeble and the drunk, but the solid and strong'. He made it easy for any peasant to withdraw from the village commune and consolidate his strips into a heritable freehold farm. But the peasants felt safe in the *mir*, and only about a tenth of them took the opportunities which Stolypin offered. In any case the reform had come too late; there simply was not enough land to share out among a peasant population of the size to which it had now grown, while techniques still remained backward, and agricultural yields in most provinces were as low as ever.

The bureaucratic machine remained in control of national life, and Maurice Baring wrote in 1910 that 'as a general rule the local administrative officials, by the manner of their interpretation, are completely successful in sacrificing the spirit to the letter of the law'. The Government, he said, was flooding the Duma with trivial matters for consideration, in order to keep it away from more serious affairs. Madame Jarintsov, writing in English in 1914 to explain the state of her country to the fortunate British, said: 'It must be remembered that not only what is on the lists of prohibited things is regarded as a crime, but also what is not on the unwritten lists of things that are allowed.' 'The slightest breath of criticism', said Maurice Baring, 'is held to be subversive and detrimental.'

The Church, as usual, was too closely identified with the Government to offer any independent leadership; Madame Jarintsov spoke of 'the striking absence of any moral bond between the clergy and the rest of the population'. The intelligentsia, apart from some convinced and persistent Marxists and liberals, tended to turn away from politics to the arts. This was the exuberantly brilliant period of Scriabin and Rachmaninov, of the first works of Stravinsky and Prokofiev, of Stanislavsky and Meyerhold and Andreyev in the theatre, of Chaliapin at the opera, of the poetry of Blok and Akhmatova and the Symbolists, of the stories of Gorky and Bunin, and of the circle of all the talents which was gathered around him by that emperor among impresarios, Diaghilev.

The country was getting a little richer, but it was still a country of a limited number of grands bourgeois; Russia never had much of a cheeseparing petty bourgeoisie. Fortunately some of the grands bourgeois had excellent taste, and their money supported the great flowering of the arts: Stanislavsky and Diaghilev both came from the merchant class, and there were millionaires who bought the works of Picasso and Matisse (now in Soviet national collections) before these painters were much appreciated in the West. But Russia was a poor country overall, and under the flourishing of the arts, and behind the brilliant life of Petersburg society, a terrible undercurrent was growing stronger—a sense either of tragic, unavoidable spiritual decadence, or of inevitable and maybe even welcome revolution.

I have heard it argued by economists that if there had been no First World War, capitalist Russia (with State support, of course, as always) would in fifty years have reached about the same overall economic level as Soviet Russia today. In strict economic terms this may just be true, since the Communists made such brutal and expensive mistakes, but it is difficult to believe that the standard of living of the submerged 90 per cent of Russians either could or would have been raised fast enough to relieve the tremendous head of political pressure in the country. Poverty-stricken though the Russian masses were, their political pressure was not solely the result of their economic poverty, but also of their social and political subjection. It is impossible to believe that the almost universal opposition to the régime would not have erupted again, that other ministers besides Stolypin, and probably Nicholas II himself, would not have been assassinated, and that the remnants of frightened authority would not have reacted with despairing repression on such a scale that it would have backfired: Russians in uniform would have refused to use their weapons any more against Russian civilians—which is exactly what happened in 1917.

An impartial outsider in 1914 would have been more likely to conclude that Mother Russia, with her marshy and forested spaces stretching endlessly into the distance, with her grey burden of poverty, her social and cultural backwardness, her tradition of doctrinaire government, her inheritance of procrastination and delay, and her immemorial mistrust of the average man's initiative and spontaneity, was an impossible country to run.

6. Making Revolutions

The Russian people, to the surprise of their rulers, joined in the First World War with enthusiasm. They felt their country was in danger, and they had never liked Germans anyway. (The name of the capital was de-Germanized and became Petrograd.) Russian soldiers in their coarse grey uniforms fought and endured with stoical bravery, and were sacrificed in large units by commanders who apparently cared nothing for human life. They were sacrificed because the whole army was short of weapons and equipment, short even of rifles, boots and maps; and they were sacrificed particularly in offensives which were undertaken at the request of France and other Western powers, to relieve German pressure on their own forces.

The Russians had some successes at first, while at home there was, by Russian standards, comparative prosperity. But after a year or so the overworked railways were unable to serve both the front and the towns, which began to run short of food. Industry was inadequate, and it ran short of materials too; it became clear, as Witte had prophesied long before, that Russia was in no condition to fight a full-scale war. There was unemployment, then strikes, food riots, and massive demonstrations, which the police and Cossack troops with sabres, whips and lances could barely control. The armies were increasingly ill-supplied, and reserve troops, kept idle in the rear, began to desert and go back to their villages, where at least they expected to find food. The actual direction of the war was in the hands of one incompetent minister after another; for some months it was virtually run by the Tsarina and Rasputin. Responsible people of all classes talked of revolution and the necessity of ousting the Tsar. Then the huge garrison which was kept in Petrograd to maintain order began to see itself as a collection of ordinary Russians who just happened to be in uniform: the Governor of the city had to report that regiment after regiment refused to use their arms against fellow-citizens who were demonstrating for food or were on strike. Late in February 1917, all support for the régime simply disappeared.

An English governess, Marguerite Bennet, wrote in one of her letters home: 'The real fight began because the soldiers refused to fire on the people, and so the police fired on the soldiers. Then, of course, the fat was in the fire. I believe the Cossacks were about the first to go with the people. Near the station there was a crowd, and a man got up on the statue there and began to say what they wanted—the chief thing being BREAD. On one side were the Cossacks, and on the other mounted police. They all listened, and the Cossacks agreed that they would help them; but as the crowd was moving peacefully off, a policeman attacked a Cossack. You can imagine the result. The Cossack chopped up the policeman. Then it grew and grew—each regiment that was sent against the Revolutionaries fought with them. The fight went on all Monday night and Tuesday for the mastery, but eventually the Revolutionaries, the army and the people became one against the police and the late Government. Now we have no police at all.'

A British agent living in Petrograd tells how there was no heating in many of the flats, but everyone joined in the enormous crowds in the streets: 'there were so many of us that we soon felt warm'. The cheering crowds surged towards the Duma, or down the Nevsky Prospect, or perhaps it did not much matter where so long as they kept warm— the soldiers a grey mass in ankle-length coats and peakless caps, all mixed up with drab workers waving red flags, middle-class women in fur coats and Edwardian hats, working women in quilted jackets and felt boots, intellectuals in pince-nez, all excited, many incredulous, nearly all exhilarated without any clear idea of the future. The February Revolution was spontaneous—one might almost say 'unconscious'; it was not planned like the October* Revolution made by the Bolsheviks; it was not a *coup*; in fact it is difficult to say exactly when 'it' happened. It was not a revolution *for* the establishment of any rival régime or party or faction; it was a revolution *against* rather than *for*—against the

---

* The two Revolutions are just as often called the March and November Revolutions, because of the change from the Old Style or Julian Calendar to the more accurate New Style or Gregorian Calendar, which had been worked out by Pope Gregory XIII in 1582. By the time England adopted the New Style, in the middle of the eighteenth century, the discrepancy between the calendar years and the actual years, based on the earth's passage round the sun, had become so great that eleven days had to be dropped, to the alarm of simple people, and when Russia, under the Bolsheviks, fell into line with the rest of the world in 1918, she had to make a jump of thirteen days. So although the Bolshevik seizure of power is now celebrated as of November 7th, it took place on October 25th, Old Style, and has continued to be known as 'the October Revolution'. 'October' has become a semi-sacred adjective, and the Soviet equivalent of Cubs and Brownies are called 'Octobrists'. The Orthodox Church still keeps to the Julian Calendar, and celebrates Christmas on January 7th.

Tsar personally, all his administration, and all the arms of his authority. No one bothered to support the Tsar. There was not even any minority loyalty or local loyalty to the old régime—not even among the aristocracy; they retired to the country to guard their estates, but they no longer carried out the duties of their rank as local officials, and so administration fell to bits in the countryside as well. The police disappeared into civilian clothes, and for many months, until after the Bolshevik régime was established, there was no authority to enforce civil order except for some voluntary civilian militia, who were of very varying efficacy.

The Duma was so unused to having responsibility that it dithered for several days, and then the leaders of its chief parties nominated a Provisional Government, consisting of Cadets and some conservatives, with one left-winger, Kerensky. They got the Tsar to abdicate, proclaimed Russia a Republic, and made a declaration of civil liberties for all, promising free, universal elections for a Constituent Assembly. The Western Allies, the United States and free countries everywhere applauded: Russia had at last cast off her chains. (No foreigner foresaw the Bolshevik Revolution eight months later.) Russia was presumably going to have liberal institutions at long last and enter the family of civilized nations; she would become a more reliable ally against Germany. One needs to stress that this was the reaction of Western countries in February, because fifty-odd years of loathing for the Bolsheviks have now obscured the fact, for most people in the West, that all through the reign of Nicholas II or Alexander III Russia was thought of by the average Englishman as a tyranny, kept in being by Cossacks with whips, merciless flogging of peasants, and long chains of prisoners clanking their way to Siberia.

However, February was only the brief honeymoon of revolution. If the constitutional change had come about earlier, in peacetime, a new government might have started to build a new Russia. The Provisional Government was indeed liberal minded: it released political prisoners, abolished capital punishment and exile, set up an independent judicial system again, and proclaimed freedoms such as Russia had never had in all her history. But these were paper rights for the moment; the urgent problems now were: how to get the food from the countryside to the towns, how to get fuel for heating, how the factories were to be run (whether by the workers or the employers), how the peasants' demands for land were to be satisfied, and how the mass desertions, which now began to affect even front-line troops, could be stopped before it became impossible for Russia to continue with the war. For the working class these problems naturally had priority, from their own pressing point of view; they at once showed their suspicion of the Provisional Government which had grown out of the old, restricted, pusillanimous Duma. They set up their own Soviets again—one member for every thousand workers in a factory, and usually one member for every company of soldiers. It was all rather chaotic, like everything else in Russia at this time, but the Soviets became the authority with which the Provisional Government had to compete. The Petrograd Soviet was so influential that the Government could do little without its tacit approval. By April the first All-Russian Conference of Soviets had met. Yet the Soviets were not all that revolutionary at this stage; it was rather as if the Revolution had taken political parties and leaders unawares, and after all the years of suppression they were not sure what to do with it.

The Soviets were spontaneous enough, and so were the trade unions; they both now sprang up everywhere. They were composed mainly of Social Revolutionaries and Mensheviks, with very few Bolsheviks at first, but their membership was constantly changing. It was not until April that the Germans, hoping to sow further dissension, gave a passage home to Lenin and other Bolsheviks from their exile in Switzerland, by means of the sealed train which has become so famous. The history of events between April and October is the history of the rise of the Bolshevik Party, building on the industrial workers, and driven by the phenomenal organizing genius, political judgment, and daring of Lenin. Profiting by the dilatoriness and nervousness of all other parties and bodies, and choosing the moment to strike, Lenin enabled the Bolsheviks to seize power easily—and they have held it, of course, ever since. But—and this is part of their creed—they could never have seized power without the 'revolutionary situation' created by the overthrowing of the old régime.

The October Revolution was very much a Revolution *for*—for leadership and domination by the Bolshevik Party. It soon turned out to be *against* any other form of government and any other political party whatever its programme, but it was also a revolution *for* the industrialization and modernization of Russia. The Bolsheviks were a kind of organization which had not been seen before. Their severe internal discipline, imposed by Lenin, their bold strategy and ruthless tactics, and their special dogmatic version of Marx's ideology, also developed by Lenin, were not only the characteristics which helped them to victory; they are the characteristics which have largely conditioned the Soviet system, the attitudes of the Soviet Government, its colossal successes and its colossal failures. The Bolsheviks did not develop all their severity and ruthlessness until after the October Revolution, in which they were the victors largely through Lenin's genius at taking advantage of situations. But it is also true to say that the October Revolution has proved to be one of the very few successful revolutions founded on an ideology—that is, Marxism.

Karl Marx, who lived from 1818 to 1883, was brought up a Christian, by parents who were converted Jews. Although he later rejected all religion, it has often been remarked that his writings have a great deal of the fire and also the exclusiveness of one of the Hebrew prophets. Fiery though he was, however, Marx was no 'mere' prophet, evolving doctrine from his own passionate inward convictions. Very early in life he showed an enormous appetite for learning and for comprehensive schemes of philosophy. As a young man he studied the economics and the conditions of the working class in France and Britain as well as his native Germany. He was moved by the miserable state of the early industrial workers in those countries and took part in the brief revolutionary movements of 1848 in both France and Germany, but in the reaction which followed he had to flee. In fact he renounced his Prussian nationality and spent the rest of his life in poverty in England, where he wrote most of his works, including *Capital*.

Marx despised 'Utopian' Socialists who were content to picture ideal societies without working out how they were to be reached; he toiled away all his life at facts and analysis to produce what could be regarded as irrefutable 'scientific socialism', with a scheme of thought behind it which could be used to explain all history and be applied to all phenomena. Though he obviously felt sympathy for the oppressed, historical change for him did not depend upon sympathies and feelings; it was a matter of scientific inevitability, both in the processes which he observed and in the processes which he foretold. Industrialization, as a 'law of history', he held to be everywhere in due course inevitable. It must take the form of capitalism at first, under which the misery of the industrial workers, according to Marx, is bound to increase, and capitalist oppression is bound to become more severe, as free competition develops into monopoly. Eventually the workers, at the end of their tether, will break out in inevitable revolution. They will then overthrow the capitalists and take charge of industry 'themselves', through the State ownership of the principal means of production, distribution and exchange—that is, through the nationalization of all major industry, agriculture, finance and communications.

After a period of 'the dictatorship of the proletariat', so as to annihilate any capitalist resistance or counter-attack, a 'classless society' would ensue. By a classless society Communists mean a society composed exclusively of those who work (and their dependants), whether they are professors of mathematics, fitters, sewer-men, ballet-dancers, or racecourse jockeys. The theory is that after the elimination of capitalists and private employers no one will live by the fruits of another person's work, and thus there will be no one to 'exploit' him. A classless society, it is held, would be a more admirable society, the most admirable society that has yet existed, not because workers are personally more admirable people than capitalists (though Marx did tend in practice to idealize the suffering working class of his own time), but because in a classless society no one, it is alleged, can suffer oppression, and all the talents and abilities of men and women will be spontaneously released. It is also alleged that, presumably as a result of this release, a classless society will be perfectly organized for production. The triumphant workers will, by degrees, even get rid of the machinery of State control, which will no longer be needed, and finally the State itself will 'wither away'—a Utopian idea if ever there was one!

However, Marx had very little to say about Utopia; his exposition of the classless society is a mere drop in the ocean of work which he did in examining the conditions of his own time. His analysis of capitalism (and hence also his view of the future) must have looked a good deal more convincing in the middle of the nineteenth century than it may do in some of the advanced industrial countries today. Here the workers have not become poorer but better off, largely through their own efforts; trade unions and other workers' movements are powerful, they have persuaded or obliged governments to provide social services, and capitalists have discovered that it is in their own interest to reward their workers well, so as to provide an adequate or even a greedy consumer demand. However, there are many countries where very little has yet happened along these lines, and modern developments do not invalidate the work that Marx did in exposing so dramatically the miseries and imbalances of his own day; he was the first to point out, for instance, the inevitable results of uncontrolled trade cycles. Marx's work on his own period was not just a remorseless amassing of economic facts and building up of logical demonstrations. He was concerned not only that the workers were oppressed by long hours, miserable pay, filthy, overcrowded housing, and other conditions such as we read of in Dickens, or Zola, or Charles Reade; he was also concerned that through industrialization men were being 'alienated' from their true nature. As he said in *The Communist Manifesto* of 1848: 'Owing to the extensive use of machinery and the division of labour, the work of the proletarian has lost all individual character and consequently all charm for the worker.' Like his contemporaries, Marx was full of admiration for the concrete results of the new industries—the repetition methods that meant more and more cast-iron stoves exactly alike, unlimited miles of cotton print, steam haulage, steam printing, steam cranes—it requires an effort for us today to realize the triumph, the delight, even the romance there was for our ancestors in all this. But unlike most of his contemporaries, Marx was also moved by the effects which the new methods of production had upon the relations between man and man—reducing the workers to robots, he would have said if the word had been invented then. Capitalist industry, he said, had left 'no other bond between man and man but callous "cash-payment" '; it had 'dissolved personal dignity into exchange value'. Though Marx was perhaps inclined to romanticize about old-fashioned small-scale craftsmanship, the whole *Communist Manifesto*, which he wrote when he was only twenty-six, is so brilliantly expressed and in such human terms (whatever the defects in its analysis) that it can still sound like a trumpet call to rouse the oppressed and those who take up the cause of the oppressed—in some Latin American country, perhaps, where there is a black-and-white contrast between a handful of the rich and the mass of the poor.

An original and essential feature of Marxism is the conviction that history is basically determined by economic factors alone, and that the typical characteristics of the politics, the religion, the literature and arts, and even the moral system of a period are conditioned by its economic characteristics. For example, a predominantly bourgeois, that is, a middle-class property-owning society, would have political institutions and art forms strongly influenced by bourgeois ideas of the rights of property, and its moral system would rate crimes against property more severely, perhaps, than crimes against the person. The economy, which is what characterizes society as feudal, or capitalist, or socialist, Marx called 'the base'; the rest he termed 'the superstructure'. Marx produced plenty of evidence for his concept of the superstructure, and it has proved an extremely illuminating and fruitful standpoint for the study of history. In fact one might say that in respect of this concept Marxism has proved more prophetic than in its economic analysis, since

8

the power and influence of values formed by capitalist enterprise are today greater, relatively to the power and influence exerted by values derived from other sources, than they were in Marx's day. The idea of the superstructure has been assimilated by historians and philosophers who certainly would not go all the way with Marx; they value his contribution as a point of view, not as a closed system.

But Marxists treat Marx's analysis as a completely embracing and overriding interpretation of history, because they take his view of history as in the main a conflict between broad economic and social classes, to the quasi-exclusion of the influence of individuals. Marx practically ignores the power of individual human defects as a formative force in history. The earliest capitalists, for instance, were often men who had begun as workers but who, with greed and avarice, presumably, as their strongest motive, had made themselves exploiters of the labour of their fellows. As a class, certainly, they were responsible for the evils of the early Industrial Revolution, but why was it that certain individuals, and not others, behaved in a way which made them into this 'class', and that Robert Owen and a few others with a social conscience were merely a minority? About the motives which impelled the majority of the early capitalists Marx has really nothing to say. And Marx seems to have excluded in particular the tremendous desire of many men for power as an end in itself. According to Marxist theory, a tyranny such as Stalin's should have been impossible, in a country with a socialist economic system, and during the period of 'the dictatorship of the proletariat'.

Marx overlooked, or at least was very disinclined to stress personal factors, because he was, unlike most other philosophers, preoccupied with the material world. He believed that matter, not 'spirit' or ideas, was the driving force in the world; struggling with concrete situations was what influenced people and changed them. In fact it was not until people were engaged in action with reference to things that they could be said really to have knowledge of those things. 'So far as I know,' says Bertrand Russell, 'Marx was the first philosopher who criticized the notion of "truth" from this activist point of view.' From this attitude of Marx two of his most famous sayings are derived: 'Philosophers hitherto have sought to interpret the world; what matters, however, is to change it'; and 'It is not the consciousness of men that determines their existence, but on the contrary, their social existence determines their consciousness.'

It is easy enough to bring evidence to refute the latter statement: one could adduce, for a start, the enormous power which Marx's ideas have exerted, as ideas, in almost every country, in influencing men to change the conditions of their social existence. All the same, it has been salutary for many of us to have Marx point out how men's ideas often are in fact derived from their circumstances, when they fondly imagine them to arise exclusively from some 'ideal' source. The fact is that, whether one regards his whole scheme as defective or as invulnerable, Marx has probably been the most influential social thinker in modern history, and some of his ideas have filtered through to influence and change the attitudes of many to whom the name of Marx himself is anathema.

The outline of Marx's thought which I have given here has been extremely brief. My intention was to try to show why Marxism was able to exert such a tremendous influence on most working-class movements and thus, through Lenin and part of the Russian working class, on the Soviet State. Marxism offers a scientific description and a scientific interpretation of the workers' plight at the same time that it inspires them with a vision of a rationally predictable future, guaranteed to those who will brave the fires of revolution. Marxism can appear to provide the certainty of a religion combined with the impeccable reliability of a science.

It may be useful here to mention certain things which Marx did not say, but which in the Western world he is widely supposed to have said. He did not advocate owning things in common as in a primitive community or a kibbutz, or in the old Russian tenure of land under the *mir*; he preached ownership by the State or by co-operatives. He did not advocate 'the abolition of private property'—only the expropriation of private property *in the means of production*, that is, privately owned factories, mines, banks, land, etc. He did not favour an equal wage for all. After the defeat of capitalism there would be a period to be known as 'Socialism' in Marxian terminology, during which the principle would be 'From each according to his abilities, to each according to his work', so there would be considerable inequalities of remuneration. In the final ideal state of society 'Socialism' would develop into 'Communism', when the principle would be 'From each according to his abilities, to each according to his needs'; there would be such plenty that 'inequalities' or 'rewards' would be meaningless terms; people would have pretty well what they wanted. The terms 'Socialism' and 'Communism' are used in these special senses by Communists (and only by Communists), so that every Soviet skyline today bears slogans urging citizens 'Forward to Communism!'; at present the USSR admits only to being at the 'Socialist' stage. Finally, Marx did not advocate the dictatorship of a single party, only the dictatorship of the working classes as a whole over the exploiting classes, so long as the latter continued to exist.

Russia was one of the last countries in Europe where Marx expected a revolution of the kind envisaged in his analysis, because capitalist industry in Russia was comparatively small and undeveloped, and the industrial working-class consequently should be far too small to have reached the stage of being able to make a revolution. Late in life he did suggest that the life of the peasant commune was a basis which might possibly enable Russia to avoid the full capitalist stage and 'proceed directly to socialism' (after a revolution to overthrow Tsarism, of course), but only on condition that successful socialist revolutions were already established in several of the more advanced Western countries, which would show Russia the way to industrialize, and bring support to her comparatively backward proletariat.

This is where Lenin came in, to adapt Marxism to Russian circumstances.

Lenin—the short, red-haired man in the Norfolk jacket, the world's first and greatest professional, dedicated, highly trained revolutionary, the founder, almost without knowing it, of the Soviet State—was born into a comfortable, liberal-minded, middle-class family where he seems to have had a normally happy childhood. (His father was an inspector of schools, and the family name was Ulyanov; 'Lenin' was a later, 'underground' name.) He must have been one of those boys who from a secure background take on, early in life, a rather independent, even solitary existence. Steeping himself in study, and inspired at an early age with devotion to the idea of seizing power for the benefit of his oppressed fellow-countrymen, he developed into the leader who mastered all his colleagues in argument, wore them down and was always at least one step ahead in practical policy and in daring: 'What can one do', said one of them, 'with a man who is occupied with the Revolution twenty-four hours a day?' The secure background of his childhood continued to be reflected in Lenin's more private relationships, which were gentle and considerate when politics was not involved. Many people report how he was 'always ready to listen'; his wife wrote that when he smiled, which was often, it was neither a smile of mere politeness (a rare thing with Russians in any case), nor a sardonic smile—it was a genuinely good-natured smile. He liked country life, and occasionally allowed himself the luxury of a walking tour or a spell away from cities. He took pleasure in singing, and not only revolutionary songs; in fact he enjoyed music, and later in life said: 'One can't listen to it too often. It makes you want to say nice things and stroke people's heads.' If he resisted the temptation most of the time, at least it was a more worthy temptation than some that have assailed other great leaders.

Lenin was far more ordered in his life and his studies than the average Russian intellectual; there was not a scrap of bohemianism about him. He was a typical Russian intellectual in his devotion to study and to theory, but untypical in his impatience with argument for the sake of argument: he wanted argument for the sake of action, and action according to his own ideas. The Ulyanov family were devastated, when Vladimir was seventeen, by the execution of his elder brother Alexander who, unknown to any of them, had belonged to a terrorist group at the university and joined in an attempt to assassinate the Emperor Alexander III. If it was this which set Vladimir so resolutely on the path of educating himself and others, under his leadership, to bring about the necessary revolution, it can only have been the result of the reaction between the effect of his brother's death and his own remarkably orientated nature—orientated always towards action, although even as late as January 1917, in his Swiss exile, he still doubted whether he would see the Revolution in his own lifetime.

As a student, and even as a schoolboy, Lenin belonged to several small political groups, not all of them Marxist, and it was from one of these, probably, that he first absorbed Tkachov's idea of the seizure of power by a small disciplined party. By the time he was twenty he was already a convinced revolutionary Marxist. Marx's work had long been known in Russia and discussed in little groups where politically-minded Russians, inhibited as always from political action, argued from a Marxist basis in widely diverging directions, just as people outside Russia did and have continued to do ever since. When the Russian Social Democratic Party was founded in 1898, as a small party of intellectuals and industrial workers, it soon had a left-wing of severely 'orthodox', revolutionary Marxists, and a right-wing who believed that policies of gradual reform could be a practical way to Socialism and could, as a matter of theory, also be deduced from Marx. Lenin was implacably opposed to 'reformism' or any other deviation from or dilution of what he considered to be the essential revolutionary gospel of Marx. As leader of the chief Marxist group in St. Petersburg, undertaking propaganda among local workers, at the age of twenty-seven he earned himself three years' banishment to Siberia, where he continued to write and to study. After his return, most of his life until 1917 was spent in refuge in Western Europe, several times in London, with only brief and occasional visits to Russia. But in spite of his having to live abroad, foreign visitors to Russia after the 1905 outbreak reported that Lenin was looked up to by the more militant workers as their most important leader, along with Trotsky, who was also in exile.

Lenin saw his first task as the need to educate the workers politically. The 'economic struggle', to win concessions from employers or the Government, was a matter for trade union secretaries, not true revolutionaries, he said, and he was soon proclaiming that the workers by themselves could not attain to more than a state of 'trade union consciousness'. In order to reach the level at which they would make a revolution, they needed to be led by a profoundly conscious and politically educated party which would, for example, expose to them the class factors in every possible situation, for example, in the censorship under which they all suffered, or in the systematic floggings of the peasants, or in the persecution of the minority religious sects, as well as in the strikes and the fight for better economic conditions. 'We are the party of a class', Lenin wrote, 'and therefore almost the entire class (and in times of war, in the period of civil war, the entire class) should act under the leadership of our Party, should adhere to our Party as closely as possible. But it would be smug complacency to think that at any time under capitalism the entire class, or almost the entire class, would be able to rise to the level of consciousness and activity of its vanguard, of its Social-Democratic Party.'

By advocating such a party as the ultimate weapon of revolution Lenin, as has repeatedly been said, was 'standing Marx on his head'. He was declaring that political ideas, spread with sufficient force and conviction, could bring about a revolution, whereas Marx had taught that it was the 'material conditions of production' which must drive the desperate masses, ultimately, to spontaneous action.

At the Congress of the Russian Social Democratic Party in 1903 Lenin fought to have it reorganized as a small, even a very small Party, consisting of a devoted band of experienced revolutionaries, skilled at dodging the police,* and all subject to discipline from headquarters, in both their ideology and their activities. Other delegates wanted a party

---

* They dodged them so well that practically all the Bolshevik leaders inside Russia seem to have avoided military service in the First World War; Stalin had an injured arm and was exempted.

like the Western Social Democratic Parties, with as large a membership of sympathizers as could be got, and a policy more democratically arrived at. But such a party, Lenin pointed out, 'would be a very paradise for the police', who would easily infiltrate it through their agents, and either neutralize it or destroy it. He was right, of course, about the Russian police; his opponents were trusting more to the strength of spontaneous mass action, such as Marx had expected to triumph eventually in Western Europe. Lenin's powers of persuasion won the day, and the majority who sided with him were henceforth known as *Bolsheviks* (from the Russian word for majority), while the others were known as *Mensheviks* (from the word for minority). It was a strange occasion. The RSDP was a small, persecuted party which was unable to hold its Congress in Russia; many of its leaders were already perforce in exile, and they met first in Brussels, and when they were chased away from there, in London. A typical group of Russian exiles they must have seemed, meeting in a Nonconformist hall in London (where the rent had been paid by a British well-wisher), arguing and arguing about theory, with only 'underground' means of communication with their scattered followers in Russia. England was traditionally hospitable to such little gatherings; there was, of course, no report in the British press—anyway they were all speaking Russian, the language of East End tailors and bakers. If Lenin had died during the next few years, little more might have been heard of this meeting. Yet insignificant, almost laughable, as it may have seemed at the time, the 1903 Congress which fathered the Bolshevik Party has proved one of the important dates in the history of the world.

The Bolsheviks did not split off right away; in fact at the next Congress of the RSDP Lenin was outvoted, and the Mensheviks became the majority. A little later, Lenin was actually expelled for a short time, for interfering too much in the organization of the RSDP. But he argued his way back again, and with the help of underground leaflets and the beginnings of the underground newspaper, *Pravda*, besides a few Bolshevik members in the Duma, and Bolshevik trade union officials, he began to get support in Russia. Though the interesting thing is that right up to 1917 the Mensheviks had more support inside Russia than the Bolsheviks did.

The Mensheviks had a good deal of strength among the skilled workers, and especially in the south and west of the country, which had long been more open to Western influences; they also had some middle-class support. The Bolsheviks drew their strength more from unskilled workers, from young men who had recently come from the villages, and particularly from the industrial centres of old, traditional, central Russia and the capital. In the two greatest centres, Petersburg and Moscow, they controlled most of the trade unions as the First World War was breaking out. Thus the Bolsheviks were more of a strictly class party, their membership was younger, less educated on the average, and probably more ready to accept the plain and downright analyses of situations which Lenin put before them. They were not, many of them, likely to be the kind of people who value the abstraction of 'individual liberty' above certain concrete goals which look attainable, and they must have been happy in a leadership who seemed determined and knew their own minds. The Mensheviks were the more 'Western' of the two factions, the more democratic in the normal Western sense —and there were plenty of Russians at this time hungering for democracy. Lenin was more in the old Russian tradition of minority or autocratic government, but also his policies were usually nearer to practical politics in the immediate Russian situation.

The form and tradition of government which he created, and which is rigidly incorporated in the Soviet Union today, was no sooner formulated than it was attacked by Trotsky and several other Bolsheviks. On the very morrow of the Party Congress in 1903 Trotsky made a tragically accurate prophecy: 'Lenin's methods lead to this: the party organization at first substitutes itself for the party as a whole; then the Central Committee substitutes itself for the organization; and finally a single "dictator" substitutes himself for the Central Committee.' So long as Lenin lived the danger probably was not too great; he remained accessible to people of all ranks, modest in his personal dealings, an expounder on the platform rather than a rousing orator like Trotsky. What is more, there is no evidence that he evinced greedy, or sadistic, or even complacent enjoyment of power when it finally fell into his hands. All the same, power was what he pursued, for more than twenty years, and in pursuing it and exercising it he remained the same inscrutable solitary, behind the ready smile and the decent private relations, that he was when he started out. He was a dictator by virtue of being nearly always right in his *ad hoc* judgments, and by his startling and often unscrupulous opportunism in tactics. That was the position he wanted, and he could not have changed his nature had he even wished to do so.

If I have seemed in the last few pages to be inordinately occupied with political theory rather than events, I can only repeat that in Russian

7. Second-hand
   boot market, early
   twentieth century
   (Novosti)

8. Seasonal worker,
   1912 (Novosti)

9. The Politburo in 1929. *From left to right:* Ordjonikidze (suicide 1937), Voroshilov, Kuibyshev (d. 1935), Stalin (d. 1953), Kalinin (President of the USSR, d. 1946), Kaganovich (expelled 1957), Kirov (murdered 1934) (John Freeman)

10. Raisa Vladimirova, secretary of her factory's Young Communist organization (Novosti)

11. Soviet worker (Novosti)

12. Outskirts of Bratsk, Siberia (John Massey Stewart)

circumstances it was bound to be mainly theory which occupied Russian politicals over their glasses of tea and long-tubed cigarettes, and that to a considerable extent it was theory which eventually decided what happened in Russia.

Lenin found his fellow Bolsheviks in an agony of theory when he came back from Switzerland in April 1917: should they try to make the Soviets declare themselves the true and effective government of the country? That the Soviets had more support than the Provisional Government there was no question, but—they were dominated by Mensheviks and Social Revolutionaries; the Bolsheviks would be in a minority in such a Government. And more fundamentally, since the middle-class, 'bourgeois' revolution had overthrown the old autocracy, ought not good Marxists to wait until the now dominantly capitalist Russia had risen to something like the West European level of industrialization? In due course there would then be a large and politically conscious proletariat of industrial workers, whom the Bolsheviks would lead to the 'inevitable' workers' revolution. Lenin himself had at one time thought it would be necessary to wait for this stage, but now, quickly sensing with his lively political antennae the general lack of order and organization in Russia, and the fact that no body or party seemed to have a grip on what the mass of people wanted, he determined that the Bolsheviks should be that Party, and that there was a chance to go straight on to the second, crucial revolution which should put the industrial workers in power. At the beginning he was laughed at for this interpretation, even by many in his own party. But he was right about the fluidity of the situation; the rank and file were pushing their own leaders hard. They were pushing them hard, for instance, for workers' control in the factories, and before long the Bolsheviks had seized their opportunity and had won a majority on most factory committees. They were also pushing the Soviets, whose membership was frequently changing. Lenin drove his colleagues to work vigorously in the Soviets, so as to take leading positions in them, capture them and use them eventually as part of the means to seizing power—a method which has been typical of Communists ever since.

No one but the Bolsheviks, apparently, was prepared to take a firm position on the two questions which mattered most: whether to continue the war or not, and how to get bread for the towns. For getting bread meant getting the grain out of the peasants, who were now so out of hand that they would only co-operate if the land were to be confiscated, by decree, from its existing owners and given to those who worked it. It was a twin problem, really, because if the Government decreed that the peasants were to have the land, it was feared that the bulk of the soldiers (who were also peasants) would simply desert. There were still nine million men under arms, and they were not always even getting food. At the front they had given up fighting, and the Germans had given up attacking, so as to encourage fraternization and pacifism in general. Some of the nine million were reading the Bolshevik *Pravda*, which urged them not only to give up fighting but to encourage German soldiers to revolution as well.

However, few people, beyond some of the Bolsheviks, could yet bring themselves to face the idea of a separate peace with Germany, and in Petrograd some members of the Soviet joined in a compromise coalition with the Provisional Government, whose grip was weak enough in all conscience. This increased the gulf between the moderate socialists and the Bolsheviks, who of course stayed out of the coalition and gathered more support from militant workers by doing so. They were going from strength to strength—from a membership of 20,000 in February to 240,000 in August. The Provisional Government was very unwilling even to announce a date for elections to the promised National Assembly, because it feared that support for the Cadets and right-wing parties would turn out to be minimal. In June and July there were local elections, completely free and democratic for the first time, for the municipal councils, or dumas, of the principal cities, and in many of these the Bolsheviks got a majority. Over the whole country the Social Revolutionaries did best, but the Cadets did badly.

The peasants, who had been comparatively quiet, were beginning to break out and seize the land and the forests for themselves—and this time there were no military units which could be used to hold them back. Lenin at once saw the possibilities of support from the peasants, who had previously been thought of as too politically backward to be counted as forces of revolution. In fact there was so much disorder everywhere that, against the advice of the Bolsheviks, there was an unsuccessful rising against the Provisional Government in Petrograd, led mainly by sailors from nearby Kronstadt. It failed, and a short period of reaction followed, during which Trotsky was in prison for a while, and Lenin in hiding.

The commander-in-chief, General Kornilov, now proposed that the Government should break up the Soviets altogether, and reintroduce the death penalty so as to restore discipline in the army. The Western Allies had naturally been nervous for some time about the anti-war tendencies in Russia, and their leader-writers now hailed Kornilov's move as the inevitable military takeover after a revolution. But Kornilov was no Cromwell nor Napoleon; the war had gone on too long already, and he was a complete flop. His forces melted away, and even if they had stuck to him they would never have reached Petrograd, because the railwaymen had torn up the lines ahead of them. Kerensky, who was now Prime Minister, in fact dismissed Kornilov. He was arrested, and this successful riposte against 'the forces of counter-revolution' brought further great reinforcements to the Bolshevik side. The food situation in the towns was all the time getting worse, the value of money was unpredictable, and the peasants were vociferating that the land question must be settled at once, or the ploughing would not get done before the winter.

Lenin now called for 'boundless audacity'; the Bolsheviks at last had a majority in the principal city Soviets and in many of the army Soviets, but most of the Bolshevik leaders still hesitated to follow Lenin's call for an armed uprising. Then the Germans, after a long lull, took the offensive again, and their advance towards Petrograd caused the Petrograd Soviet to propose a 'military revolutionary committee' to defend the revolution—a heaven-sent opportunity, seized by Lenin, for the Bolsheviks to create a military organization dominated by themselves. They turned it, of course, into an organization for insurrection, and fifteen days later, under the brilliant leadership of Trotsky, all the key points in Petrograd were seized by the Bolsheviks. The only fighting of any consequence was at the capture of the Winter Palace; in fact other Russians were going to the opera the same night and had no idea of what was going on. But slight though the conflict was, it was conclusive. Fighting in Moscow lasted several days, but all the cities were very soon won.

Two leading Bolsheviks, Kamenev and Zinoviev, striving urgently to preserve some respect for the principle of democracy, had urged that the rising should wait until it could be backed by the Second All-Russian Congress of Soviets, which was due to meet in November. Lenin, relentlessly pursuing a different principle, wrote to the Central Committee of his Party: 'To "await" the Congress of Soviets is absolute idiocy, for this means losing *weeks*. It means timidly to *refuse* the seizure of power, for on November 14–15 it will be impossible (both politically and technically), since the Cossacks will be mobilized for the day of the foolishly "appointed" uprising.' (It may be doubted how effective the Cossacks would have been, but it may also very much be doubted whether the Congress, in which the Bolsheviks did not have a majority, would have wanted to launch an insurrection.) Lenin went on, in rather curious language: 'The people have a right and a duty to decide such questions not by voting but by force; the people have a right and a duty in critical moments of a revolution to give directions to their representatives, even their best representatives, and not to wait for them.'

Lenin's conception of 'the people' shows clearly and ironically enough in this last-minute document, but tactically he certainly chose the right moment. Some of the Bolshevik rank and file had already been killing off conservatives and Cadets, while Kerensky could find no troops to fight for him. The Cadet leader Nabokov said afterwards: 'The ease with which Lenin and Trotsky overthrew the last coalition government of Kerensky revealed its inward impotence. The degree of this impotence was an amazement at that time even to well-informed people.'

On the morrow of November 7th Lenin issued two decrees, one declaring an armistice with Germany, the other nationalizing the land. The Gordian knot of Russia's twin problem was cut at last.

The foreign press, somewhat mystified, reported the Bolshevik Revolution rather briefly, under such headings as 'Another Upset in Russia'. In Britain a single journal only, Marxist and of tiny circulation, recognized the Revolution for what it was.

There was reason enough to suspend judgment, even for those who were on the spot. Some of the Bolshevik leaders were themselves not sure how long their Government could last, and in the south, Cossack generals were raising anti-Bolshevik cavalry from among the independent peasantry. When the expected Congress of Soviets met, the day after the Bolsheviks seized power, 270 out of its 650 members—Mensheviks and right-wing Social Revolutionaries—denounced the takeover and walked out. The remainder of the Congress—Bolsheviks and left-wing* Social Revolutionaries—gave their support to the new Government, the Council of People's Commissars. (The Commissars were nominated by the Bolshevik leaders to head the old ministries, or what was left of them.) At least one Bolshevik, Kamenev, thought that

---

* The left wing of the Social Revolutionary Party was more concerned about the smaller or landless peasants than the right wing was, and it also had some Marxist leanings. It was a small faction, but it made a useful ally for the Bolsheviks at first; later its members reverted to their old party tradition of assassination, and disagreeing with Lenin's peace policy, one of them, Dora Kaplan, tried to shoot Lenin and wounded him in the head. In 1921 the left S.R.s, as well as all other political parties, were declared illegal and their leaders arrested. Some of the S.R.s, still stiff-necked in their opposition, were found languishing in prison, at least as late as 1940, by newcomers, the victims of Stalin's purges.

his Party ought to form a coalition Government with the Mensheviks and S.R.s, but he was brushed aside. The endorsement of the new Government by the Congress of Soviets, even though it was a mutilated Congress, gave the Council of People's Commissars some sort of legality in the eyes of a large part of the population, and it is typical of the times that the 270 Mensheviks and S.R.s who walked out had no luck at all when they tried to set up an alternative Government on their own. News travelled slowly to the provinces, which was where they had support, but it was what happened in the capital and a few other cities, where the Bolsheviks were in a majority, which mattered just then.

Eighteen days after the October Revolution the long-postponed elections for the National Assembly at last took place—with many misgivings on the part of the Bolsheviks, who feared that the result would be little help to them. Only about half the electorate voted, but the elections were, for the first time, based on a universal and equal franchise. The Bolsheviks got only about a quarter of the votes and 175 seats, and the left S.R.s 40, but the right S.R.s got 380, with the Mensheviks and Cadets nowhere. The triumphant S.R.s marched through the streets of Petrograd, the day before the Assembly was due to open, in order to celebrate the victory of democracy, but the Bolsheviks gave out that this was 'a counter-revolutionary demonstration', and they got some of their most trigger-happy young men to mount an armed guard over its passage. The Assembly, the first and only representative parliament in Russia, did meet, on a day in January 1918, but at the end of that day it was dispersed by Bolshevik Red Guards, and it was never allowed to meet again.

So the Rubicon was now crossed into one-party dictatorship. The whole democratic part (according to our ideas) of the Social Democratic tradition, which had been the ideal of many for several generations, was thus suppressed in Russia, and it has stayed suppressed. The very name of 'Social Democrat' disappeared, and the Bolsheviks were now calling themselves the Communist Party. Yet at the time, the extinction of the elected parliament raised singularly little stir.

Once again, it was partly the great size of Russia which made democracy difficult to work. The S.R.s had a majority in the Assembly because they were the peasant party, and most Russian constituencies were peasant constituencies. (Probably most of the non-voters were peasants, too.) But apart from the seizing of estates, most of the political activity was concentrated in the towns. And the situation in the towns now was that people were queueing for hours to get a little food, that many of them were unemployed, and many already grey with bad feeding, though there was a plentiful diet, varying from day to day, of political leaflets and fly-posted appeals, orders and announcements. People were already cowering back as Red Guards patrolled the streets —young men in working clothes carrying rifles, with red stars sewn on their caps. If people were thinking politically, they were thinking first about the peasants who had the grain, and how it was to be got out of them by the townspeople, who had practically no goods that the peasants wanted, only paper roubles; or they were thinking of the Germans, and whether the armistice was to be trusted; or perhaps they were thinking of the old régime and the old culture and fearing they might be by no means dead; and a minority, certainly, were thinking, in fear, of the rise of the crude, enthusiastic young men with red stars for badges. They were thinking in helpless fear, because they were themselves a minority—in Petrograd, in Moscow, in all the cities—and because they did not see how the young men could be stopped. But what they feared most was what almost everyone feared—the menace of a chaos bubbling up from below which would be worse than any tyranny. All these fears were more urgent than any concern for the principle of equal, popular representation which ought to have been realized in the Assembly, and if any disgruntled S.R. members of that Assembly stayed on in Petrograd they had to share the same life and the same fears; communications with the provinces were bad, and few in the city would be interested in their protests.

Any viable government at this time would have been bound to be authoritarian, and it is difficult to see what party, faction, body, or organization could have seemed at that time willing and able to take on responsibility and be authoritarian enough, other than the Bolsheviks. One can hardly say that all their methods were either necessary or inevitable: Lenin's idea of a dictatorial party subordinated to its own dictatorial leadership was not inevitable; his rejection of coalitions was not inevitable—but one can be pretty sure that what most people demanded of any government just then was that it should be above all effectual; they had had enough of discussion. Authority was not merely what they had been used to and understood—it was badly needed; however enthusiastic people might be about either or both of the Revolutions, the shops were empty of nearly everything, the trains were few and slow, the factories could not get their supplies, and life seemed to be running down altogether. The peasants had indeed benefited;

they had the land; but if the Revolution was going to make townspeople better off materially, that could only be in an uncertain future.

In March 1918 the Germans consented to sign a peace with the Russians—the Treaty of Brest-Litovsk, whose appalling terms sliced off a third of European Russia, nearly all her best agricultural land, and most of her coal. Even the Bolsheviks were split over accepting such conditions, and it was typical of the ruthlessness of Lenin that he insisted on signing. Further resistance was in fact impossible; to persist for the sake of either territory or ideology would have imperilled the future, and he 'knew', as a Marxist, that the Bolsheviks' hour must come again. Most of the lost territory, actually, was recovered after the Western Allies had defeated Germany in November 1918, and when the Second World War began the first Soviet war aim was to recover the remainder—the Baltic Republics, and what had become Eastern Poland.

The Civil War of 1917–21 broke out by degrees, in a piecemeal fashion; it consisted of a number of campaigns undertaken for so many reasons that non-Russian historians today are often reluctant to allow them the name of a civil war—'more a collection of adventurisms'. It did not break out in the cities, where there were sizeable groups of the middle class—and it is important to remember how small and politically subdued the Russian middle class, even the business class, had mostly been. The Whites raised most of their support from the better-off peasants in the south and in Siberia. Some of the White generals—Denikin, Kolchak, Wrangel—certainly desired the good of their country, others were mere adventurers. The Denikins and Kolchaks hoped to reimpose a more old-fashioned type of authority than the improvised, apparently unpredictable Bolshevik version. (Some of them, incidentally, raised the standard of Nicholas II again, though to little advantage.) The British, French, Americans and Japanese intervened, but halfheartedly, since most nations by now had had enough of war. They intervened at first to support any Whites who might go on resisting the Germans, and they intervened also because the Bolsheviks had repudiated all the foreign debts of Tsarist Russia, and because Bolshevik nationalization meant the loss of a great deal of foreign investment. The intervention was not tremendously significant, but it left a bitter hatred which had not died out when Britain and America became allies of Russia against Germany again in 1941. Trotsky trained the new Red Army, with the help of former Tsarist officers for whom loyalty to their country seemed more important than loyalty to the Tsar—or maybe because they could find no other occupation. But the Red Army was built up largely of workers, and officered by them too. (One youth from a textile factory who fought and survived is now Chairman of the Soviet Council of Ministers: his name is Kosygin.) The Reds eventually had ten times as many men as the Whites, but they took a long time to win. There was a great deal of brutality on both sides, but particularly from the Whites, who did not understand the change that had come over most of the peasants, while the Reds treated them, on the whole, more considerately. The southern regions had also to endure the 'Green' Armies, who plundered, murdered and raped in the interest of Anarchism, or of no cause at all. In the end there was no doubt, says the British agent Sir Paul Dukes, who was doing underground work at the time, that when people had to choose between Whites and Reds, they preferred the Reds; besides their more sympathetic political attitude, the Reds were officered and led by men like one's own mates.

The campaigns of the Civil War were terribly improvised on both sides, like everything else in Russia in those years: medical services were almost non-existent, and finally there was famine, cholera and typhus. Four million Russians had died in the Great War, another million died in the fighting in the Civil War, but seven and a half million more, all of them civilians, died through starvation or disease during the Civil War years and the famine just after. Farms were derelict, the area under grain shrank to half of what it had been, animals were destroyed, towns were depopulated, the industrial working population depleted, and manufactures were barely ticking over, at one-eighth of the pre-war rate. Russia was in far worse plight than she had been when the First World War began.

1921–2 was the nadir, the year from which one should begin to count Soviet progress, not 1917. It was not very long ago. The Soviet Union is still mostly run by men of about sixty years of age, or coming up to sixty, who had a childhood of semi-starvation and insecurity, when they were being dragged, without fathers, from one spot to another to escape the fighting or in the hope of finding food, with corpses and disease part of the everyday scene. No wonder they are today an ultra-conservative generation, nervously anxious to preserve discipline quietly and avoid any kind of 'trouble' or the appearance of trouble. In fact nearly all the Soviet men and women of similar age are conservative today, and fear any lapse into the disorder which as children they knew.

Yet it was these men and women, and their fathers and mothers, who carried out the Bolshevik Revolution, not merely in the sense of seizing power or winning the Civil War, but through all the grinding of the twenty-odd years that it took to make the Revolution effective and change the old Russia. The October Revolution would probably never have taken place without Lenin and Trotsky, yet they and the brilliant circle of intelligentsia round them, and afterwards Stalin himself, would have been powerless without the energies and enthusiasms— and there was enthusiasm even under Stalin—of several million workers who were near-peasants, or who were pure peasants newly arrived in town.

What is one to understand by 'peasant', or by the near-peasants who were industrial workers—the two classes who provided men who are now in key positions all over the Soviet Union, and who together made up more than 90 per cent of the nation in 1917?

It is a pity one has to use the word 'peasant'—certainly not if it suggests picturesque, 'merrie' peasants living in quaint old cottages. For one thing, there are scarcely any old cottages in Russia; the wooden huts burn down too easily, and there have been far too many occasions for them to burn down. In the north and centre of Russia people lived in one-room log huts at most fifteen feet by twenty or thirty (the same as one still sees from the train); they rarely ate meat, and besides the full-grain black bread, they fed mostly on potatoes, buckwheat, cabbage and beet. In the treeless steppe they had (and often still have) one-room huts of whitewashed earth, with the floor scooped out below ground level. Whether north, centre, or south, they usually slept on the earthen floor or on benches, but in the steppe they were mostly better off for food, with pigs or even sheep and cattle, and oil to cook with, from the sunflowers which waved taller than their little cabins. They distilled illicit spirit from potatoes, or drank the government vodka when they had a little money. They were half-starved at times, they were hardy and enduring beyond our ideas of any rocklike northern fisherman or sailor, they were patient and usually acquiescent because they had no alternative, but underneath, they always felt that a man had a right to what he could win with his own spade or scythe or axe—especially, perhaps, with his axe. They were immensely conservative on the whole, because keeping to the simple ways they knew, and the few simple possessions they had, was the only kind of security they could hope for. But there was nothing romantic or sophisticated about their conservatism. They were superstitious about house goblins and the spirits of drowned maidens: to appease the one and avoid the other seemed common sense, like the observation of the Church rituals, which they

9

accepted as guaranteeing part of the everyday scene, but most of them did not know the Church services and were quite likely to talk while they were in progress; they also had a fund of obscene stories about priests. They had a great capacity for Christian charity and for Christian, or probably pre-Christian, brotherliness; they preferred working in comradeship to sweating it out on their own. They were not burdened with an elaborate code for living, like the Jews or Hindus. They were realistic and practical—realistic in the sense that the best Russian literature is realistic, facing things and people as they really are. They could be original, they could be independent, and it is remarkable how little they had been cowed by all the centuries of serfdom and oppression. In the seventeenth century several million of them flouted their Patriarch and their Tsar, who were changing some details of Church ritual, and went into the wilderness as persecuted 'Old Believers'. By the time the Revolution arrived, probably 25 million of them had forsaken their traditional Church, either as Old Believers or as members of various later independent sects, some of them, such as the Baptists, imported by Germans, while others, such as the Flagellators or the Doukhobors, grew up around local prophets.* The Church did not retain much of a hold on the other hundred million or so; according to no less an authority than the Orthodox theologian Berdyayev, who was in Russia at the time and originally sympathized with the Revolution, the majority of the people gave up their Church when they gave up their Tsar: the two loyalties had been, apparently, of a similar kind.

The 90 per cent of peasants and near-peasants, in 1917, were the storehouse of at least 90 per cent of the nation's energy, 90 per cent of its moral goodness as well as its moral turpitude, and probably also 90 per cent of its potential talent. They were so many, these 'peasants', they cannot all have been those slower, simple-minded but calculating types who narrow their eyes at you, the types who in other countries get left to till the land while the smart ones exploit town life. They included the 'simple soldiers' who so astonished Maurice Baring, when he was a war correspondent in 1904, because they could cook an excellent dinner, mend a watch, make fireworks, paint scenery, or sing in a quartet at the standard of a European opera house. They included the highly intelligent, the stupid, the quick-witted, the coarse-grained, the fine-grained. It is perhaps particularly difficult to realize how in this mass of the rough-skinned and primitively dressed there must have

* New faiths still appear in country districts, even in quite recent Soviet times.

been, at least potentially, every kind and grade of sensibility, from the crudest to the most discriminating, from the commonplace to the most enterprising. The coarse one can readily believe in, especially in view of the more brutal features of Soviet life later, for which there were bullies and bosses ready made; there must also have been some of the suspicious, ferret-like types whom the system eventually needed, though these were not recruited from one class alone; plenty of former middle-class or even upper-class people turned themselves into such types to save their skins. But also, among the 90 per cent, there was that reservoir of fine but undeveloped sensibility from which, during the next twenty years, were drawn surgeons, violinists, singers, ballet-dancers, and so forth, of world class. To appreciate the infinite variety of potentialities one needs perhaps to have seen the Russian people as I saw them myself no longer ago than the Second World War, when the whole civilian population seemed bundled into shapeless clothing, they were grey with malnutrition, their faces bleeding from scurvy, banging their clumsy mittens together in the iron cold—yet when we spoke together, here were also the poets and the architects and the enthusiasts for Shakespeare as well as the crane-drivers and electricians and lathe hands—and sometimes there were both kinds in the same person.

The peasants and near-peasants brought all this variety of talent and character to the Revolution, and they brought also a combination of characteristics which it is crucially important, if perhaps difficult, for us today to comprehend: they brought an ancestral stoicism *along with* a capacity for leaping at opportunities. This was the stoicism which Maurice Baring, for instance, found among the soldiers, where it meant the uncomplaining missing of a meal, the uncomplaining enduring of a beating, and equally the unquestioning inflicting of a beating when it was ordered. There were the Russians of whom Gorky wrote, in *My Childhood*, just before the Revolution, that 'through the poverty and squalor of their lives, suffering comes as a diversion, is turned into a game and they play at it like children and rarely feel ashamed of their misfortune'. These were the Russians who used to sing, as my old Bolshevik friend told me:

> '*Sevodnya v traktire,*
> *A zavtra v mogile.*'

(In the boozer today, in the graveyard tomorrow)—and not with any music-hall irony, but meaning just what they sang.

It was for these Russians, to these Russians, and through these Russians that the Revolution seemed to open. As Gorky also wrote— out of the brutalities and beastliness of *My Childhood*:

'Life is always surprising us—not by its rich, seething layer of bestial refuse—but by the bright, healthy and creative human powers of goodness that are for ever forcing their way up through it. It is those powers that awaken our indestructible hope that a brighter, better and more humane life will once again be reborn.'

Two of the most distinguished living psychiatrists have written about the character of the men who helped to make the Bolshevik Revolution. 'The outstanding trait of the Russian personality', says Henry V. Dicks, 'is its contradictoriness, its ambivalence.' But further: 'All revolutionary motivation, at the pre-rational level, must include some themes like that of supplanting, or stepping into the dead father's [Tsar's, landlord's, etc.] shoes.' The Revolution must have been made, says Dicks, by men capable of 'maniac denial'. (This quality, says Berdyayev, was the traditional Russian asceticism turning secular.)

Erik Erikson, in *Childhood and Society*, says: 'In the Bolshevik psychology, of outstanding importance is a determined *"grasping"*, paired with a resistance against sinking back into dependence . . . a kind of delayed Eastern protestantism.'

Delayed it was, but it had been latent all the time, perhaps ever since the establishment of serfdom. Turgenev saw and described it seventy years before the Revolution, in one of his peasant sketches, *Hor and Kalinitch*: 'The Russian is so convinced of his own strength and powers that he is not afraid of putting himself to severe strain; he takes little interest in his past, and looks boldly forward.'

7. How Long Does a Revolution Take?

So much squalor and disease has been swept away by Soviet governments, so much enlightenment spread over the whole of their territory, so much talent fostered, so much initiative frozen and killed off, so much monotony imposed, so much intellectual and spiritual freedom suppressed; there has been such bulldozing of the sleepy old landscape and such bulldozing of the labour of millions (many of them, till recently, unto death); there has been such launching of Tupolevs into the air and astronauts into space, such twentyfold and hundredfold growth to make the USSR second in the world for industrial might; there has been such upheaval, terrorizing, blossoming, shackling, fructifying and forcing into straitjackets that it seems difficult to know how to begin the story of Russia after the Revolution.

It has all taken place in so short a time: the Soviet Union celebrated its fiftieth anniversary, elaborately and at great length, in 1967, but that was only the anniversary of the Bolshevik seizure of power; it could not be reckoned more than the thirty-ninth anniversary of Socialist industrialization, which began with the first Five-Year Plan in 1928.

The political tyranny, the tremendous industrialization, the education and public health programmes are all aspects of the same gigantic Bolshevik drive—to bring Russia out of her backwardness, fast; to cast off her history in which advances had always been too few and too late. The aim of the Five-Year Plans was 'To overtake and outstrip the leading capitalist countries in technique and economic organization'. Half-way through the agonies of the first Plan, in 1931, Stalin made a speech to industrial executives, some of whom had been asking whether the tempo could not be slowed down. He said: 'To slacken the pace means to lag behind, and those who lag behind are beaten. We do not want to be beaten ... Russia was ceaselessly beaten for her backwardness. She was beaten by the Mongol Khans, she was beaten by Turkish Beys, she was beaten by Polish-Lithuanian gentry, she was beaten by Swedish feudal lords, she was beaten by Anglo-French capitalists, she was beaten by Japanese barons; she was beaten by all—for her backwardness. For military backwardness, for cultural backwardness, for political backwardness, for industrial backwardness, for agricultural backwardness ... We are fifty or a hundred years behind the advanced countries. We must make good this lag in ten years. Either we do it or they crush us.'

Witte had not been able to industrialize fast enough because he was held back by a hopeless political system whose chief aim was self-perpetuation: the Bolsheviks, in the course of a few years, forged a ruthlessly effective political system which had aims involving the whole of Russian life. From Marx they drew an almost religious belief in the virtues of industrialization and the virtues of the industrial worker. And from Marx they drew their conviction that not only the political and economic system but every feature of the old 'superstructure' must be changed—the old culture, science, morality, the family, and religion. As time went on, however, it became clear that the Bolsheviks drew strength not only from a Messianic confidence in their mission but also from the living root of Russian patriotism, indeed from Russian chauvinism. And eventually not all the old 'superstructure' was rejected, and it was seen how potent some of the deeper, less conscious Russian strains remained. Revolutionaries are bound to have some base of inherited and largely unacknowledged stability from which to launch change: the intensity and assertiveness of their extremism, as individuals, is pretty well a guarantee of the intense conservatism of their self-protective core, and the more drastic and successful the Revolution which they are able to carry out, the more likely it is that some features of the older society may remain for a long time fossilized or not open to question. They are preserved—to make a symbolic comparison—like the little green Victorian lampshade in the portraits of Lenin, which is still copied in millions of lampshades all over the Soviet Union. During the Second World War—the Great Patriotic War as it is so often called in Russia—it became particularly obvious what a powerful cement the old Russian communalism could be. I shall have something to say concerning its survival when I write about contemporary Russian society: after two generations and more the communalism is not so strong as it was, and this weakening is one great cause of difficulty, under the Soviet system, in solving the main domestic problems of the 1970s. Many of the early Bolshevik goals have been reached —in heavy industry, in power and in public health, for instance —but the political system which secured them remains almost unchanged, and it is very ill-adapted to coping with a better educated society and its demands for consumer goods. The political system badly needs to be modified, but no one in authority seems to know how this can come about without an unthinkable surrender of a good deal of power and of the principle behind such power, and this impasse, one need hardly say, is the other great cause, indeed the major cause, of Soviet difficulties at the present time.

In the beginning, however, it was unlikely that any of this should have been foreseen. The Bolsheviks were not even sure that they would succeed, or how they would succeed. They had to give up two cherished articles of faith, at least for a time. The Russian Revolution had not acted as the torch to set alight revolutions in Europe; the Communist Governments in Hungary and Bavaria had been extremely short-lived, and though a strike of Glasgow dockers had helped to end British intervention in the Civil War, only sporadic encouragement was to be had from European workers' movements in general. Secondly, there turned out to be little evidence for the naïve anarchistic belief that the workers, now they had been freed from capitalism, would naturally act in the ways that new industrial development was going to require. Not that they were unwilling to work, but they wanted too much independence, they wanted to organize the work themselves. In 1921 Red sailors and Red Army men led a revolt at the naval base of Kronstadt under the slogan 'Soviets Without Communists!' At the same time the peasants over a very large part of the wheat-growing provinces were rebelling against the requisitioning of grain by over-zealous Communists—and this in March, too, in the period of the 'hungry gap'. The Kronstadt affair was sternly suppressed by Trotsky, but to suppress the peasants would have been much more difficult and, in any case, suicidal in effect. Russia in 1921 was exhausted, and Lenin now decided on a complete change of policy. If the industrial workers could hope for no help from outside, then the Bolsheviks must adopt the other alternative which Marx had hinted at for a revolutionary party in Russia: they must lean on the peasants, petty-capitalist though the peasant outlook, for the time being, might be. To the scandal of some of his colleagues, Lenin introduced his New Economic Policy (NEP). The peasants were encouraged to sell in the open market and even to 'enrich themselves', subject only to a government tax on what they produced; small-scale capitalist produc-tion was allowed and encouraged, and along with it small-scale capi-talist commerce, so as to get the products of the towns out to the peasants again, and to bring peasant produce into the half-starved towns. Heavy industry, transport, foreign trade and banks—'the commanding heights'—remained nationalized, but the NEP men soon brought small-scale manufacture back to a prewar level, while some of the peasants began to grow rich, and the NEP merchants swilled champagne in the restaurants that had started to flourish once more.

The NEP period improved food supplies and introduced a mild general relaxation, but the industrial workers as a class did not benefit much from it. Large-scale industry was far from being organized yet, and the result was unemployment, to the tune of two million at its highest point. The Bolsheviks, like other Russian politicals, had no experience of actual government behind them, and no idea at first of the immense bureaucracy which would be required in order to set up and maintain a Socialist economy in Russian circumstances. The very profession of economist was still something new, in the 1920s, and the only practical help available came from some of the remaining members of the Tsarist civil service, a class which had always included a proportion of public-spirited men. Lenin foresaw a national economy planned from the top, on similar lines to the planning of the German economy during the First World War —the first example in history of such overall planning. Applying this model to Russia, he said that the new economy 'demands unquestioned obedience to the single will of the leaders'. But in 1922 he suffered his first stroke, and in 1924 he died.

Debates about the next course for Russia continued for four years after Lenin's death, while the Nepmen and the *kulaks* grew ever more prosperous, and the country looked to be drifting uncomfortably far away from Socialism. Meanwhile, however, the Soviet Government was laying the foundations of a welfare state, with some new housing, hospitals, sanatoria, some good industrial medicine, social insurance, and the fostering of education at all levels, though there were not enough teachers to make it practicable to introduce compulsory education until 1930. This was the golden age of the Revolution for its intelligentsia. They were attracted into all branches of the welfare work: they tried out educational experiments, particularly in the handling of orphans and delinquent children, of whom the Civil War had left a sad number; they explored child psychology and produced delightfully illustrated, gay little children's books— a field in which the Russians were world pioneers for many years; they developed psychological tests so as to pick out the more gifted children; and they tried to apply Marx's idea of 'polytechnical' education, so that every Soviet youth should master the skills of a number of trades. The Communist Party Programme of 1919 had laid down that: 'The treasures of art, formerly the property of the exploiters, are all to be made accessible to the workers.' Some of the intelligentsia were needed at first merely to protect art treasures from sabotage—(one of my older friends had a hand in this under the Commissar for Education, Lunacharsky, dashing from room to room in the Winter Palace to preserve priceless works)—but afterwards they brought their wholehearted Russian enthusiasm to the job of trying to introduce workers, some of them almost illiterate, to works of art and works of literature. It was not always easy at first, though audiences seemed willing: Miss E. M. Almedingen has told (in *Frossia*) how she taught French to rough workers who wanted to learn this language of the old cultured class. 'The French alphabet', she began, 'has 26 letters', to which her class objected that they were not illiterate, they knew their alphabet, and the alphabet (the Russian alphabet, of course), has 32 letters! Stanislavsky has described, in *My Life in Art*, how the Moscow Art Theatre, producing Chekhov and other classics in its old manner, was faced with a full audience of workers on free tickets, talking and cracking nuts, arriving late and going away as though they might have been at a fair, but after he had addressed them, and persuaded them that they owed it to the actors to keep quiet, he soon had a devoted following.

It was anyway the golden age of the Soviet arts. In part it was a continuation of the age immediately before the Revolution—the age of artists who still inspire the West and of artists so original that their work has even yet not been assimilated. It was the age of Meyerhold and Stanislavsky in the theatre, of Blok and Akhmatova in poetry, of Kandinsky, Naum Gabo, Chagall, Lissitsky, Tatlin and Malevitch in art. Tatlin, a powerful painter, was one of the first, if not the very first, to reject the artificiality of two-dimensional painting for the directness of three-dimensional constructions 'with real materials in real space', and Malevitch, in his school of Suprematism, took abstract art to a peak beyond which one could go no further. Kandinsky, Chagall and others already had established reputations in Munich or Paris, but as patriotic Russians they returned to their country on the outbreak of war in 1914, and under the Soviet régime Kandinsky was for a short time in charge of art museums, and both Chagall and Malevitch were professors of art. But soon Kandinsky was tempted back by the Weimar Bauhaus, and Chagall and Gabo and many artists and writers found the Soviet atmosphere too restricting and exiled themselves to the West. For many artists in all fields, however, the Revolution was the dawn of unlimited new inspiration: they exulted in the prospect that art was no longer to be segregated from everyday life. There was 'street art' of all kinds; the poet-artist Mayakovsky said: 'Let us make the streets our brushes, the squares our palette.' He designed one series of the new posters which brilliantly appealed to the illiterate or stabbed home the point of government campaigns. There was a powerful new use of lettering, both in posters and in book covers—especially by Rodchenko, who was the first to use the now familiar device of photomontage on book covers. In the theatre Meyerhold, Tairov and others put on productions which tried to involve the whole audience in the action, or in which, perhaps, the cast entered from the back of the auditorium on motorbicycles. Curtains, flown scenery and all traditional stage machinery were often dispensed with, and inventive designers of the 'Constructivist' school erected strange abstract constructions on the stage so as to shock spectators out of any conventional reactions. There were also eccentric productions such as the concert of factory sirens and whistles, conducted with flags by a man on a rooftop, or the play produced by Eisenstein, uncomfortably but with proletarian intentions, inside a gasworks. Mayakovsky was declaiming his verses 'At The Top Of My Voice' in rough new forms meant for mass listeners, while the self-taught peasant boy Yessenin was writing poetry of a more old-fashioned kind which brought the old Russia into the new.

Some of the intelligentsia—probably those who knew the workers least—had fantastic ideas of creating a new 'proletarian' art and 'proletarian' literature, divorced from all bourgeois traditions, but Lenin rapped them down, insisting that Marxism, 'far from refusing to acknowledge the greatest accomplishments of the bourgeois era, has assimilated and reconsidered all that had been valuable in human thought and culture for more than two thousand years'. The creative arts would be 'prompted by experience of the period of proletarian dictatorship' but on the basis of the best that had gone before; only in this way would 'a truly proletarian culture' arise.

Lenin is said to have regarded the cinema as the most important of all arts for the revolutionary cause, and he nationalized the film industry in 1919, putting it under the charge of the Commissariat of Education. The film suddenly flourished, and with Eisenstein,

Pudovkin and Dziga-Vertov it quickly reached some of the greatest heights in its history. Scarcely anything in the world of entertainment was untouched by the Revolution, and it was only partly owing to Party directives that the theatre was so transformed; it was because the new audiences and the new social relationships called forth new conceptions, new attitudes, new forms of presentation.

The architects, of course, had the biggest horizons before them in this socially-minded State. Turning their back on the ornamented, over-aesthetic architecture, the last debasement of Renaissance neo-classical, which was still rampant in every European country at that time, they designed bold blocks of concrete in shapes and proportions not seen before, of the kind that were developed a little later (and better) by Le Corbusier, Gropius, or Mies van der Rohe. The Vesnin brothers, Ginsburg and others sketched plans for new kinds of town, with linear planning or radial planning, while Ladovsky proposed an extensible garden city—an idea which has been taken up and propagated recently by the Greek architect Doxiades, the leader of ekistics, or the study of the human environment.

These Russian pioneers in all the arts—and they were truly pioneers —won great admiration and have retained great admiration from foreigners who are far from being Communists. Consequently, everyone knows how the new tendencies were nearly all suppressed in the 1930s, and replaced by the dull Victorianism of 'socialist realism' and by the vulgarity of over-ornamented Stalinist megalomania. What is less well known is that admiration for this inventive period survives healthily among professionals in contemporary Russia, and although the most advanced paintings of the early period are still kept from public view, the professional magazines freely quote Tatlin and Lissitsky, for instance, and in general the period is officially accepted as a part of the Soviet tradition 'from which we can gather impulses for new research'. The newest 'unofficial' artists have kept up the originality of the early period, and although such men as Neizvestny have no official status as artists—that is, as members of the Union of Soviet Artists—they are at least not prevented from selling their work to foreigners and to a few discriminating Soviet collectors. The newest public buildings in Russia are often much simpler in design and slenderer in feeling—the best sometimes have a springy lightness about them—although there is a deadly monotony about the average mass-produced flats which are being put up with such speed: they make it difficult to tell one Soviet city from another. The originality of the early book jackets is continued (by Neizvestny, among others) in a minority of magazine and book covers today; what is lacking is a recognized base for its use.

The suppression of so much of the work of the first Soviet artists was only a small part of the Stalinist suppression, and it is not always realized how many other features of the period were at the same time reversed and have stayed reversed. The experimentalism in education, for instance, was cut short and reviled as 'Pedagogics'; psychological testing was considered a source of undesirable class distinctions and has remained completely taboo; and 'polytechniza-tion', for all its Marxist origin, has been replaced by specialist technical training, because once the Five-Year Plans began, what the country needed was 'specialists', and of these, at the technician or craftsman level, it still has not enough. In the early days the institution of the family was attacked because it was likely to perpetuate the old 'bour-geois' attitudes, but in the 1930s this position was entirely reversed. The family has since been regarded as one of the pillars of Soviet society. (It is many years since Soviet children were elevated to heroic status for denouncing 'counter-revolutionary' or 'anti-Soviet' tendencies in their parents.) As part of the campaign against the family, divorce and abortion were made easily obtainable in the early period—divorce on the demand of one of the partners alone—but under Stalin they were made much more difficult. Only recently has divorce again become more accessible, and abortion, apparently, available with very little question.

It is still often supposed by foreigners that the Soviet State in its early days operated on a principle from which it has since fallen sadly away—the principle of equal wages for all. Alternatively, it is often supposed that if there has been a privileged class in Soviet Russia, the manual working class has been that class—or at any rate that it was intended to be so in the beginning. Neither of these assumptions is true. Before the Revolution the Bolsheviks had discussed the desir-ability of equal rewards, but after they came to power there was no principle, even in the earliest days, of equal wages or equal rations: doctors and scientists, for instance, very soon had priority in rations and in housing, and Lenin ordered the ordinary rations to be quad-rupled for the psychologist Pavlov. Party membership in itself brought no material advantage—it still does not—and in the first few years after the Revolution paid Party officials were supposed to receive wages no higher than those of the average worker. Nowadays, of course, many of them are paid a great deal better, and it is perhaps this discrepancy which has given rise to the mistaken idea of an original equality for all citizens. Manual workers did have some advantages in the early period when, for example, the sons and daughters of former bourgeois and upper-class families were excluded from higher education and from many civic rights. For a brief time theatres were even reserved exclusively for workers, but this restriction soon disappeared, and the last of the statutory disabilities for 'former' people and their offspring were removed when the Stalin Constitution was enacted in 1936.

The features of the early period which foreigners admire, such as the experimentalism in education, ought not to be thought of collectively as 'liberal': they arose from a Marxist rather than a liberal ideology, or one could say that they were liberal only in so far as Marxism itself is liberal, to the extent that it seeks, in principle, to free men from their social chains. When Stalinist totalitarianism followed (as a perversion of Marxism), from 1928 onwards, some of the early features which foreigners class as 'liberal' still remained, in particular the complete equality of the sexes—equality before the law, in wages and salaries, and in social rights. (If any inequality exists now the balance is in favour of women: they may draw their pensions at fifty-five while men must wait until they are sixty, and the divorce laws are weighted so far as is practicable in their favour: Soviet maintenance orders are heavy and seem to be well enforced.) Illegitimate children are treated as having equal rights with those born in wedlock, and this also dates back to the early days.

In retrospect the twenties may seem the age of the golden dawn, and inside the Soviet Union itself many of the younger intelligentsia nowadays have this feeling about the period. But in most respects it was a time of hardship and discomfort; it only seems to have been bearable, in terms of everyday life, because the period of the first Plans, from 1928 onwards, was in most ways so very much worse. The arts, or education, in the early period could not fill up all of people's lives, and they often had to be enjoyed on a diet of tea, black bread and the odd salt herring. The fundamental and all-pervading facts about the period, the facts which pressed upon ordinary lives all the time, concern the state of the economy, and the building up of Party control over the national life. If one can grasp this, and can accept how inappropriate much of the early experimentation was to the country's immediate needs, one is well on the way to understanding how it was that Stalin's tyrannical rule came to be accepted and admired by so many for so long.

During the NEP period Soviet industry reached the prewar level of output once more, and in some branches it surpassed that level. To the amazement of most foreign observers, this was not due to the NEP capitalists, but to the nationalized industries, for they were responsible for 85 per cent of Russia's production. They employed some foreign specialists and a little foreign capital, but the possibilities of new technology and the enthusiasm of running things themselves were what drove the former workers who now had the managerial jobs. The Tsarist level of production, however, was inadequate for a growing country, and the peasants—which still meant the majority of the population—were now dissatisfied for several reasons. The Revolution had given them the land, with the result that there were far too many individual farms, many of them too tiny to provide any surplus for the towns, while on the larger farms the richer peasants, who were producing most of the country's food, wanted higher prices for it. They also wanted consumer goods—a comfortable bed, perhaps, instead of the old benches—and they wanted farm implements and fertilizers, and all this was beyond the capacity of Soviet industry until it had very much broadened its base. Education and the welfare state could not grow without the expenditure of a lot more money, and the chief source for that must be from the profits of a much-expanded industry. And overriding all, the Bolsheviks had a deadly fear of foreign attack—partly on account of Marxist principle, which warned them that the capitalists would 'fight to regain their lost paradise', and partly owing to the foreign intervention they had experienced in the Civil War and the continuing outside threats against 'the growing menace of Red Russia'. The Soviet Union needed an armaments industry, and the base for that had to be a huge primary expansion in coal, iron, steel and electric power.

In the four years after Lenin's death in 1924 the Communist Party leadership endured more controversy, uncertainty and intrigue than at any time in its history. There were genuine hesitations over the pace at which industrialization could be attempted, and over the concomitant pace at which the Party could afford to control or to collectivize the peasantry. But these were not public debates. In 1921, when the introduction of the NEP brought a partial retreat from Socialist doctrine, the Party had not only proscribed all non-Bolshevik groups and associations; it had also thought it necessary to stiffen its own ranks by forbidding the formation of any groups or factions, even loose or temporary, to favour one policy or another, such as had previously existed among its own membership. Trotsky's prophecy, that power would be concentrated in the top leadership, was already coming true. The unity of the Party became a fundamental article of faith, and it inspired a narrow but earnest devotion in the membership, which numbered half a million in 1921 and grew to 1·3 million by 1928. With a good deal of experiment and error, the Party built up an official machine to run the country: before the Revolution there had been about 600,000 officials; by 1928 there were four million of them, out of a population of 150 million. These were, of course, not simply bureaucrats and police to see that Party lines were being followed, though the Cheka was already at work against 'enemies of the people': they were the organizers for local and regional government, for trade unions, for the co-operatives, or for control of the armed forces, they were the magistrates, and they included the equivalent of the whole staff side of capitalist business, the men to run the nationalized industries. Most of these four million had to be recruited from a population totally untrained save for brief courses in Marxism, because the élite of the original working-class Bolsheviks had either been killed in the Civil War or already promoted to higher office; indeed to some of the highest offices in the land. There were *ad hoc* courses of various kinds for the four million as time went on, but many of them who survived the purges stayed in the administration until the 1960s or even the 1970s; they have been replaced by men who have had more education but who, owing to the way they were selected by their seniors, are often as politically blinkered as their predecessors.

But in the 1920s the new recruits to the Party were mostly young and mostly town workers newly come from the country; Party membership gave them a feeling of comradeship in place of the village community they had left, and of comradeship in an élite. As for the rest of the town population, they wanted to be left to recover after the Civil War and the famine; they were crowded into the already overcrowded housing, and they were full of complaints about the poor quality of the goods turned out by the regenerated industries. Untrained management could drive untrained or part-trained workers to achieve quantity: quality was a more difficult target, and this problem has stayed with Soviet manufacture ever since. In 1925,

according to the Soviet press, five out of six new pairs of shoes were
so poorly made that they lasted only a few weeks. There were not
likely to be many objections to a great leap forward in industrialization.

The national slogan, after all the in-fighting in the Party leadership,
was to be 'Socialism in One Country'. To the ordinary man and
woman this seemed much more like common sense, much more
promising of improvement, than the defeated Trotsky's policy of
'permanent' (i.e. continuous, international) revolution. It was a
slogan to raise convinced Communists to a pitch of Messianic intoxi-
cation: their country, the rejected of Marx, was to be the chosen
land for the first realization of Marxist Socialism. Even the less politically minded, in all their deprivation and depression, had not quite
lost the old feeling that Russia was a chosen land and the Russians
were a chosen people; for the working class, at least, the slogan
kindled a new hope even among those who were suspicious of the
Communists.

'Socialism in One Country' was Stalin's slogan and Stalin's policy.
In general he invented few policies, he knew little of economics, and
he tended to keep to the middle way; his extremism all went into the
carrying out of a policy. He had sided first with one tendency and
then the other in the leadership, trading always on the need for unity,
until he had been able to isolate Trotsky and get him deported from
Russia. He had managed to expel most of Lenin's original associates
from the Politburo,* replacing them by secondary characters such as
Molotov, until he had manoeuvred himself into an impregnable
position. The debates inside the Party had been about genuine issues,
but Stalin had made them also into stark manoeuvrings for power;
he had concentrated more and more of it in his own hands, so that now
the final stage of Trotsky's prophecy had been realized: 'a single
dictator substitutes himself for the Central Committee'. How had this
happened?

Joseph Stalin (born Djugashvili, at Gori in Georgia) came from
origins more plebeian than those of any other of the founders of
Bolshevism. His parents were freed serfs: a kind of serfdom had
lingered on in Georgia after it had been abolished in Russia. His
father was a cobbler, and his mother, anxious for Joseph to rise in the
world, put him in a seminary to train for the priesthood—the only

---

* Politburo means Policy Committee. It is the highest body in the Communist
Party for the discussion of policy, and in fact policy is never determined, and
not even much debated, anywhere else in the Soviet Union.

way up for a poor man's son. The discipline and education were ridiculously harsh and narrow, and Joseph was expelled for repeatedly introducing forbidden books—such as the works of Victor Hugo or Darwin—and reading them to other students. While in his teens he had joined a Marxist group in Tiflis, and after leaving the seminary he was soon editing an underground periodical. The whole of the rest of his life was spent in political work, including the organization of bank robberies to get funds for the Bolsheviks, and four sentences of exile; he escaped from the first three and the war released him from the fourth. By 1906 he was already one of the Bolshevik leaders, disagreeing often with Lenin. When not in prison or exile he was in the thick of labour organization and underground Party work in the Baku oilfields or elsewhere in Transcaucasia, while Lenin and the Party's central leadership were living in Europe—'aloof from Russian reality', said Stalin, who never went abroad in his life apart from two brief visits on political missions. He educated himself a good deal, on Marxist lines, and was well-read in the classics of Russian literature, but he remained suspicious of intellectuals and frequently contemptuous of them. Marxism, as the faith of an oppressed class, suited him perfectly, and when the Party came to power he could not but be aware that out of the fifteen members of the first Soviet Government, only four came from the working class, while in the Party's Politburo there was but one—Tomsky. (Stalin became a member of the Politburo a little later.)

The tremendous chip on Stalin's shoulder did not seem to be due to his being a Georgian, a member of a minority, and under the Tsars a despised people. It was being a member of the oppressed working class which counted. In Georgia before the Revolution Georgians were either small-time aristocrats (probably called 'Prince'), or they were peasant labourers: the middle-class jobs were done by Russians, Armenians or Jews. Stalin soon merged his Georgian identity in the cosmopolitan world of the industrial workers in such cities as Baku. Eventually he became thoroughly accepted, not only by this minority of Azerbaidjanis, Tatars, Armenians and a dozen other races, but by the Russian working class, or by a large part of it at least, as their spokesman and leader, even their adored leader, once the policy of 'Socialism In One Country' had begun. This is the more remarkable since Stalin never lost his Georgian accent—the soft, slurring, burbling way of speaking which Russians contemptuously call the 'Kinto' accent. I heard Stalin speak over the radio several times,

and I have heard a recording of his address to the nation on the outbreak of war, and it seemed to me impossible to believe that this
unimpressive, even hesitating, delivery could be that of a terrible
dictator or, indeed, of a leader of any great importance. However,
the public heard, and saw Stalin very rarely: the all-pervading image
of the all-wise father figure was built up by the organs of propaganda,
not by his personal appearances, and this being done, possibly his
people may have felt that there was something reassuring in the
paternal softness of his speeches.* The early newsreels show Stalin
as confident and pushing, with a blunt simplicity of address, underneath which perhaps only those who are used to the ways of public
figures would detect an unpleasant, calculating slyness.

Western diplomats who dealt with Stalin during the war said the
face he showed to them was polite and friendly; he did not radiate
personal magnetism but dominated by cruder means—he was so
brusque and rude in his behaviour to all his subordinates that he
made visitors feel extremely uncomfortable. As his assiduous bio-
grapher, Isaac Deutscher, says, he was 'a man of very ordinary stature,
with middling thoughts, but the fists and feet of a giant'.

Stalin was capable of prodigies of work, particularly of administrative work, of attention to significant detail—the amassing of information
in files, the sifting of reports, the drafting of laconic summaries and
recommendations, the selection, deployment, reprimanding and
redeployment of personnel. When the first Soviet organs of government were formed, the intellectuals took most of the top jobs: Trotsky,
for instance, became Commissar for Foreign Affairs, and Bukharin was
Politburo member in charge of press and propaganda. But there
remained the unglamorous jobs concerned with looking after the
machinery of government and Party—the kind of staff positions that
are inevitable in any large organization and that easily earn the oppro-
brious label of 'bureaucrat' for their holders. It was Comrade Stalin,
modest in bearing as he so often could be, who took on these responsi-

---

* It has never been Communist policy to depend upon oratory to fire the
people, except in the days immediately before the Revolution. Lenin was an
incisive plain speaker, excellent at exposition, and thousands of 'agitators', as
they are called, try to model themselves on him when they convey Party policy
to factory and other meetings even today. Trotsky indeed had a first-class gift
of oratory, but this was one of the reasons why he was mistrusted by his colleagues. There has never been anything in Soviet Communism resembling
the Hitler rallies in Nazi Germany. Probably it has been thought too dangerous
to arouse passions which might get out of hand; the avoidance of oratory is also
an indication of the immense, old-fashioned, even child-like Communist faith
in the power of rationality.

bilities, and the intellectuals were suitably grateful to him for doing so. He was made Commissar in charge of the Inspectorate, whose staff (recruited, of course, from the untrained) were to watch sternly over the work of every branch of government, and had considerable powers of entry, audit and examination. Then he became General Secretary of the Party, responsible for all the machinery of Party organization and for the appointment, the records, the promotion or sacking of Party officials all over the country; at the same time he was the link between the Central Committee and the Control Commission, a sort of popular court set up by Lenin for examining and judging things from below: it was this Commission which started the first purges. Within two years, and before the death of Lenin, Stalin was in effective charge of the whole machinery of government and Party, and was perhaps already packing key positions with men who owed everything to him and would follow him.

One need not leap to the conclusion that Stalin already had total dictatorship in view at this period; he was such a practical administrator, so good at making *ad hoc* decisions, that all through his life he does not seem to have looked very far ahead to the distant consequences of his actions. But Lenin saw the danger, and in his 'Testament', composed after he had suffered his second stroke, he wrote character sketches of all his colleagues. He singled out Trotsky and Stalin as the two ablest men in the Party, but expressed doubts about the use Stalin was making of 'the enormous power in his hands'. A few weeks later he added the famous postscript: 'Stalin is too rude—an unbearable fault in the office of General Secretary', and he proposed that 'the comrades' should replace him in that office by someone else. In the last days of his active life Lenin attacked Stalin openly, and if he had lived he would certainly have persuaded his colleagues to demote him. But his Testament was never published nor, mainly through a series of accidents, was it even given wide circulation inside the Party, and Trotsky was more generally mistrusted than Stalin; in the manoeuvrings to expel Trotsky, Stalin's position soon became unassailable. None of this dissension within the leadership was known to the public, of course, and whenever there was a clear-cut group in the leadership who were opposed to Stalin, they were hamstrung by their deep, inalienable attachment to Party unity. It is on record that they found it difficult to believe, at first, that Stalin was intriguing against them in pursuit of power alone. The minorities would have thought it blasphemy to form a faction or 'appeal to the people', though

Trotsky's followers did make one public demonstration, just before his expulsion. Gifted men such as Bukharin would take up grovelling attitudes in order to ensure that they were still trusted by their comrades—one must emphasize that it was 'by their comrades' and not just 'by Stalin'—after they had temporarily diverged over policy. They would, for instance, accept that although they could not be received back into the Politburo, the best service they could render the Party was to work hard in support of policies which previously they had so mistakenly opposed. Eventually even these submissive attitudes did not save Bukharin and a dozen other leaders from execution, during the purges.

The deep Russian need and talent for comradeship, the sense of being one of the elect, and the genuine devotion of some of the country's best men and women to the betterment of Russia all thus fused in loyalty to the Party. The same attitude spread right down through the membership, so that by the time the big purges came in the 1930s, Party members on the whole seemed unable to believe that the Party could be wrong, and when arrested, as so many of them were in the senseless campaigns of Stalin's political police, they would submit to every kind of humiliation, to public confession and punishment, 'as a last service to the Party'. All of this one may read, again and again, in accounts by some of those who survived. One of the best is *Into The Whirlwind*, the account of her arrest and eighteen years in prison camps by the stalwart Evgenia Ginsburg, who after her release now apparently lives a life no more restricted than that of any other Soviet citizen, and still regards herself as 'a Leninist-Communist'. She says of herself when she was twenty-seven: 'I don't want to sound pretentious but, quite honestly, had I been ordered to die for the party, not once but three times, I would have obeyed without a moment's hesitation. I had not the slightest doubt that the party line was right. My only—I suppose, instinctive—reservation was that I could not bring myself to deify Stalin, in spite of the growing fashion. But if I had this guarded feeling about him, I carefully concealed it from myself.'

A great deal of the history of Russia, one could say, is essentialized in the character of the Party—the peasant communalism, the almost total lack of a tradition of representative government, the view of government purely as *authority* (a view held by people of all classes, except for a few elements, who were mostly destroyed by Lenin or Stalin), the concentrated symbolizing of authority in one superhuman personage,* and finally the religious emphasis of the Orthodox on right observance and the necessity of participation in the collective, without any of the Protestant or Catholic insistence on individual responsibility for one's own fate in this world and the next. The Orthodox frame of mind persisted among the Communists, as an unconscious basis for their way of looking at society and in spite of their rejection of religion, just as the Protestant or Catholic tradition of responsibility has persisted and continues to form some of the attitudes of humanists and atheists in the West. Stalin's early formal training in an Orthodox seminary may well have helped, paradoxically, to shape the habit of mind which he applied to the suppression of the Orthodox religion and its supersession by a new collective faith.

Traditional though it may have been in much of its spirit, the Communist Party organization was a great deal more effective than any Tsarist government had been. If the Party had been in the hands of someone more humane, more receptive, and with less of a chip on his shoulder than Stalin, it might have achieved the industrialization of Russia with rather less suffering, though its methods could hardly have been anything but blunt. The Party at least was (and still is) run on the principle of 'democratic centralism', which roughly means that policies are decided at the top, but are supposed to be explained to members patiently and at length, until the recalcitrant or faint-hearted take them up with enthusiasm. The same principle was applied to the nation at large: a vast amount of Party members' time went into expounding and defending Party policies to the public, and although in the end policies were ruthlessly applied in any case, and neither Party members nor outsiders had any choice but to accept them, the policy of explaining did mean that what I have called 'the Rise of the People' found some response and some expression, in Russian terms. If Russia still had a dictatorship, it was a dictatorship operated by people of more or less one's own kind (or so they seemed, and indeed were, at first), and certainly by people who, underneath the Marxist jargon, talked the same language as oneself. In general the explanations from Party members were often brief, doctrinal in content, and expressed in a crude, raw manner because there was so

* This deification, at least, disappeared after Stalin's death and the exposure of his tyranny by Khrushchev, and it has never been renewed. Today one can say that all these historical influences seem to be much weaker: it is only the Party bureaucracy which is unable, or unwilling, to acknowledge that forces striving towards greater individualism are at work.

often no one but crude, raw young Party workers to do the talking —while, of course, the political police were only too exempt from any obligation to 'explain' their actions.

Stalin's rule generated such horrors later on that it is often forgotten, in Western countries, that the terrible concentration of Party power was intended for a purpose other than the universal consolidation of that power. It was intended for nothing less than the bringing about of a second Revolution—the industrial, agricultural and educational Revolution.

The Communist Party faced exactly the same difficulty that every backward, that is, every agricultural, country faces when it tries to industrialize fast—namely that it is agriculture, and agriculture alone, which can supply the raw hands for industry, yet the swollen industrial force, old and new, has to be fed by farm labour whose numbers may be depleted perhaps by half, and very little can be done to increase their productivity until industry is able to provide them with machines and fertilizers. Unless there can be a large injection of foreign credit, peasants and factory workers alike have to pull in their belts unpleasantly tight—tighter than they were before—for years. Few capitalists were willing to extend much credit to Soviet Russia; in any case, for ideological reasons their help was not trusted and, apart from a very few exceptions, not used. The peasants seemed to be the most intractable obstacle. Most of Russian agriculture was extremely backward, and it was for practical as well as doctrinal reasons that the Party had agreed in principle, from the outset, that the individual farms should be collectivized, their land being thrown together into large units where a few men with machines could do the work of double or treble the number working in the old ways. A few thousand collective farms (*kolkhozes*) were started, and some peasants saw their advantages and joined them. A few thousand government farms (*sovkhozes*) were also started—very large units, in virgin lands, run on industrial lines with labour imported for the purpose. But the bulk of the farmers who supplied the towns were still the *kulaks*, and if they were encouraged they would hold out for high prices and become a nation of petty bourgeois proprietors, wielding a dangerous amount of economic and political power, inside the Socialist nation. Bukharin thought that while industry grew at a moderate pace, the *kulaks* could be 'contained' and eventually absorbed into a collectivized system— 'like capitalists turning into good Communists?' queried Stalin sardonically. The peasantry—*kulaks*, subsistence farmers, and landless labourers together—still amounted to over 80 per cent of the population, and for four years the Party leaders hesitated to impose full collectivization lest it should disorganize food production entirely, and alienate four-fifths of the nation.

It took Stalin many years to reach a position of unquestioned power, even in the top circles of the Party: there was opposition which might possibly have deposed him in 1927, in 1930–31, during the most horrible period of the first Five-Year Plan, and again in 1934. But it was Stalin in 1928 who jumped in with both feet—those 'feet of a giant'—and brought the NEP to an end (without any compensation, of course, for the small-scale traders and producers), and it was Stalin who started up the first Five-Year Plan of industrialization (for which the preliminary work had long been preparing) in 1928, who gave it some impossibly high targets to fulfil, and who in 1929, to the amazement and horror of his colleagues, plumped for full and immediate collectivization of all the farms, adding an order for several thousand machines which the young tractor industry was quite unable to supply. Some of the small-scale peasants joined the collective farms voluntarily and even with enthusiasm, but over the whole country collectivization was enforced at a destructive pace, in a single season, by a body of ardent, ignorant young Communists who could call on armed force to back them up if they needed it. As the whole world knows, the general disintegration, the deportations, the killing of livestock by their despairing owners, and the famines of 1931 to 1934 brought the nation into a situation which was for a time so severe that, as Stalin told Churchill twelve years later, it was as threatening as any of the worst periods of the Second World War.

And yet, during the same few years, however unbelievable it must seem, Russia's industrial production, through the smoking chimneys and mines and electric plants of the Five-Year Plan, through the labour of half-starved millions, grew to a figure four times higher than it had ever been before the Revolution.

8. The Reign of Stalin (1928–1953)

Indelibly ingrained in every Soviet citizen older than about thirty-five are the effects of having lived through four colossal upheavals—agonies—transformations; what words can be powerful enough to encompass the almost mortal strains of fifteen years which saw the Second World War and the reconstruction after it, the first Five-Year Plans, the collectivization of a hundred million peasants, the great purges and the Stalin Terror?

It was also during those fifteen years that Russia underwent another, more welcome, transformation, which in any other country would have been counted a revolution in itself: the whole nation (except for a few of its oldest inhabitants) was made literate; all its children went to school; higher education, science and research institutions grew immensely, if lopsidedly; and the nation's health was safeguarded through universal medical care and the beginnings of other social services.

Today, talking with average Russians, with those who have done well out of the system as well as those who are exasperated by its repressions, I have always been given the same answer when I asked what meaning there was for them personally in the slogan which one sees on every rooftop—'Forward to Communism!' 'It means', they say, 'in the first place, peace.' (What they look for in the second place is rather surprising, and I shall return to it later; it has little bearing on the present chapter.) But they mean 'peace' in a way in which it is impossible that any Briton or American can mean it.

Twenty million Russians died in the Second World War. (I thought at first of asking the printer to head every remaining page of this book with that bare statement.) They died in masses in battle, because manpower was for long more expendable than weapons. Some of them died in that first month when the Germans advanced 150 miles, but more—half a million on one front alone—were taken prisoner, a fate which comparatively few survived. Several million soldiers and civilians died in Nazi slave camps or in the occupied areas, all of them regarded by the Nazis as a lower form of life to whom no Red

Cross or other standards of treatment need apply. During the siege of Leningrad, which lasted nine hundred days, over a million civilians died of starvation, or cold, or in air raids.

Yet to the surprise of both enemies and allies, and on the whole to their own surprise, the Russians were victorious. And the causes behind their victory, apart from the phenomenal Russian powers of endurance, and Russian patriotism, and the Russian winter, lay in the first three Five-Year Plans. Without them the Soviet armies could scarcely have been armed at all.

The first Five-Year Plan raised great enthusiasm both inside the Soviet Union and abroad. Familiar, even over-familiar though the concept of planning is today, this was the first time that a nation—and a huge nation at that—had set out to explore and exploit its resources on a national scale. The geologists sweated in the Asian deserts, made light of winter, worked under face-veils against the swarms of mosquitoes in Siberian summers, to map out the country's coal, iron, oil, copper, gold, and every kind of mineral resource. (They are still doing it, pushing further into the most inhospitable parts of the USSR.) New railways were built, such as the Turksib line (the subject of one of the most famous Russian documentary films), to link up industry with nearer sources of coal. As early as 1920 Lenin had set up a body to plan electrification as the magic wand which Socialism must wave, and now at last the power lines were spreading across the steppe from great hydro-electric dams such as Dniepropetrovsk, at the falls of the Dnieper in the Ukraine, where the Cossacks had their refuge in the old days. The whole nation was kept informed, and not infrequently was inspired, by the progress of great schemes and of the whole Plan, through striking posters and giant graphs displayed everywhere—a great publicity campaign which also won admiration abroad. The little book for children, *Moscow Has A Plan* (illustrated in the Russian manner in the English edition, by William Kermode), is still a classic of its kind and fit reading for older readers too, to catch some idea of the excitement of the time.

The enthusiasm was needed indeed: in fact it was a staple element in the bare survival diet on which the swollen industrial population had to exist: 'Tea and bread only, in the barracks of the Elektrozavod'; 'At the sulphur mine we sometimes didn't see bread for two weeks at a time—we had soup, buckwheat, green plums and green apricots to eat.' At Magnitogorsk, the city by the enormous iron ore site in freezing Kazakhstan, a month's rations in 1932 were: 'Bread 30 kilos, meat 3 kilos, sugar 1 kilo, butter ½ kilo, grains 2 kilos, potatoes as available', but also (and they were unusually lucky in this) 'milk 15 litres'. Clothes were almost unobtainable. To keep warm in a Russian winter one needs *portianki*—strips of linen to wind round the feet and calves, which are then inserted into the large, shapeless felt boots or *valenki*. At Magnitogorsk, in temperatures of minus 35° Centigrade, some workers had to go about in *valenki* with holes in the soles, and *portianki* which were mere rags. In summer people were glad if they had a good pair of plimsolls to wear.

These reports come from three American engineers who worked in Russia during the First Plan. The most informative and objective of them, John D. Littlepage, was chief engineer of a gold mine from 1928 to 1937. In his book, *In Search of Soviet Gold*, he wrote: 'If this was the second Revolution, the Revolution of 1917 can hardly have been worse . . . They tried to do thousands of things at the same time, before they had prepared one-tenth of the necessary personnel of managers and skilled workmen; under the circumstances it is a marvel that they came through at all. They might not have done so if the Soviet peoples were not so long-suffering and willing to put up with any amount of discomfort and even with food shortages over long periods.'

Littlepage 'had to teach each individual worker at the gold mine drilling, timbering, blasting, the operation of the milling machinery, and especially, *the care of the equipment*'. But he was an extremely adaptable man, his physique could stand the conditions, and he says he was satisfied, after six months' training, with the work of his labour force, who were mostly *kulaks* expelled from their farms, and totally inexperienced in industry. In the factory where Andrew Smith worked the labour was better trained, but the tempo of the work was terrible: he describes, in *I Was A Soviet Worker*, how all the machinery was being driven to death, and men were often injured through drilling large pieces too fast, or because they 'had not time' to screw down the pieces they were working on. Piece-rates for repairs were worked out by an almost untrained girl, so that fifteen minutes might be allowed for a job which could be done in three, while only five minutes was allotted for a job which would need an hour and a half.

But somehow, in weariness and in manic enthusiasm, the novices —the men and women who when they began had never seen a screwdriver, and could not understand the need for regular hours of work— somehow, driven and organized and persuaded by other novices, they more or less completed the Plan. Half-way through its course Stalin stepped up the tempo, and the slogan became 'The Five-Year Plan in Four Years!' Not all the targets were reached in four years: steel, for one thing, was well behind, but the output of coal, and pig-iron, and electric power was doubled (though electric power was supposed to have been quadrupled and pig-iron quintupled); industrial production, taken overall, was doubled. Machines of many kinds poured forth, and among them were the tractors which the new collective farms desperately required. But the little independent businesses which used to supply consumer articles had gone, and the nationalized industries did not start to supply more than a trickle of these until well through the Second Plan; in fact it was not until 1937 that the ordinary citizen saw much of an improvement on the bare shelves of the shops—an improvement at last considerable in quantity, but still leaving a great deal to be desired in quality. Food could hardly be called plentiful until the beginning of the Third Plan in 1938. When I went on excursions in 1934, in the company of young volunteer labourers who were building the Moscow Metro, they were surprised and delighted to find a wayside kiosk which actually sold one article of food—hunks of black bread. But by 1939, when I visited Russia again, supplies were quite different and, at least in the cities, there were plenty of rounded cheeks and fat bellies to be seen. In the smaller towns, however, I heard of very irregular distribution, with long queues for inadequate supplies of tea or even bread: the mere size of the country has meant, and still means, very patchy distribution of both indispensable necessities and dispensable trivialities.

The figures of national investment show clearly enough the main intentions of the Plan. At the beginning of the first Plan, in 1928, out of a national income of 25,000 million roubles only 14·3 per cent was devoted to investment, all the rest being absorbed in consumption, though that was at a low enough level. At the end of the Plan, in 1932, 44·2 per cent of a very much larger national income (40,000 million roubles) was being invested to develop the nation's resources, while the total sum allotted to consumption had hardly increased at all.

The general verdict of foreign economists on the early Plans is that they would, of course, have been more efficient at a slower and more humane tempo, that they could have been more realistically prepared, and that a modest supply of consumer goods, if the small NEP enterprises had been left in being, would have been a useful incentive to add to the slogans and the general atmosphere of unbearable drive. But the skilled craftsmen in the NEP enterprises were the very people most wanted in the new industries, and perhaps, if the crude, raw personnel had not been driven so hard by equally crude, raw managers and Party men, the Soviet Union might never have built up an armaments industry in time to resist the Germans. It was a period as hard and cruel as our own Industrial Revolution, but looked at in retrospect, it now seems to Russians a heroic time, though a time to which none of them would want to return.

The clumsiness, the unpunctuality, the untidiness, the inability to see the point of working to arbitrarily organized hours—all these failings had similarly to be got over in the early stage of our own industrialization (though it is rather extraordinary how rarely they are mentioned in our history books). The material conditions in the two Industrial Revolutions were not so similar, though in hardship and misery perhaps quantitatively about equal, but the Russian workers could have, and a majority at times probably did have, an enthusiasm which was only occasionally aroused in Britain, in some paternalistically well-run mill or factory. The Soviet worker had the beginnings of some social services, while the early British worker had only charity, but on the other hand the British worker had every incentive to build up his own organizations, his own response to oppression. The Russian workers were beginning to do this in the last decades before the Revolution, but the mass of Soviet workers, in the industrial revolution which began in 1928, had no such possibilities and not very much incentive: they were being bossed by people exactly like themselves and not much better rewarded; their complaints were handled by the new Soviet trade unions, which are not much more than social welfare organizations, and which the Soviet authorities had had in many places to build up from nothing, so slender a base was there in the pre-revolutionary working class for them to work on.

The Stakhanovite workers—the men who invented simple ways of speeding up work by a better division of labour, besides breaking records with their own efforts—these were mostly spontaneous innovators; some at least of the industrial workers felt a heroic pride in their own contribution, and some of the young were still volunteering for double shifts and Sunday work when I saw them in 1934. The material standards of life were wretched, the housing conditions meant that two families often had to share a single room, but what with the new plants and new transport which people could see being built up, and what with the paid holidays and sick pay, the maternity leave, the universal free schooling, the evening classes for nearly everybody if they wanted them, and the increase in cinemas, libraries and medical services—they all added up to a better and more hopeful standard of life, *for town workers*, than under the Tsars. The cinemas mostly showed propaganda films, but some of these were the classic works of Eisenstein or Pudovkin or Turin; the libraries were full of propaganda works, but they were full of technical books too, and they also contained the Russian classics in all their wealth of pre-Bolshevik humanism: the Soviet authorities have never, I believe, issued doctored editions of the classics, and although they suppress and imprison contemporary authors whose work they find too liberal, they have suppressed, I think (unlike the Nazis), no classic authors, except for the major works of Dostoevsky, which were more or less unobtainable during the later years of Stalin. The accommodation and the variety of fare provided in these new cultural institutions might be poor, but they did at least come into being where often no cinemas, libraries or schools had been before. The enthusiasm for Stalin was not wholly whipped up by propaganda: a lot of it was perfectly genuine.

For most of the peasants, in contrast to the town workers, life at first descended into chaos under the Plan. Stepping up his targets as usual, Stalin demanded 'the liquidation of the *kulaks* as a class'. (Who was a kulak? 'I was a *kulak*,' an old pensioner told me: 'I was eleven years in Kamchatka* because of it, and 90 per cent of us died there. I was a *kulak*—because I had a cow!') Out of the 25 million peasant households perhaps two million were better off than their neighbours, they owned some horses and stock, and some of them employed the labour of other peasants or got them into debt—both heinous crimes under Communism. These richer ones were now savagely attacked, and the poor peasants and landless men were encouraged to vent their envy on them, although in many cases communal solidarity and Russian good nature proved too strong, and the village would refuse to single out its own '*kulaks*'. The *kulaks* were not even allowed to join the collective farms if they wished, but were exiled to till the harshest regions of Siberia, or rounded up as forced labour to dig canals or build embankments; it is estimated that about three million of them died. The lesser peasants were sometimes forced into the collectives at gunpoint—and yet during the four months between November 1929 and February 1930 half the peasants

---

* People willing to go and work in Kamchatka are nowadays offered 70 per cent above normal wage rates.

in the whole country had already joined of their own accord, seeking safety in the new communities, and fearing the requisitioning of their produce if they stayed out of them. The climax came when some of the crude young Party 'activists', totally ignorant of agriculture, began to force the peasants to surrender their livestock—their treasured cow or pig or pair of goats—into a common pool. A few of these Communists got killed, but the peasants knew the odds were hopelessly against them; there was no escape, and in violent resentment and despair they started killing their own animals. (For a week or two, at least, whole villages gorged themselves on meat.) Stalin had to call a halt, in his speech to Party workers, 'Dizzy With Success'. But the damage had been done: the country was left with half the number of horses, half the pigs and cattle, and one-third the number of sheep and goats it had had before collectivization, and it was not until after Stalin's death that stocks rose above their prewar, Tsarist level.

One can read of the primitive barbarities of the collectivization in Sholokhov's novel, *Virgin Soil Upturned*, published after the death of Stalin. One can read of the free rein given to natural envy, greed, good nature, brutality, brotherliness, gluttony, and despair—how the poor peasants shared out the clothes chests of the *kulaks*, and one poor woman at last got a second garment, after managing for years with a single skirt transparent with many washings, and how in another village they could get no soap, and shirts grew stiff as a board with dirt and sweat. Sholokhov does not tell of the Communists who were murdered, nor of the famine of 1932–3 when, after a bad harvest, another million persons died, but then he is an officially approved novelist, a one-time favourite of Stalin. In consequence the brutalities which he does describe—and they are plenty—are the more convincing.

But the collectivization, though it was slowed down, was not called off, and by 1938 only one per cent of peasant families stayed outside it. After the first paralysing shock, it became possible to realize that the new system could be more productive than the old network of tiny farms. In 1938 the Soviet Union was no longer a nation which was four-fifths peasant; the people on the land now numbered just under half the population, and yet they were growing more grain, twice as much sugar beet, and three times as much cotton as before.* The

---

* This is not to say that large private farms, properly run, might not have been more productive than the collective system: the United States, where only 5 per cent of the population is on the land, today gets four times the average agricultural yield of the Soviet Union, where 30 per cent of the people

Soviet Union had become the largest manufacturer of agricultural machinery in the world, and the MTS—the machine and tractor stations which had been set up to serve groups of *kolkhozes*—had a staff of over a million with a modicum of mechanical training.

What made life tolerable for the peasants was the law of 1935 which allowed them to keep a small private plot (of not more than one and a quarter acres), with one or two animals, for each household. They were allowed, and are still allowed, to sell the vegetables, fruit, milk, honey, eggs and meat raised from these plots in the open market, where prices go up and down according to the scarcity and quality of the food in the government shops (which have fixed prices); even in the heart of Moscow there is still a large covered peasant market where housewives drive bargains with dirty-fisted peasants for a chicken, eggs, tomatoes or spotty apples, or a bunch of asters or sweet peas.

The official complaint always was that the peasants spent too much time on their own plots and not enough on the collective fields, yet small though the total area is of all these plots, the country simply cannot do without them. They are cultivated so intensely that they yield, on the average, about eight times as much as a collective field of the same area, and in the late 1960s they were still producing about two-thirds of the country's eggs, one-third of the meat, and one-third of the milk. After the fall of Khrushchev their usefulness was at last officially recognized, the peasants were encouraged to produce even more from their own plots, and the public were encouraged to buy from them. For years, under Stalin, the peasants had had to wait until the harvest was in and the compulsory deliveries of grain, flax, vegetables, etc. had been made to the State, before they got any money at all for the 'labour days' which they had put in through the year. Part of their payment was in kind, and by the time they received any money they were naturally deep in debt to the collective. The payments, at official prices, for the compulsory deliveries were cruelly small: in the later years of Stalin the management of a *kolkhoz* had to sell 238 tons of grain in order to earn the price of a truck; ten years later, when Khrushchev had raised agricultural payments to a proper level, they could buy a truck for twenty tons of grain. Since 1966 the peasants have been getting fortnightly regular payments, like other workers, and since 1969 they have, for

are still in agriculture. The average quality of American soil, it must be admitted, is better, but what has been lacking in the USSR, at least until the 1970s, has been capital investment in agriculture.

the first time, the right to pensions, while their earnings at last, in the 1970s, are reckoned to be only about 15 per cent below the average of the town worker.

But all through the Stalin period the peasants, the people who fed the nation, were the exploited and neglected half of the population, in many regions barely keeping themselves alive, and then only through their private plots. Any potentiality they might have had as a political opposition—as inheritors of the tradition of burning manor-houses and killing officials or landlords—was completely crushed out of them: the suppression of their politico-economic independence was of course one of Stalin's chief aims in carrying out the collec-tivization so mercilessly. It is only fair to add that in many districts the peasants soon found themselves materially better off than before, though the old contrast between the poor patchy forest soils of the north and the rich rolling black earth of the south remained. For all peasants there were now schools which gave their children at least a four-year education, there was some sort of medical care in most places, and electric lighting was beginning to go on in the villages. But resentment rumbled beneath the surface in a great many districts, and it was hardly to be wondered at that some peasants welcomed the invading Germans in 1941.

One advantage, at least, the peasants did have: after all the agonies of the collectivization, they were on the whole left alone under the Terror.

What is to be made today of this still incurable, searing wound in the nation's immediate past—the Purges and the Terror of 1935 to 1938, and the resumption of them after the war so long as Stalin lived? When one gets friendly nowadays with a man of middle age or over, one soon asks him, perhaps with a grin, '*Vy sideli?*' (literally, 'Did you sit?', or in the English idiom, 'Were you "inside"?') almost as one might ask 'Where were you during the war?' And if he replies '*Ya ne sidel*' ('I was never in a prison or a camp'), one feels suspicious of him, because he may have been one of those responsible for putting other people 'inside', or one of the innumerable informers and denouncers who saved their skins and climbed into their present positions by getting someone else put away. But even if he is a bone-hard Party type who never 'sat', he will at least shake his head solemnly and say: 'That was a black period in our country's history.'

These, however, are the ones who survived. How many were the others who were silenced for ever? A very distinguished Soviet scientist, Academician A. D. Sakharov (the leader, behind the scenes, of several bold campaigns for liberalization), wrote in 1968: 'At least 10 to 15 million people perished in the torture chambers of the NKVD from torture and execution, in camps for exiled *kulaks* and so-called semi-*kulaks* and members of their families and in camps "without the right of correspondence" (which were in fact the prototypes of the Fascist death camps where, for example, thousands of prisoners were machine-gunned because of "overcrowding" or as a result of "special orders").'*

Subtracting the estimated three million *kulaks* whom I mentioned before, there were, apparently, something between seven and twelve million others who for various allegedly 'political' reasons were executed by shooting (in the back of the neck so as to render the face unrecognizable), or who died as a result of their treatment in prison, or of starvation, thirst, or suffocation in the weeks of locked-up journeys, crammed into goods wagons or the holds of 'death ships', or who died in the camps from dysentery, tuberculosis, or simple heart failure, sawing timber or shifting loads beyond their strength, and being punished, when they could not keep up their quota, by a reduction in their already totally inadequate rations, so that they wasted even faster to death. These were the ordinary run of deaths: there were some even more arbitrary types of murder, such as the slaughtering, when the Germans were approaching, of the whole population of camps in western Russia, because it was believed that any camp inmate would become a collaborator if given the chance.

But why had the miserable victims been sent to the camps? *'Zashto?'* 'To what end?' they asked again and again. Two who were released and escaped from Russia, Beck and Godin, published a short book, *Russian Purge*, in 1951 which seems to me, though short, the most comprehensive view of the Terror which I have read. They give a list of seventeen theories which circulated in prison to account for the Terror. Leaving aside the two eccentrics—the man who put it all down to sunspots, and the other who felt it was a retribution for his own lecherous youth—it is maintained by Beck and Godin (who are respectively a historian and a scientist by training) that there is some truth in all the other fifteen.

One can acknowledge in the first place a few excuses, or reasons,

* Quoted from Sakharov's essay, and programme for a sane Soviet future, circulated privately in the Soviet Union and published in England under the title *Progress, Coexistence and Intellectual Freedom*, by André Deutsch—Copyright The New York Times Company.

which might be held valid cause—if not by British standards then by those of many other countries—for a new government such as the young Soviet Government to put some of its citizens away: they might be genuinely fomenting counter-revolution, seeking to restore the old régime; or after expulsion from the Party they might be trying to organize a faction of their own or to split the Party; or they might, like many people during the British Industrial Revolution, be trying to sabotage the process of industrialization which they did not understand and for varying personal reasons resented. And finally, every country deals severely with any of its citizens who act against its interest, as agents for a foreign power.

Some few Soviet citizens must have been guilty on one or other of these four counts, and quite a large number, probably, committed minor acts of sabotage. Mere hamhandedness often ranked as sabotage and was punished with quite inappropriate severity, but some foreign engineers who worked through the Five-Year Plan were convinced that there were other acts which were deliberate, and that some of these involved men very high up indeed in industry or in the Party, who might, for instance, be trying to cover up their own bad mistakes in ordering materials. Littlepage quotes one industrial chief who had made a good thing out of buying German cast-iron parts instead of the mild steel which was scheduled in the Plan. But as to other types of anti-Soviet activity, the Civil War had been so devastating in its effects, and the Bolshevik victory so complete, that nothing was left which could be called 'counter-revolution'. Lenin called off 'mass terror' against remnants of the old régime and abolished the death penalty early in 1920; at most there remained a few 'Whites' as highwaymen and adventurers in the wilder parts of the country for a few years. As to Trotskyists, Khrushchev recalled later, in his 'unmasking of Stalin' speech to the 20th Party Congress in 1956, that as early as 1927, inside the Party, 'only some 4,000 votes were cast for the Trotskyite–Zinovievite Opposition, while there were 724,000 for the party line. During the next ten years', he said, 'Trotskyism was completely disarmed; many former Trotskyites had changed their views and worked in the various sectors of building Socialism. It is clear that in the situation of Socialist victory there was no basis for mass terror in the country.'

The fantastic, completely implausible aspect of the Great Terror was that everyone arrested was accused of at least one, and usually all four major crimes—counter-revolution, working against the Party and against Stalin, sabotage, and working for a foreign power. 'Confessions' on these lines were extracted, by order; the few who held out and did not confess were never brought to even the semblance of a trial and were probably shot out of hand. The charges were laid against such huge numbers—estimates vary between seven and fourteen million* (out of a population of 170 million) as the number of prisoners at any one time—that incredulous though the public might be concerning cases which they knew of, they were led to feel that in general 'there must be something in it', and a great many foreigners felt this too. But while foreigners were free to condemn or not, Soviet citizens were being organized in 'protest' meetings to 'demand' the death penalty for all these 'enemies of the people'.

There was 'something in it' to just about the same extent that the British Government might feel justified, for instance, in preventing all of its subjects from visiting the Soviet Union, corresponding with Soviet citizens, or obtaining Soviet publications, on the grounds that they might 'come under Communist influence' and be recruited as spies. In the past a few people with British passports have been recruited in this way, and the Soviet Government might well expect rather more of its subjects to be susceptible to foreign temptations. But the proofs of an actual temptation, or of the yielding to a temptation, were not the essential element in the charges against prisoners during the Terror. Mere association with a foreigner on a single occasion, or even receiving a foreign letter, would be enough. How could the victim prove that he had not in any way at all been impressed by his foreign acquaintance and been inclined by contrast to denigrate some aspect of the USSR? That granted, he was at the top of a slippery slope that led to the abyss of 'treason', and it was impossible for him to prove that he might not some day, in some imagined circumstances or other, slide the whole way down.

Or to quote, as an example of anti-Party charges, from one of the public confessions by leading Party figures: Radek and Bukharin, on trial, admitted that they had overestimated the difficulties of collectivization. They had in fact advised against it, in the precipitate form adopted by Stalin. They were thus 'guilty', among other 'crimes', not of an error of judgment, of over-caution, but of opposition to, and hence 'sabotage' of, the true line of policy, the line which circumstances, it was alleged, had by 1927 already proved to be the 'correct' one.

* At the end of the Tsarist period there were only about 5,000 political prisoners.

Foreigners have often been touched by the compassionate way in which a sense of sin can easily be aroused among the Russian Orthodox. All of us, they hold, have sinned, *often without being conscious of the fact*, and the acknowledgment of our universal guilt brings us nearer to the more apparently blatant sinner, even to the murderer, who seems to be more readily forgiven, less rejected of his fellows among the Orthodox than among, say, Protestants who can so rigorously divide the righteous from the unrighteous. The same susceptibility to being shown, by one's fellows, that one had inadvertently sinned was retained by many of the early Communist Party members (in spite of their having rejected the Church), and this helps to explain how many of the country's best men and women were led by NKVD prosecutors to make extravagant confessions and to believe that their cup of coffee with a foreigner, for example, was potentially or, as the Party used to say at this time, in a disgusting perversion of language, 'objectively', as guilty a matter as the act of a saboteur who accepted foreign gold to run grit into a new turbine.

I spent an evening once with a former NKVD prosecutor who had chosen to defect abroad rather than face a capital charge: he kept the attitudes of his old profession so firmly after twenty years that I could only feel that they expressed something deep in his own nature, and in the nature, probably, of many other Russians of his generation. 'Everyone', he maintained, 'is guilty of something', so that he had little use for the principle of *habeas corpus*; it was better that innocent men should be jailed, 'if that would help the community', than that the guilty should go free.* In interrogation, he said, the point was not to discover *what* you had done (which was usually of small importance), but *why* you had done it, and *who* had helped you. We know from dozens of sources that the essential part of a prisoner's miserable existence, in the months spent under interrogation, was first to construct a suitable 'legend'—a fictional admission of guilt which would satisfy—and secondly to denounce one's 'associates', real or imaginary. Most prisoners gave way in the end

---

* Times have changed a good deal since this prosecutor left the Soviet Union. A handbook on *Examination of the Accused (Taktika Doprosa)*, published in 1970, shows a much more humane and equitable attitude, on the whole closer to Western principles. It points out, for example, that a refusal to give evidence must not be taken as proof of guilt. Such principles, or some of them, are still violated in political trials, but these trials have shrunk to a very small percentage compared with the years under Stalin, and they usually meet with a certain amount of protest from some members of the public—which in Stalin's day would have been unthinkable.

when confronted, perhaps, with one-time dear friends who, under repeated and unbearable pressure, had already signed denunciations involving themselves.

However, although all these attitudes and practices may help to explain the atmosphere of the Terror period, and why such a large number of totally innocent people were put away, they do not account for the mass scale on which arrests were eventually carried out. Was it, perhaps, to procure slave labour for such projects as the Baltic–White Sea Canal, or the giant Bratsk hydro-electric station? The NKVD were in charge of all the arrests, and they were also responsible for many of these labour projects, but it can hardly be maintained that unskilled prisoners, on starvation rations, were the most economically useful labour force that could have been shanghaied into service by a government as all-powerful and terroristic as Stalin's. The prisoners of the Terror were put to work, on the whole, because nearly all prisoners in the Soviet Union have always been—and still are—put to work.

It is more revealing to ask '*Who*, on the whole, were the prisoners?' And also 'Who in particular were arrested?' Why were the President of the Soviet Union, Rykov, and others of Lenin's original comrades, why were three out of the five Soviet Marshals, all the Admirals, about half the army officers, and finally 70 per cent of the Central Committee of the Party who were supposed to be responsible for these people—why were they all arrested and shot? It is clear nowadays, from the revelations of Khrushchev and others, that Stalin deliberately set out to destroy all possible rivals, both individuals and potential groupings, including Kirov, the popular Leningrad chief, and a likely rival, whose arranged murder was made the first excuse for launching the whole Terror; all those who had ever opposed Stalin in the Politburo or the Central Committee; all senior army officers, so as to forestall any remote possibility of a *putsch*; senior Party officials and most of those who, if promoted, might conceivably be in a position to oppose Stalin—especially the 'Old Bolsheviks', the stalwarts who had been in the Party before the Revolution and might be a nucleus of independence; and striking more at random, a vast assortment of local secretaries, officials, intelligentsia, distinguished scientists and writers, people who had had foreign contacts (whether at the orders of the Soviet Government or not), and men and women in positions of minor and very minor authority.

Only the most important prisoners were given a public trial, and then only if they had been reduced to a state where they 'confessed'; Stalin needed the 'confessions' to lend credibility to what was in plain fact his massacre of leading personnel. Political advantage having been secured from the confessions of the leaders, it presumably became important to extract confessions also from the lesser fry, in order to give the whole nightmare some grim air of plausibility. It would not have been sufficient merely to announce that, say, 10,000 Party officials had been shot for such a generalized offence as 'plotting to restore capitalism'; they must be shown to be guilty as individuals, guilty in several and particular ways, and guilty out of their own mouths. It seemed apparently unimportant that so many accused 'confessed' to impossible crimes, such as 'constructing artificial volcanoes to blow up the whole country': the NKVD, according to Beck and Godin, 'required clear proof of individual guilt, not only for foreign consumption, but also for their own people, to satisfy their own ideological sense of justice'. Though 'justice' is not here in quotation marks, it must serve as a perverted label for the whole rationally irrational web of lies in which prosecutors as well as accused were caught. 'One is reminded', say the same authors, 'of the Inquisition and the witches' trials, with the precise instructions for the extortion of confessions, handed down to us in the *Malleus Maleficorum*.'

Every prisoner wanted to get his confession accepted and sentence passed, because he might then be sent to a camp—he could hardly hope for release—and might for the first time since his arrest be allowed some communication with his relations. Prisoners found helpful old hands in their cells who would advise them on the kind of 'legends' that might be accepted, but presumably it would not do for the investigators to accept a confession and get rid of a man until, through underfeeding and many kinds of moral pressure, with loss of sleep and often beatings, he had been reduced to a state of total acquiescence. No investigation took less than two and a half months, and it is thought that perhaps 100,000 officials were used for interrogating and guarding prisoners under examination, during at least the three worst years.

Finally the NKVD machine acquired such a momentum of its own that it became gruesomely ridiculous even by the Soviet standards of the time: thousands were swept in for the 'crime' of having failed to denounce some mythical 'enemy of the people', or on the principle of guilt by association—through marriage, through blood relationship, through being second in command to an arrestee, or through having at some time or other worked with an arrestee—but even these blanket categories could hardly bring in enough victims when the lower NKVD grades in the localities were given such orders as 'Find 150 Trotskyites and arrest them', or 'Exterminate five hundred enemies of the people'. By the end the network of informers—the *seksots*—had probably composed incriminating reports on the greater part of the town population (including, of course, each other) for the files of the NKVD. The NKVD chief,* Yagoda, was himself denounced and executed and succeeded by the even more loathsome Yezhov, who himself fell to Beria, and in 1938 the whole thing at last slackened off.

After that year, according to John Scott, working in Magnitogorsk, 'hundreds were released', often 'with terse apologies for mistakes', and most people in Magnitogorsk began to take an optimistic view of the future. Some examining magistrates were prosecuted, and a general impression of an about-turn in policy was cultivated. Those who were released, however, were usually prisoners who had been under investigation: few releases from camps took place until much later, and arrests, on a much diminished scale, continued.

In so far as the Terror set out to destroy the Party and military leadership, it can certainly be laid at the door of 'the cult of personality' —the smooth phrase under which Stalin's personal excesses have been more recently condemned; but it was also, of course, a deliberately mass Terror. Those who feared the régime were thought, during this perverted period, to be more reliable citizens than those who might be devoted to it, for if the latter had used their own judgment in exercising their devotion to the Soviet state, they might on another occasion use their own judgment to oppose it: such was the poisoned reasoning not only in the mind of Stalin but in the minds of thousands of his near associates and tens of thousands of his officials. The mass Terror, in fact, was only a monstrous exaggeration of a principle which had already been acted on, in a limited way, long before Stalin's paranoia—and it is a principle which is far from having disappeared from the Soviet system, though its application today is both milder and less frequent as well as much more limited in scope, and it is accompanied, fortunately, by more rational principles, which operate powerfully if uneasily alongside it among the leadership. Young men who are called in today for 'warning' by the KGB (the successors to the NKVD) are sometimes bold enough to argue with its officials

* Members of the NKVD, or examining personnel, were just about as liable to arrest as other people; Beck and Godin tell of one prisoner who outlasted, during his interrogation, ten examining magistrates, all of whom had been arrested in their turn.

and even to be cheeky—an attitude which would have been incredible
in Stalin's time. (When I asked, in the 1950s, why my old acquaintance K, a devoted Party man and hard worker, had been shot, the
only excuse his surviving friends could think of was that 'perhaps he
had been too rude to "Them" '.)

It should never be forgotten that the Terror fell most heavily on
the intelligentsia and on officials: the rank-and-file manual workers
and the peasants, though frightened, were not so often its victims.
The first-hand accounts which we have of the Terror are all written
by former officials or members of the intelligentsia, and it is a most
valuable revelation in Mrs. Mandelshtam's harrowing memoir, *Hope
Against Hope* (published in 1971), that she tells how when she worked
in a cotton mill (being barred from work for which her education
fitted her) she found the working people 'talked much more freely
than we did in intellectual circles', that many were contemptuous of
the show trials—'See what they are doing in our name!'—and though
they thought 'any kind of resistance futile and dishonest', they showed
a practical, old-fashioned sympathy to her and to all prisoners or
persons threatened by the régime.

She helps to explain that mystery so incomprehensible to people
in the West—'How could so many acquiesce in injustice on such a
scale?' There was a general fear, she says, of chaos after the anarchy
which they had all lived through fourteen or fifteen years before, so
that even the intelligentsia 'prayed for a strong system'. There was
also a longing for unanimity and even for self-abasement among too
many of the intelligentsia, because they had cast off so many of the
values in which they had been brought up, and had pinned their faith
to the new Soviet world. The poet Yevtushenko says in his autobio-
graphy that there was a great reluctance to believe that a trusted
leadership—the only possible leadership, it seemed—could be guilty
of such crimes as everyone in the end came to know of: 'It would be
too terrible.' Evgenia Ginzburg says that during her eighteen years
in the camps 'many managed strangely to combine a sane judgment
of what was going on in the country with a truly mystical personal
cult of Stalin'. Such people were carrying on the pre-revolutionary
attitude—that the dictator was sacrosanct, but his officers were merely
imperfect creatures like oneself. Beck and Godin say that when NKVD
officials were arrested and put into crowded cells 'the attitude of the
other prisoners towards them was completely friendly, and feelings of
vindictiveness towards them were exceptional'. Outside the prisons

there were many merely credulous souls, especially among the workers, who were only too relieved to be able to fasten on scapegoats among the persons denounced, whom they could blame for the shortages and breakdowns in their daily life. And finally, at the same time that the Terror was in progress, Nazi Germany was gathering strength, and the menace of all foreign enemies of the Soviet Union was played up so strongly that many felt grateful to Stalin, in spite of all, for apparently guaranteeing them protection.

By no means everyone acquiesced. Rudzutak, for instance, one-time head of the Central Control Commission and a Party member since 1905, retracted in open court the confession which had been forced from him, and attacked the NKVD, alleging that it had been penetrated by 'an as yet unliquidated centre which forces innocent persons to confess'. This allegation was ignored, and Rudzutak was shot, as were other prominent Bolsheviks who protested.

Rudzutak was the sort of Bolshevik who was needed—the sort who might have stood up to Stalin. Still more, the country needed all those executed senior officers, from Marshal Tukhachevsky downwards, who could have prepared the armed forces better for war. But Stalin had had such successes (and not all of them to Russia's harm); he had built up such a pyramid of power in every domestic field; he had, as is truly said, 'invented totalitarianism', so that he came to trust his own judgment in the dangerous game he played with Nazi Germany. Fearful of war, he bought time for developing war industries through the Ribbentrop–Molotov Pact, and kept faithfully to his own side of the bargains it involved, even to the expelling of refugee German Communists, whom he handed over to the Gestapo. The Nazis were far less scrupulous on their side, and Stalin soon received warnings from many sources that they were preparing to attack the USSR. He obstinately refused to believe these reports about his newly-negotiated 'ally', he blundered catastrophically in his interpretation and in his timing, and so the Russian people, dogged by ill fortune almost as if they had been the Jews, found themselves plunged, after a brief interval of false security and comparative prosperity, into the Second World War.

Twenty-four hours after the German offensive had begun, Stalin was still ordering his frontier forces not to retaliate; the reports were 'a provocation'. Troops who might have faced the Nazis, even though poorly officered, had not been properly mobilized, and now planes were destroyed on the ground, while weapons and armour were terribly short; the forces defending the Leningrad front had only 9 per cent of their complement of tanks. In a short time the Germans overran a huge territory which had been the home of 40 per cent of the Soviet population, and which had produced 65 per cent of the country's coal and 68 per cent of its iron. For the only time, apparently, in his career, Stalin seemed to be in despair. He had a few generals shot for retreating, but for some weeks he could not be communicated with; defeatism was rife, and in the occupied or threatened areas some peasants were collaborating with the invaders. In December the Germans were at the last approaches to Moscow, most of the Government was evacuated to the Volga town of Kuibyshev, and for a few days there was dangerous panic in the capital. But at last, after six months of continuous retreat, Stalin was able to launch a counter-attack, in icy weather, and for this the Germans were completely unprepared. They had to give way. For the first time in Hitler's advance over Europe, one of his armies had been forced to retreat, and it was Soviet soldiers (with some help from 'General Winter') who had done it. Soviet morale recovered a little, and it was seen that Stalin was not among the evacuated: in fact he stayed in the Kremlin throughout the war, exercising now, after his unpardonable early blunders, his talent for understanding and organizing a mass of detail, and leaving most strategic decisions to the new Marshals under his chairmanship—men like Zhukov, Rokossovsky (who was fetched from a prison camp), or Malinovsky.

With great difficulty the plant and personnel of 1,360 factories were evacuated, ahead of the German advance, to industrial centres in the Urals and Siberia. It was two years before the evacuated plants could reach full production, but eventually the whole industrial out-put of unoccupied Russia was doubled, and towards the end of the war it was operating at the rate of 40,000 planes and 30,000 tanks and armoured vehicles a year. The types were very few and their equipment of the simplest, but the T34 was said to be the best tank in the world, and the little Ilyushin fighters, made mostly of plywood, were 'more manoeuvrable than a Spitfire', or so I was told by a French pilot who had flown both. America and Britain sent some planes and tanks, but their great contribution was motor transport.

The Germans continued their advance in the south until they were held up by the Volga and by the tenacious heroism of the defenders of Stalingrad. The Russian command then used the old strategy practised by Alexander Nevsky against the German knights

in 1242, and by Kutuzov against Napoleon: they made their defending forces hold on almost to the point of exhaustion, and then when
the enemy thought victory was easy, launched a savage surprise
attack upon his flank. Stalin guessed that Hitler's paranoia would
make him overrule his marshals when they wanted to retreat, and the
result was the catastrophic encirclement—the worst blow the Germans
had suffered.

The Russian people had rediscovered patriotism for themselves, as
they did when they destroyed Napoleon's Grande Armée in 1812,
and Stalin (who may well have been surprised at such loyalty) encouraged the nation with reminders of past defenders of Mother Russia:
the victorious generals of Tsarist campaigns were held up as heroic
models, the Napoleonic invasion was constantly recalled, and the
Church, to which so many people still seemed to cling, was spared the
attacks of militant atheists for a while, was allowed to elect a Patriarch
(for the first time since the reign of Peter the Great!) and was tacitly
allowed some respect as a national and patriotic institution. (In fact,
anti-religious propaganda had been relaxed beforehand, in anticipation
of the war.) As the Soviet victories increased, even the aristocratic
old ladies who survived in Leningrad became enthusiastic for this
Government which was so much more successful against the Germans
than Nicholas II had been.

However, this is hardly to say that the home front was in any way
cheerful. I spent two of the war years in Russia as a civilian member of a British mission, and I had many weary days in which to observe
life in Kuibyshev, or Moscow, or some of the villages: practically
no shops were open anywhere except for the sale of the severely
rationed food, in winter there was sometimes neither heat nor light,
and grey-faced women and old men shuffled through the streets,
never expecting their men home on leave, and only occasionally raised
to delight by the rare letter in purple ink on coarse green army paper.
The atmosphere was not quite despairing, but it was monotonous
and long-suffering and *serious*—not solemn, but serious in a simple
way which I found hard to explain in my letters home. Jokes and
cups of tea after the air raid were not the mood: the direct and simple
Russians would have thought the London attitude unnecessarily
flippant, showing courage but suppressing any expression of natural
grief or the natural desire for revenge. They greeted the final victory, when it came, with a surge of child-like joy such as the British
don't give way to, though if the British had been in the Russians'

shoes they might perhaps have found themselves able to express it: victory for the Russians, with so much of their land barbarously occupied, and all their resources strained to the utmost, had for long seemed not merely far off but impossible.

As a result of the war Soviet national pride was vastly strengthened and the dominant role of Russia in the Union of Soviet Socialist Republics was more emphasized than ever, because of the play that had been made with her glorious past for the sake of war propaganda. The Internationale, which rouses 'starvelings' of all nations 'from their slumbers', was downgraded from its position as the national anthem and replaced by a new hymn (still in force) which celebrates the 'indestructible union of free republics *established by great Russia*'.

The Party was now in an immensely stronger position, too. Individual Communists had taken such a lead in resistance—they had always been the first to be executed by the occupying Germans— and on the home front they had done so much simple encouraging and keeping up of people's spirits. A couple of million men and women applied to join the Party, as a sort of patriotic act, during the war, and their enthusiasm, and the enthusiasm of millions of others outside the Party, increased the adulation of Stalin the victor and fed 'the cult of personality'. Government was arbitrary, had always been arbitrary, but at least this Government was effective. Its tyrannies were in quite a different category, as occasions for suffering, from the horrors of foreign invasion.

But the nation was terribly, terribly tired. 'Their backs were bent', wrote Yevtushenko, 'and their eyes despaired of ever understanding anything. And yet these people were not embittered or sullen, there was a timid kindness in them and the expectation of an answering kindness from the world. They were poorly dressed but there was in them a sort of majesty, perhaps unconscious and therefore the more proud.' They expected relief and relaxation. They did not get it. If twenty million had been killed, how many millions more were wounded and handicapped or permanently disabled? Of the population that remained between the ages of twenty and forty there were but four men to seven women, including the disabled. Agriculture had been as badly damaged as industry, so that almost everyone was underfed, and the survivors were weakened, many of them for life. In 1946–7, after a bad harvest, there was once again a famine in the south, and many thousands died of starvation. Yet it was impossible to do much about food or consumer goods until heavy industry, which had been worked to death during the war, was renewed or reconstructed. It was seven years before the country regained its prewar standard of living, and even then the housing situation remained worse than before, since people from the villages continued to crowd into the towns, where they had to live in communal dormitories or improvised shacks, just as in the days of the first Five-Year Plans.

There was no avoiding any of these miseries, nor the long-delayed postponement of relief. Stalin added to the burden by one of his most obscenely inhuman policies: anyone who had been a prisoner of the Germans was regarded as a possible traitor—because he might conceivably have had some anti-Soviet motive for allowing himself to be made prisoner. So that all who survived the brutality of a German camp, or who had been forced labourers under the Germans, were sent to Soviet camps for screening, after which large numbers of them were sentenced to a term in a labour camp. Some of the smaller Soviet nationalities—the Chechens, Balkars, Kalmucks, Crimean Tatars and others*—were rounded up to the last man, woman and child and deported to Central Asia, on the grounds that some of them had collaborated with the Germans.

Stalin was probably well aware that far too many Soviet soldiers had seen Nazi Germany and found its standard of living, to their amazement, much better than their own. (Twenty-five years later, the contrast is still remembered by ex-soldiers who, of course, never went abroad again.) There had always been an 'iron curtain' between the Communist homeland and the capitalist countries, and after the war Stalin reinforced it with what one can only call pathological severity. He refused help from the Marshall Plan (and blackmailed the Czechs into refusing it too), he kept foreigners away so that they should not see the sorry plight of the Communist homeland, and he sent his own people to labour camps if they had the slightest kind of foreign contact. This was the period when Russia's past was glorified to the exclusion of most of the rest of world history, and when Russians whom no Westerner had heard of were exalted as the originators of great inventions such as the steam engine. Stalinist chauvinism became so exaggerated, and the barriers against foreign influence so forbiddingly high, that the intentions of this policy were to some extent defeated: the ordinary man's curiosity about foreign peoples and foreign countries tended to overcome his crude sense of Soviet uniqueness

* All of these peoples have since been rehabilitated, and all except the Crimean Tatars allowed to return to their homes.

and superiority. Stalin's death left a huge legacy of unsatisfied Soviet desire for knowledge and contact of all kinds with Western countries. How to contain or reduce the pressure of this great head of desire constitutes one of the biggest problems for post-Stalin governments, for all that they have already opened a good many chinks in the iron curtain.

The grim greyness of life in the reconstruction period, from the material point of view, was inevitable: the pathological greyness of its intellectual life was the culmination of a process which had begun about 1930, when Stalin wrote in the Party magazine, *Bolshevik*, that nothing ought to be published which did not accord with the official points of view. In a country which was pulling in its belt as tight as Russia was during the first Plans, and under a Party dictatorship, it was probably inevitable that the arts and intellectual life must go through a period of Victorian-style puritanism, stressing simple moral values and excluding wider or more subtle characterization or speculation. For one thing, the public might hardly have endured to see artists and writers spending their time on experimental work, or work for minority tastes, when they were being supported basically by the State, even if only on the same half-starved level as the workers themselves were living. But what with the growing paranoia of Stalin and coarse Party leaders ignorant of the arts, and some self-torturing intellectuals who betrayed their own kind through a mistaken obeisance before crude political aims, the period became increasingly depressing, severe and vulgar for all the arts. New music, for example, was only allowable if it could be easily appreciated at a first hearing and was on the whole 'in a major key', so the young talent of Shostakovitch suffered a sad setback; novelists and playwrights were supposed to be 'engineers of the human soul', and writers who were too bold or too original to fall in with the senseless censorship were put away in camps where they died, like the poet Mandelshtam and the novelist Pilnyak, or were hounded and forbidden publication, like the poetess Akhmatova. Mayakovsky had already committed suicide in 1930 and Yessenin in 1928, and it is estimated that the potential works of at least six hundred gifted writers were lost through their execution or death in the camps. Some less original or merely pliable writers managed to survive by repulsive adulation, producing fulsome odes and other tributes to Stalin. Stalin liked blowsy 'wedding-cake' architecture, and so when great new 32-storey buildings were required, they not only had to observe this style, but they had to be praised as a monument to the dictator's taste. (Many gross and enormous examples unfortunately remain, all too solidly built, such as the Ministry of Foreign Affairs or the Ukraine Hotel in Moscow.)

Not only the arts but the sciences suffered serious injury. In physics it was impossible to accommodate the Heisenberg principle of indeterminacy, because according to Marxist philosophy everything can be explained through laws of prediction. The charlatan Lysenko, on the basis of a few experiments which others were unable to verify, alleged that characteristics acquired from the environment could be transmitted in the evolutionary process: ordinary Mendelian genetics therefore became anathema, its professors were dismissed and persecuted, and one of the world's greatest biologists, N. I. Vavilov, was removed from his post and died in a camp. Most surprising of all, economists had to fly in the face of the facts they had observed about the capitalist world after the war, and had to agree that economic disaster was imminent in the West, because the Stalinists, in their coarse application of Marxism, said this must be so. A few clever physicists, biologists and economists, however, managed to put up a façade of conformity, behind which they pursued more genuine researches and even instructed students.

Millions of plaster casts, all over the Soviet Union, now reproduced the features or the figure of the 'genius'—a genius, it was alleged, in almost all fields—who after the war carried on a more and more arbitrary one-man dictatorship in the Kremlin. During the war Stalin had been careful never to sign orders of the day unless things were going well; according to the American diplomat, George Kennan, he usually had two alternative policies running at the same time: if one of these succeeded, it was attributed to 'Stalin's genius'; if the other failed, it was pinned on someone else, like the 'Molotov Pact'. After the war, however, Stalin was much more the single-handed operator and much more unapproachable. He had long since treated the Congress of the Party itself with contempt: according to the rules it should have met every year, but after 1927 it was summoned, during Stalin's lifetime, only in 1930, 1934, 1939 and 1952. Inside the Politburo, Stalin had involved all the other members in so many of his crimes against the Soviet people that it was impossible for any of them to break away or to oppose him; by their own account, during his last years they lived in constant fear. And Stalin himself lived in fear, changing his sleeping quarters every night, and eating nothing that had not first been tested by someone else in his presence. Solzhenitsyn's portrait, in *The First Circle*, of the last stage of the dictator—self-congratulatory, nervous, isolated and afraid—must be based on reliable information; it would have been quite inappropriate for Solzhenitsyn to draw upon his novelist's imagination, when there are so many people alive who had contact with the Kremlin in Stalin's day. Behind his back Stalin was referred to as 'the Asiatic'. Had Russia fallen under an 'Asiatic' system of tyranny? The adjective is too vague; though as a derogatory word it relieved the feelings of those who employed it, they might more suitably have said 'Byzantine' or 'mediaeval', but actually there was no adequate word to characterize the first totalitarian régime in modern history.

Stalin was in command of the Soviet Union for twenty-five years. His abilities were a mixture of the canny and the clumsy: his character was obstinate, secretive, vindictive, suspicious, in many ways vicious, and eventually despotic. When his second wife, Nadezhda Alliluyeva (mother of Svetlana), denounced his methods in the collectivization and committed suicide in 1932, this seemed to him an unforgivable act of treachery. The Jugoslav Communist Djilas, who knew Stalin well, sums him up as 'a monster who, while adhering to abstract, absolute and fundamentally utopian ideas, in practice had no criterion but success—and this meant violence, and physical and spiritual extermination'. Stalin saw and knew practically nothing of his own people during the greater part of his life as dictator. But when he died, in 1953, he had transformed the country: he had made it one of the world's two super-powers; he had made it fundamentally urban, industrial and literate; he had made it, willy-nilly, a politically working whole (of a sort), and more effectively centralized than ever before in Russian history; he had forced it through changes which, for the most part, must be regarded as basically irreversible in any plausible Soviet future.

What makes Soviet life tolerable in the 1970s—and any Soviet citizen would agree that the differences are really considerable—lies not in any changes in the basic institutions and organizations created under Stalin, but in changes in the detailed methods by which they are run, and in changes in attitude, interpretation, atmosphere, and even in basic intention. To outline these changes will be for the next chapter.

The unmasking of Stalin, and the violent reaction against him and his methods, initiated by Khrushchev, did not go quite so far as was at one time promised: his body was removed from the tomb in the

Red Square where it had lain embalmed alongside Lenin's, but there was also talk of expelling him posthumously from the Party, and of not only rehabilitating his victims but of erecting a monument to them. Neither of these ultimate condemnations has been carried out, and the official attitude with regard to all the crimes of the Stalin period is still uneasy and inadequately defined. But the pendulum does not seem, at least, to have swung so far in his favour as is often supposed outside the Soviet Union. The latest appraisal of Stalin, at the time of writing, is in a new volume of the Soviet Encyclopaedia of History: this reproduces Lenin's 'testament' which criticized him, gives him credit for work in the early revolutionary years, but says: 'Extreme measures were taken and mistakes were made in carrying out collectivization, the responsibility for which Stalin must bear.' The article goes on to attack 'the adulation of his person which turned his head and brought about the personality cult', and says he 'violated the principles of collective leadership, restricted democracy, grossly violated Socialist legality, and waged massive repression against outstanding Party, State and military leaders which caused great harm to the Party, State, army, and nation . . . He committed serious miscalculations in estimating the timing of a possible attack by Nazi Germany which were fraught with severe consequences in the first few months of the war.'

The buses in Tbilisi, the capital of Stalin's native Georgia, still exhibit his portrait, and among the older part of the Soviet population there is a fair minority who still admire him because he gave them a job or a career or because he 'made the country stable' or 'made it great'. But the younger half of the nation—and that means by far the larger half—are still waiting for a complete and comprehensible account from their leaders, an admission, in fact, of all that was blackest in that crucial period of Communist Russia. A large proportion of them are alienated from Communism without being actually opposed to it (since they can see all around them the advantages it has brought): to rekindle their faith, they would need to be offered opportunities which no Soviet Government has yet dared give its people, but first their rulers would have to have the courage to indulge in a full confession, and a full and frank explanation of the crimes committed in Communism's name.

9. Living with the Party Today

When I was asking Russians, sixteen years after Stalin's death, what they expected from the slogan 'Forward to Communism', and they unanimously replied 'First, peace', they were equally unanimous in their second expectation. Communism, they said, should mean *'More and better goods in the shops'*. They sometimes added, if they were themselves in a skilled or professional job, 'Better quality work from the craftsmen.' So far, apparently, had the concept of 'Communism' ceased to operate either as a lodestar or as a Moloch.

The life of the average Soviet citizen today is not—and I should like to repeat, is not—taken up with looking over his shoulder for the KGB. There are a few subjects, but only a few, which he would not discuss in a public place without first looking round—political subjects which some people rarely mention, but which a great many others discuss privately and without fear. He is almost certain to know a number of people who spent years in camps during the Terror: he is unlikely to know anyone who is in a camp now. His life is full of irritations, frustrations, and occasions for grumbling or for petty scheming—his wife's life more so than his own, and they may occasionally lump the whole lot together in one big grumble at 'our system', but they don't seem to spend much time thinking or talking about the larger issues of policy.

They do not live and work as neat little cogs, though 'the system', in theory, accounts for them in groups, and in practice it tries to keep tapes on them as individuals. They are cogs in the same sort of way that most of us are in an industrial society, and the Soviet Union today is quite as complicated as other industrial societies, more complicated in many particulars, and more unpredictable, because attempts are always being made from above to predict too much. The ordinary townsman is not so much caught in a machine as moving within a loosely all-pervading mesh: it is there all the time, but sometimes one or two meshes can be wriggled through, and very often they can be stretched—indeed, how stretchable they can be! In other places the tangle may clog and hamper him at every turn, but it is not so often that it pulls him up with a jerk.

Leaving metaphors aside, I should like to outline over the next few pages the principal ways in which life in the Soviet Union, during the last decade or so, differs from life in the Stalin period. I do not propose to recapitulate recent political history, to tell once again the story of Khrushchev's rise to power after Stalin's death, nor how he was deposed in 1964, and two years later it was decided to slow down the de-Stalinization process which he had so vigorously initiated. One feature of Soviet political life which has remained much as it was in Stalin's day is the alternation of periods of comparative repression with periods of comparative relaxation. This seems inevitable under a régime where so few endeavour to dictate to so many, and the few must often disagree among themselves. It also serves to keep the people guessing, but the swings today are not wide; it would be truer, perhaps, to speak of policies of repression or relaxation being given the upper hand from time to time, while the opposite policy remains discernible, and hinted at, underneath.

The features which I am about to mention seem to me least susceptible to 'swings', and most likely to be characteristic of life in the Soviet Union in at least the short-term future. To arrange them in an order of importance seems impossible: they are all significant.

RULE BY OLIGARCHY

To begin at the top of the national hierarchy: one-man dictatorship has clearly now been superseded by the principle of rule by oligarchy, that is, by the Politburo of the Party, which at present has fifteen members, and the Party Secretariat of ten members, which is concerned more with Party organization and personnel than with general policy. (At the time of writing four leaders are members of both bodies.)

Each member of the Politburo is responsible for one or more—usually more—sectors of national life, so that conflicts and complicated balances of interest must arise, between the needs, for instance, of heavy industry, consumer industry, defence, agriculture, public order, the earning of foreign currency by trade, scientific research, funds for social welfare, and so on. Similar conflicts must arise within the Council of Ministers, a body which is more like a council of Whitehall chiefs than a cabinet in a democratic country. The Ministers, who are perhaps eighty in number, and whose appointments are vetted by the Party, cover almost every branch of national activity, e.g. the coal, petrol and food industries, light metals, or agriculture, besides public health, foreign affairs, culture, etc. The Council wields a great deal of day-to-day power in detailed matters, but on matters of basic policy it is directed by the Politburo (though on paper it is responsible to the Supreme Soviet). The Chairman of the Council of Ministers, Kosygin, is in fact a member of the Politburo, and there are other interlocking appointments which make it easier for the Party to control what is called 'the Government'.

All this machinery existed in Stalin's time, and in theory its powers were the same as now, but there was apparently no end to the number of issues, great and small, which had to be referred to the dictator, of whom even the highest personnel were afraid. Today it is to the advantage of each of the powerful leaders that they should not allow any one of their number to get ahead of the others, and various reshufflings from time to time seem to show how jealously they contrive that an over-ambitious man, such as Shelepin, should not acquire too much power. (The whole Party organization is of course much more sophisticated and experienced than it was when Stalin perverted it all to be his own instrument.) It is also to the interest of the leaders—or so they judge—that they should appear to the public to preserve a monolithic unity, and so one gets the impression of an oligarchy unanimous in its dictatorship. If the members of a minority inside the Politburo should lose their case—a plea, perhaps, for more expensive missiles—they all prize the appearance of unity too much to let dissension appear; besides, if they can intrigue for a different alignment of forces, they might win next time. This method of government is one of the principal reasons for the intense, slow-moving conservatism of the Soviet Union today; a tight little committee of opposing forces does not usually come to quick decisions. In fact, by studying the Soviet press carefully a skilled reader, Soviet or foreign, can often tell what kind of major differences there may be at the top.

It would seem anyway to be established that a minority inside the Politburo is nowadays entitled to be spared to fight again for its viewpoint, instead of being hounded to expulsion or even execution, as used to be not uncommonly the case. The *Guardian*'s commentator, Mr. Victor Zorza, suggests that the habit of political debate is bound to spread to the next lower level, the Central Committee of the Party, a very important organ which has close links with the Politburo and has at present 241 members. One of the basic principles which animated the Dubcek Government in Czechoslovakia, and which they proclaimed from the housetops, was exactly this right of the minority to continue campaigning for its views. It was also one of the basic reasons why the Dubcek Government was suppressed by the Soviet Union. If they had kept quiet and allowed minorities inside their Party the privilege of dissent, while at the same time preserving a monolithic exterior in the eyes of the world, they would have kept in step with the timid internal progress of the motherland of Communism, and possibly their country might not have been invaded.

What the ordinary Soviet citizen sees is not the debating that goes on above his head, but the portraits of the fifteen members of the Politburo, in the street on the two great national holidays— May 1st and November 7th—and sometimes in the papers, when long reports of already agreed discussions are printed. The giant portraits are taken down after a very short interval, much shorter than used to be the case, and publicity for the leaders in general is on an extremely reduced scale, compared with the eczema of adulation in Stalin's time. The personalities of the leaders, in fact, seem to be played down so far as the public is concerned: when Khrushchev was obliged to 'resign' the news was given briefly, well down the front page of the newspapers, and more recently, when I asked several people about the newer members of the Politburo, they said 'We know nothing about them.'* And though almost anyone may wear a Lenin button or a button celebrating one of the Russian astronauts, there is no such thing as a Brezhnev button or a Kosygin button or a button for any contemporary political figure.

So there is no longer any living demigod on whom to lavish worship—a circumstance probably regretted by some of the older, simpler inhabitants of the USSR. Lenin's portrait is indeed to be seen everywhere, but Lenin has been dead nearly fifty years, and if his personality now bears something of an odour of sanctity, at least there is no longer any equivalent of a Tsar in the Soviet hierarchy.

FALLEN LEADERS

Though no democratic process exists to remove them, nowadays

---

* An irreverent friend alleges that, looking out of his flat on the ring boulevard early one May morning, after a heavy celebration the night before, he saw a portrait of Malenkov being marched along with the others, ten years after his disgrace. 'It must have been drawn from store with the other portraits', he said, 'but no one noticed, not even the bearer. They couldn't have named all the other fourteen Politburo men anyway!'

fallen leaders are neither executed nor impeached, but demoted, as Malenkov and Molotov were, or allowed to retire into private life (under supervision), like Khrushchev. A similar principle applies to officials who have fallen down on their job: they can nowadays expect nothing worse than to be downgraded or transferred to an unpleasant part of the country, unless indeed they have been found guilty of corruption or peculation, in which case they face prosecution and sometimes the death penalty. The same principle seems to apply right down to the lowest grades: one slip, or one grain of heresy, is no longer held to corrupt the entire human being, as in the days of the Terror, so that here another atavistic principle (perverted from the Orthodox sense of universal sinfulness) has been abandoned. Only in the matter of foreign contacts, or of openly contesting Party authority, is a small 'crime' (though not nowadays an imaginary one) still liable to be exaggerated into a serious public danger. Inside the Party there seem likely to be no more purges. The present membership, at 14·5 million, is probably thought to be too large for efficiency; it is 6 per cent of the population instead of the usual 5 per cent. There is to be a new issue of Party cards, we are told: the passengers and undesirables will presumably not get one, but they (and the Party) will be spared the ignominy of expulsions, and they will surely suffer no punishment.

THE KGB

Today this is a great deal smaller than it was under Stalin, and it is under much closer Party control; it is perhaps noteworthy that the man now ultimately responsible for it, Andropov, is not a full member of the Politburo but a 'candidate member'; this deprives him of a full voice in Party counsels, while giving him an extra incentive to keep in line with general Party policy, which seems to be that the KGB must not be allowed too much independence. The smaller KGB of today employs a smaller body of informers, who are of course easily identifiable by the people they work among, and are sometimes treated with open contempt. No one knows for certain what use is made of the mass of reports in the KGB files, but it is only infrequently that any of these result in a prosecution. Guilt by association has disappeared as a cause for conviction, and sentences are much shorter than they used to be—two or three years on the average, while eight years is regarded as heavy. In such camps as still exist, however, the deliberate underfeeding and petty humiliations, to judge by the reports of men like Marchenko, are as revolting as before. A new obscenity, or rather a revival of an old Tsarist one, is the internment of a few of the most courageous dissenters in mental hospitals —men such as General Grigorenko or the farmer Yakhimovich— on the grounds that their dissent is a sign of psychiatric disorder. But in all other cases prisoners are at least brought to the semblance of a trial, and even if the court has been 'packed', somehow or other people get to know about the trial, and the news is circulated surreptitiously: the KGB are no longer able to pass sentence in savage secrecy.

THE RULE OF LAW

Most of the trials which take place in the Soviet Union are not, of course, for political crimes. They are not trials for such offences as 'the systematic dissemination by word of mouth of deliberately false statements derogatory to the Soviet state and social system'. As in any other country they are chiefly prosecutions for corruption, fraud, theft, assault, murder, failure to pay taxes or alimony, and so on, or they are long and complicated suits between state enterprises concerning failure to complete contracts. Several legal journals appear in the USSR, and in these one may read regular reports, with comments, on exemplary or difficult cases, and on successful or unsuccessful appeals to higher courts. The cases, and the comments, show a vastly increased respect for the rule of law, and for the new rules which lay the burden of proving guilt upon the prosecution. 'Confessions must be corroborated by other evidence'—in complete contrast to the procedures of Stalin's loathsome chief prosecutor Vyshinsky, who is condemned in the latest edition of the Soviet Encyclopaedia for taking 'an erroneous view of the law and the state'. All of this makes the violation of legality and equity, in a minority of cases, the more glaring. Yet the two great authorities on Soviet law, the American professors Berman and Hazard, 'do not consider violations of legality by the Communist Party an *intrinsic* feature of the Soviet system' (my italics). Judges, they say, are required to support the general Party positions, but 'decisions in individual cases are not dictated from above'.

CRITICISM

In spite of there being no free press in the Soviet Union, the public have always had the safety-valve of criticism, when plans have not been fulfilled or individuals have failed in their duty, through wall newspapers, trade union branches, letters to the local or the national press, and complaints to Party secretaries or to members of the Soviets. Under Stalin there were so many other accusations flying about that this safety-valve had only limited value, but today the freedom for a good deal of criticism is taken for granted, and it can extend up to persons as high in rank as the Ministers. It would be dangerous for anyone to complain about 'the Party' or 'the Government' or 'the KGB' or about major lines of policy, but there are thousands of complaints about individual Government departments, or more often, about individual enterprises and officials. Part of the work of Party secretaries involves keeping an ear to the ground and estimating what substance there may be in complaints. Complaints about Party branches are published too, but much less often. Deputies to the Supreme Soviet have, to a limited extent, powers resembling those of British M.P.s in getting some of their constituents' grievances investigated.

Mrs. Mandelshtam declares, in *Hope Against Hope*, that a fundamental difference between the present and the Stalin period which blackened most of her life is that today, if there were to be a recurrence of injustice on anything like the Stalinist scale, 'people would scream'. Under Stalin they were afraid to scream, and if they did, their screams were not heard. The present Soviet Government shows itself to be well aware of the kind of public it has to do with nowadays: most of them will put up, grumblingly, with what they are accustomed to, but any tightening of the screw might produce riots and strikes such as have occasionally occurred in several places, over specific issues, in the last few years. Or such as in Poland actually forced the hand of the Polish Communist Party in 1971. In Poland the striking workers of Szczecin and Lodz actually caused a change of leadership in 1971, and the Gierek Government has since made considerable economic concessions to the nation at large. Because the revolt was for economic and not political reasons—i.e., it was not too obviously directed against the Party—the Polish Communist Party called off the forces which it had at first summoned, and the Soviet Government did not repeat its Czechoslovak *coup*. The lesson has not been lost, one may be sure, on either the Soviet leadership or the Soviet workers.

REHABILITATION

During 1953–7, rehabilitation was granted to most of the camp prisoners accused of 'counter-revolutionary' crimes, almost all of whom had already been released. Trade unions and professional organs made special recuperative provision for many of those rehabilitated. The great biologist Vavilov is now the subject of a biography in the series 'Lives of Distinguished People', his opponent Lysenko being completely discredited, but the book stops short of admitting that Vavilov died in a camp; it merely says his last work appeared in 1940, 'and two and a half years later he was dead'.

FREEDOM OF WORK

No one is tied to a job, although students in their first three years after graduation, and technicians in their first four years, are directed towards employment, usually in the more unpopular parts of the country. Everyone still has a labour book, but in Stalin's time this tied you to the job where you were, under severe penalties. There is a shortage of labour in most fields and in most parts of the country, and jobs of many kinds are advertised freely. Men leave to get higher wages, illegally offered by another factory, or because they have been badly treated, or there is too much night work, or merely for a change. A director said to me enviously: 'In England you can sack a bad worker. We can't!' The construction industry has for several years been getting only half the labour it was supposed to recruit under the Plan, and there are no means by which men can be compelled to join it, though a recent increase of 20 per cent in wage rates may have had some effect. The Moscow secretarial schools turn out only 2,600 qualified secretaries a year, but about five times as many are wanted, so some girls make more money by working as freelance typists at home.

DOCTRINAL ARGUMENT

This is carried on pretty freely among professionals in every field. The journal *Questions of Philosophy* has admitted, for instance, that the 'inevitable' collapse of capitalism and the world victory of communism are no longer axiomatic, but rather vaguely postponed, as a new 'expertocracy' takes over in the capitalist countries. The same journal also admits, after two years' discussion, the priority of mind over matter: in totally un-Marxist terms, 'the idea predetermines economic necessity'. A Georgian book on *Man As A Philosophical Problem* explained in 1970 that 'people will correspond to the character of their social system, but social systems likewise depend on the character of the people composing them'. In the same year a

scholarly book examined Kierkegaard's scheme of the world, relating
it to Dostoevsky's views, and a number of critical articles in *Soviet
Literature* have discussed, and showed understanding for, some very
un-Marxist factors, such as Jung's theory of archetypes, or the inter-
dependence of conscious and unconscious processes, as illustrated
in the work of Dostoevsky or the poet Mandelshtam.

Then there was the delightful book called *I and We* (*Ya i My*),
published by the psychiatrist V. Levi in 1969. Why, he asked, instead
of trying to make people mutually trustful and tolerant, do we prefer
'Pay your fare or you'll be fined', 'Do not overtake', and such threatening phrases? Fastening on the more sordid aspects of everyday Soviet
life, he says of his countrymen: 'We allege that we lack the time to
get rid of ugliness, carelessness, lack of deference, insincerity, because
we are preoccupied with building the future.' But the future, he says,
is only a sequence of fleeting moments like the present: why this
irrational injustice against ourselves? It might be better for the future
if we learned how to 'create significant moments' at the present time!*

Such dangerous thoughts as these are only to be found in the
specialized journals read by the intelligentsia, or in books published
in small editions. The great majority of mass-circulation political
literature for the ordinary citizen consists of dull reiterations or
variations on the old-fashioned Bolshevik Marxism taught in school,
or in the university, or in the army (60 hours for all recruits), in the
shape of compulsory courses in Marxism-Leninism, which plenty
of Russians have described to me as 'just going in one ear and out
the other'. Since 1961 the schools have had compulsory courses in
'combating anti-Communism' too, which at least shows the greater
penetration of foreign ideas nowadays among all classes. And yet,
in the course of hundreds of contacts with strangers, I have met
with only one person in twenty who tried to push Marxism down
my throat or who even volunteered any remarks about Marxism—
and that is in about the same proportion as Party members to the
general population. But why should books like Levi's be allowed? They
all have to pass the censorship, just as every other scrap of printed
matter in the Soviet Union does, down to bottle labels; it is unlikely
that any censor would take the risk of being very much more liberal
than his colleagues, and one may suspect that the Party committees
which mill over ideology have decided to allow the discussion of

---

* Most of these illustrations are taken from the invaluable quarterly digest,
Soviet and East European Abstracts Series.

some wider ideas, in restricted circles, because hard-faced though the chiefs may be, they are genuinely worried whether the old formulas can be used without modification, in a changing world: they want 'Marxism' adapted if needs must; they cannot afford to have it degenerate into a sort of prayer-wheel.

MORE MODEST GOALS FOR THE NATION

Since Stalin, and even more so since the removal of Khrushchev, the policy has been for more practical and realistic national goals. The methods used to enforce Stalin's policies were so inhuman that it is often forgotten how primitively utopian in conception those policies often were. The Soviet Union continues to be more doctrinaire than any of the European Communist countries except Albania, but Soviet plans today are neither utopian nor megalomaniac: they are so adapted to practical possibilities, or are so often merely drawn up *ad hoc*, that the spirit of the whole system has been described as 'creeping pragmatism'. It seems unlikely that there will be many more attempts to rush ahead in giant strides, as when Khrushchev brought 70 million virgin acres under cultivation in two years. He got magnificent harvests for a few years, but afterwards a large part of the new lands had to be abandoned for lack of rainfall, irrigation, or fertilizers. Again, it was admitted in 1971 that the 1966–70 Plan did not reach its targets for electric power, natural gas, or mineral fertilizers, probably because the construction of new plants fell behind. Planning is now supposed to be more flexible, with alternatives to allow for accidents or contingent failures.

All these relaxations make the ordinary man's life a great deal freer from restraint. But there are other, more positive developments since the Stalin era which are so much around him all the time, and which are changing his daily life so greatly, that they deserve to be listed in capitals: THE NEW HOUSING, THE INCREASE IN CONSUMER GOODS and THE AGRICULTURAL REFORMS outlined in the last chapter, which have at last brought the lives of the agricultural 30 per cent of the population up to a standard of living approaching more nearly that in the towns.

Soon after Stalin died, a majority in the Politburo must have decided that it was time the nation as consumers were given some consideration. This was the policy of Malenkov, it was the policy of Khrushchev, who deposed Malenkov, and it has been the policy of those who deposed Khrushchev. I shall never forget the expression on the faces of my friends in the late 1950s, when they said they were at last getting 'Something to have in our hands now, instead of working for some indefinite "posterity".' The consumer policy was begun because the nation was starved of everything but necessities, it has continued because the leadership now believes that rewards and incentives, on the whole, bring better results than punishments and crude discipline, and it has long since been developed to such a level, and so widely, that it would be impossible to reverse it. The Plan for 1971–5 is investing just about twice as much in light industrial production as did the Plan for 1966–70.

It is easy enough to denigrate and even to sneer—the Russians will do it for you—at the standards: the terrible monotony of the nine-storey blocks, the bad joins and crude finish of the huge prefabricated units they are built of, the ill-fitting doors, the lino that will not lie down, the local authorities who turn off the whole water supply for twenty-four hours without warning, the general impossibility of getting spare parts, the despairing struggles for overcrowded buses out to the new flats, and in the shops the rudeness of almost all the assistants, the piles of vulgar plastic goods, and the resignedly trudging women, padding from store to store in search of sugar, maybe, or flour, or beetroot, and finding nothing but dried fish and stacked bottles of Caucasian wine. In one large Siberian town no kettles were to be had for a whole year; in Moscow itself typing paper disappeared from the shops for several months, and as for the schoolbooks that everyone wants—in Moscow, in the small towns, in the villages—there never seem to be enough to go round. Russians would gasp with pleasure at a little English corner shop, with fifty kinds of sweets, wrapped bread, a stand of stationery, and a deep-freeze for the ice-cream and meat pies. They are faced by great formal counters of artificial marble (or maybe it is real marble); the few goods that are on display are placed behind glass ('for hygiene'); the prices are all handwritten, and the two-queue system operates—one for the cash desk to get your receipt, and a second one to get your purchase. Nowhere, not even in Moscow, are there enough shops, and people crowd in from fifty miles around to find a sweater, or a frying-pan, or soap. The villages can wait week after week for a lorry to slither through the mud of the forest and the sand and pools of the riverbeds to bring fresh stock for their wooden store; so they run short—and I quote from the Soviet press—of soap, and paraffin, and bread.

No wonder the queues in town are so slow, when women have to load themselves up in anticipation of further shortages—thirteen pounds of soap at one go perhaps, or maybe they waddle delicately home with a great string net containing exactly one gross (I know, because I asked) of eggs.

But although stories like these are true enough—I could recount dozens more of them, and one can find them all the time in the complaints columns of Soviet newspapers—one cannot rely simply on them for anything like a true picture of the situation. The basic thing about housing, for a start, is that in the last ten years 112 million people—almost half the population—have been rehoused. They were living in insanitary, bug-infested, frame-houses with earth closets in the yard, or in 'communal' flats—six families in six rooms along a corridor, sharing one tap, one kitchen, and one lavatory. Now every one of these families has a flat of its own—two rooms, large hall (for winter clothes and stores), large kitchen, separate bathroom, and separate lavatory. At last each family has a key to its own privacy. Some of the flats are clumsily designed, like Victorian tenements, but many of the newer ones are light and airy and would satisfy any Westerner. As recently as 1965, 60 per cent of people in Moscow were still living in communal flats; in 1971 the figure is only 25 per cent—among them my old friend the Professor of English Language at Moscow University, a *grande dame* among professors, who entertains you to exquisite *zakuski*, vodka and tea in a little alcove packed with books to the ceiling, and then retires behind the bookcase to wash up in a tin bowl. She could have a better flat but clings perversely to her communal one because it is quiet and conveniently placed and has a decent outlook; she is a widow, however, a 'family' of one, and any larger unit would find the space desperately restricting— yet this is the kind of flat which families of two generations and perhaps six persons were enduring until a year or so ago.

As for the shops, part of the trouble is that hardly anyone will consent to serve in them. The prosperous working class (and by comparison with Stalin's day they are prosperous) scorn the service trades, which are all undermanned: in desperation the authorities have begun to allow pensioners to work as shop assistants, or as cooks, or waiters, or hospital orderlies, while still drawing the whole of their old age pension in addition to their wages.

And as to the distribution and the local manufacture of some of the simplest goods—it may be faulty and inefficient because it is in the hands of too many people, or because none of them are allowed enough elbow room for their own initiative, or—more likely nowadays —because they are too lazy or too timid to use their own initiative. Maybe they can make more money for their enterprise (which means more bonuses), or for their surreptitious personal profit, by making or selling other things than those which are most required. Or perhaps they have already fulfilled the Plan for selling shirts, and they will now only sell you a shirt if you will also buy a sweater, because the sweaters are so poor that nobody wants them and so that bit of the Plan is in danger of being unfulfilled. So one sees maddening contrasts—a counter loaded with excellent cameras facing another with the most miserable selection of children's toys—but then perhaps the best toys are all the time under the counter, waiting for the customers who are on the assistant's list for personal tips 'when things come in'. And yet there are a few highspeed, continuously flourishing shops like the bakery cum confectionery cum café on Moscow's bright new German-style boulevard, the Kalinin Prospect, where the rolls, the buns, the twenty kinds of bread, and the cakes, the coffee and biscuits come tumbling out of hatches in apparently inexhaustible streams. Of course luxuries can be found in the foreign currency shops, or the 'closed' shops for a privileged few, but if all the goods on sale here were to be poured into the ordinary stores they would satisfy but a drop in the ocean of consumer desires.

If you are patient and persevering, as Russians are, you may get much of what you want in the end, though at present prices it will be expensive. If a woman is persistent she will eventually have a chance of some smart underclothes, or a pair of gaily-coloured plastic boots, or some exorbitantly priced length of lamé or chiffon which for a further exorbitant fee she can get made up in the store, in a state *atelier*, or—best of all—privately. The prices do not deter; many men and women are in a position to make something extra for themselves 'on the left', as they say. The foreign clothes and shoes which the Government has been importing for the last few years are snapped up instantly—a Marks and Spencer knitted two-piece for £30, or a pair of 'Career Girl' shoes for £20, are both well worth waiting for. There are a few places where the service is quick and efficient, and even polite—many station restaurants, in my experience, and the shop in Gorky Street which sells little else but varieties of tea. But this establishment has a Georgian manager, and I am told he has—or had—a conscience about the public, as well as ways—dark-eyes, sexy Georgian ways, perhaps—of persuading his staff to co-operate. As for the despairing tourists, sitting for an hour in the Astoria in Leningrad, before the snooty waitresses will deign to notice them, they might take comfort from Murray's old *Guide to Russia,* which recommended, in 1875: 'Dinner should if possible be ordered a day beforehand, although a few hours will suffice to secure most of the dishes named here.'

The real point for Russians is, first, that it is all so very much better than the bare and battered boards in most of the shops, and the watery fare in the very few restaurants, during the first forty years of Soviet rule. And the second point is that so many Russians nowadays have a little money to spend. This may seem strange in view of the high food and very high clothing prices: a Soviet worker on an average wage has to work twice as long as an average American worker to be able to pay for a kilo of white bread, for instance, and ten times as long for a kilo of pork, or a dozen eggs, or 100 grams of tea. (These figures are for 1969.) But the rent of a family's new flat, including heating and lighting, on average amounts to about only 7 per cent of income; the Soviet worker has no contributions to pay towards his pension, or the health service, or maternity and other benefits, and the education of his children is free at all stages.* They want value for money in other things, their taste has been developed rather than blunted, they will not buy the shoddy clothes or defective articles so often on sale if they can help it, and so the Soviet Union faces a minor inflation: too much money chasing too few goods with the savings bank deposits rising all the time, in anticipation of more and better goods and services in the future. There is some reason for looking forward hopefully: between the years 1960 and 1969, while the country's output of natural gas, for instance, increased four times, and of electric power

* The maximum old age pension which can be earned, at the age of 60 for men and 55 for women, is about the same as the average national wage. Medicines must be paid for, but all other health services are free. The industrial medicine service is one of the best in the world, there are more doctors and hospital beds in proportion to the population than in Britain or the USA, and the average expectation of life is 70 years, only a little lower than in the Scandinavian countries. Thirty per cent of the population are studying—in school, in colleges or institutes, in evening classes or correspondence classes. Nine million people spend their spare time in amateur dramatics or choirs or orchestras or groups for practising the fine arts. On the other side of the picture, student grants are poor, and a large proportion of schools, even in the village, are still working double or even treble shifts because of a lack of accommodation. The villages in general are badly served, particularly with doctors: official figures for the Belorussian Republic give districts where there are, for instance, only 68 doctors instead of the scheduled 150, 29 instead of 48, 64 instead of 112.

three and a half times, the factories producing consumer goods also made great advances, e.g.:

	1960	1969
Television sets	1,726,000	6,596,000
Refrigerators	529,000	3,701,000
Washing machines	895,000	5,153,000
Knitted outerwear	112 million articles	363 million articles
Full milk products	8,300,000 tons	18,200,000 tons

For 1975 the promise is 72 television sets, 72 washing machines, and 64 refrigerators for every hundred families, in this population of 240 millions.

Meanwhile, thousands of everyday commodities are scarce and the result, just as anywhere else, is a black market. There has of course always been a great black market network in Russia, and inflation has not made it any better. The notorious *blat*, the omnipresent small-time corruption and under-the-counter trading, is, one could say, the lubricant which enables an over-planned system with a basis of scarcity to work. Every now and then someone is brought to book, and so the public learns, for instance, of the elaborate conspiracy planned from Osh, in Kirghizia, which began with the misappropriation of 95 crates of lump sugar so that they could be sold privately; it was declared, with the connivance of the inspectors of the Government insurance organization, who no doubt got their share, that all this sugar had been washed away in an Asiatic downpour. In practice, many factory directors would be unable to reach their targets in time if they did not make use of the strictly unofficial and barely legal agents, the *tolkachi*. These are the operators who make a good living by finding out what surplus material there may be to spare from one enterprise which probably overestimated for the Plan in order to be on the safe side, and then arrange for its sale to another enterprise which has been let down by one of its suppliers. (Everybody's materials are part of someone else's production plan, and the occasions for breakdown in the chain of supply can be only too many!)

The Government could easily soak up most of the surplus purchasing power by increasing the output of cars. It matters not that a car costs the full year's salary of a well-paid job, or that most of the country's roads are simply dirt roads. (Only 5 per cent of the country's freight is carried by road, less than is transported by pipeline.) Nothing, after a flat, seems to be more ardently desired than a car, and yet no more than 300,000 were turned out in 1970, which is only about twice as much as ten years earlier. The authorities promise 600,000 cars a year in the current Five-Year Plan, but production at the great new works equipped by Fiat or Renault is strangely slow.

The problem is crucial. It is not one of production but of policy. The Party cannot bring itself, apparently, to launch several million citizens (with the expectation of millions more to come) into the freedom of the car, avoiding registration formalities as they travel, putting up in private houses (as they already do in summer by the overcrowded Black Sea), and escaping who knows what responsibilities. Suppose they were all to drive up to the frontier—with Finland, with Norway, with Persia, Afghanistan, or China? Suppose they were to get together in groups before anyone could keep an eye on them?

The fact is that, in spite of all the post-Stalin relaxations, there is no change in the basic authoritarian principle and the basic authoritarian system. *The individual is not trusted.* This is not just the comment of a Western liberal: it is exactly what many Russians say: 'We are not trusted to decide for ourselves—we are often not trusted even with enough information about the significance of the work we do.' The authorities are not only reluctant to entrust people with cars; they make it impossible for them to acquire duplicating apparatus of any kind, and they seem reluctant even to trust them with enough paper, the production of which climbs very slowly year by year and stays obstinately low—about 60 lbs. per head against about 250 lbs. in the United Kingdom and 500 lbs. in the USA. The underground *Chronicle of Events*, which seems to circulate widely, is thought to be produced with the help of scientists, some of whom have duplicating machines and paper at their disposal for institutional purposes. It is for similar reasons, one imagines, that there are in most places no telephone directories of private subscribers, and only about three million such subscribers in all.

A few of the young have been known to write letters to the press (which of course are never published) asking for 'proper elections, with a choice of candidates', and even 'proper political parties, as in other countries'. These protesters are very much a minority and one should not exaggerate their significance, but outside the one-sixth of the nation who belong to the Party (and even probably among some of its members), it would be hard, I think, to find a great number who are prepared to accept the authority of the Party in all its forms.

They may approve of a great deal of Party *policy* for the country, but that is another matter.

The Communist Party of the Soviet Union is still the party which Lenin founded, the party of a hand-picked minority directed from the top. It is no longer, of course, a party in the sense in which non-Communist countries use the word. Its nature might be better grasped if it went by some such name as the Spanish Fascist Party, the Falange, i.e. 'the Phalanx'. The CPSU is meant to be a directional and organizational élite. It is not mentioned in the Soviet Constitution as any part of the machinery of government. Article 3 states: 'In the USSR all power belongs to the working people of town and country as represented by the Soviets of Working People's Deputies.' The Party only appears in Article 126, which guarantees the right of citizens to unite in trade unions, co-operative associations, etc., and adds: 'the most active and politically most conscious citizens in the ranks of the working class and other sections of the working people unite in the Communist Party of the Soviet Union, which is the vanguard of the working people in their struggle to strengthen and develop the socialist system and is the leading core of all organizations of the working people, both public and state.'

There is a just discernible technical sense in which Article 3 might be considered true: laws in the Soviet Union are not laws until they have been approved by the Supreme Soviet. But the deputies to the Supreme Soviet are appointed through single-candidate, uncontested 'elections', their nomination is vetted by the Party, and the approval of the Supreme Soviet for a proposed law, like the Royal signature to a British Act of Parliament, is never refused.

Every Soviet citizen knows that power resides mainly and ultimately with the Party; for instance, complaints made to an area Party Secretary are a more serious matter and likely to be more effectively dealt with than complaints to the regional Soviet, or to the manager of any enterprise within the area. The authority of the Party is meant to be kept clearly separate from the state organizations as laid down in the Constitution. The Party does not itself produce anything (except political literature and some newspapers); it does not engage in industry or agriculture or transport or social welfare or education (except political education); it does not administer the law, although it has been responsible for many perversions of it. The Party does not even engage directly in administration or government. And yet the Party makes itself responsible for the condition of the economy, for directing the

Soviets, for the selection of the country's key personnel, for the press, radio and television, and for the whole of what may be called the country's ideology, through committees entrusted with the supervision of the arts, literature, religion, etc. It is intended to be, to use an official phrase, 'the leading and guiding force of Soviet society'.

The Party exercises its control at the lowest level through the 'primary organizations', or as we should say, the local branches, of which there are 340,000. Most of these are not based on geographical areas but upon the places where people work—factories, offices, farms, army units, naval units and so on. People can be got at more directly there than in their homes, and it is in their work unit that members can exert the influence which the Party requires. It is not so often that Soviet citizens apply to join the Party: more commonly they become members by invitation, because the Party does not want mere sympathizers, but born organizing secretaries, encouragers and leaders, and it goes to a good deal of trouble to seek out likely candidates. The kind of person wanted is the sort who in any Western society is probably not to be found in any higher proportion than the 5 per cent or 6 per cent which the Communist Party membership bears to the total population of the USSR. The rank-and-file member does not get any privileges out of his membership: on the contrary, he is obliged to give up most of his spare time to meetings and exhortations; he has to check up on others, to educate himself in Party policies and theory, and so forth; he has to pay out 3 per cent of his income in Party dues, he is supposed to lead a strictly upright life in the eye of the world, he has to abandon any religious observances to which he may have been committed, and he may be sent away for long periods on Party assignments—where indeed he gets some priority in hotel bookings, rail tickets, and so on. If he is young he may start with some starry-eyed notions—as, it is said, the boys from the villages sometimes do: but the authoritarianism and the strictness and repetitiveness of the duties are soon likely to give him a bureaucratic outlook if he becomes a secretary. Among middle-aged and older people some of the country's best, including of course members of the intelligentsia, are to be found as rank-and-file members, along with the careerists; the Party likes to recruit men and women who already have the respect of their fellows, but these are by no means necessarily the ones who get chosen as Party officials—nor do all of them want such promotion.

Every 'primary organization' has a secretary and a deputy secretary, though only if it has more than 150 members can one of these be paid. But at the next higher level, in the district organization, all secretaries are paid, and similarly in the larger regions comprising many districts, and in the Republican organizations above them, and eventually in the central organizations of the Party in Moscow. These are the men (along with a few women) who form the Party 'apparatus', the *apparatchiks*, who are well paid, enjoy many privileges and are usually hated or despised by the public. They number 200,000, perhaps 300,000, out of 14·5 million members, and it is they who are the backbone—usually a very stiff and unyielding backbone—of the country's organization. (Trotsky warned the Party at the beginning against such officials and their tendency to stasis.) The 135 regional secretaries have been described as having 'as much authority as the governor of a province in Tsarist times', and these secretaries, along with some other key people, form the Central Committee of the Party which, in theory, elects the Politburo from among its members. Each grade of the Party organization, in theory, elects the officials who constitute the next higher grade, but in practice the lower grade is not trusted; when there is a vacancy the available candidates are so carefully vetted by the next higher grade that the whole process might be called one of co-option rather than election. And this applies to the Politburo too: it is a self-perpetuating organization whose membership changes only very slowly as members become superannuated or die off, though occasionally—to the general excitement—there may be a change for other reasons. The concentration of power in their hands represents a burden which few would wish to carry: 'The buck stops with the Politburo.' They are well supplied with cars, *dachas*, and the usual privileges of high office, but they have little time to enjoy them: they have to pursue, in concert, what they conceive to be the nation's interests.

The principal job of Party members and secretaries is to see that industry and agriculture work properly and reach their monthly, quarterly and annual targets. Promotion in the 'apparatus' goes to those who can get norms fulfilled without creating any problems for the men above them and without stirring up any awkward antagonisms among the workers. The Party has very few sanctions at its disposal nowadays in dealing with workers who know they will get bonuses if they exceed the target by only a little, and have their own ingenious and pretty impenetrable ways of sharing out the small

privileges and the easier or more remunerative jobs among themselves, or of practising ca'canny if they are being pressed unnecessarily. The Party man may sometimes be able to offer such induce-
ments as using his influence, perhaps, in getting priority in a new
block of flats for the workers whom he is trying to encourage, but
to a large extent he has to use appeals to personal or group responsibility, or he has to organize bouts of 'socialist competition' between
one unit, or one enterprise, and another. A local secretary may be
able, through his Party contacts, to get rid of a bottleneck which
is holding up supplies in his own factory, or he can use his power to
decide a difficult case of conflicting priorities: it happens only too
often, in this country of shortages and over-elaborate planning, that
two bodies, say a local Soviet and a factory, may find themselves
competing for transport of materials which are needed with equal
urgency for their two respective parts of the Plan. The *apparatchik*,
if he is high enough in rank, is the man who can decide who is to have
priority in such a case.

Yet though the *apparatchiks* can sometimes cut Gordian knots,
they are much more celebrated for using their position to interpose
where they need not, for creating paperwork, and for generally
choking up the workings of the nation. The *apparatchiks* of state planning and of the Party have succeeded, for instance, in seriously slow-
ing down and limiting the usefulness of the economic reform which
was initiated by Kosygin a few years ago: there was to be much more
direct contact between producers and consumers, and the success
of factories was to be measured not by the gross value of their output without regard to 'assortment', as in the past, but by the value
of actual sales, and by the profits made. It would take too long to
describe how these apparently simple changes have been snarled
up in subsidiary regulations created by the bureaucracy, but the case
illustrates what stands in the way of any reform which tries to release
the initiative of the men actually engaged in the work. Giving them
their head would automatically make much of the bureaucracy redun-
dant. And any attempt by the practical men in the Politburo to restrict
the *apparatchiks* and the bureaucracy would of course have to be
implemented by—the *apparatchiks* and the bureaucracy.

Besides looking after production, the Party has three other main
tasks: (1) the selection of personnel by the *nomenklatura* system; (2)
propaganda to the mass of the nation, with the help of local speakers
called 'agitators', who number over a million; (3) keeping an implacable

watch against the emergence of any kind of organization whatever
which is not under Party control.

The Party keeps a nationwide list of positions—the *nomenklatura*
—which it will only allow to be held by trusted Party members:
for example judges, managers of industrial enterprises, collective
farm managers, editors, headmasters, and even history teachers
(though not other assistant teachers). Thus in most professions anyone who hopes to rise is almost obliged to become a Party member, so that he can get his name on to the list of suitable candidates
for promotion.

Every important Party branch has an 'agitprop' secretary as one
of its three full-time officers. He organizes meetings (usually at places
of work), arranges speakers for the open air, and feeds the local press
(which also comes under rigid censorship, performed by another
organ, the *Glavlit*). 'Agitators' in public places are very often ignored,
as even the foreigner may see, and at propaganda meetings questions
do get asked, and sometimes very awkward ones, but the questioners
do not seem to suffer for this, though it could be dangerous to give
the impression of being an organized faction. Party members themselves may debate matters of policy, but never after 'the Party' (i.e.
the Politburo) has come to a decision about them; thereafter they can
only 'discuss' them, which means expanding on the theme of the
new decision, what it means, and how it is to be carried out. In fact
most Party decisions are 'discussed' to this extent in the branches:
this is what is called, using the term invented by Lenin, 'democratic
centralism'.

As to other organizations, no one can start a club or society except
as part of the existing very large network of societies and clubs, which
are often run by a secretary who is a Party member, or at least under
the eye of some Party member. Forty million Soviet citizens take
part in organized sports as members of sports clubs: these are usually
organized by the trade unions, which in the Soviet Union are welfare organizations of considerable value. With these clubs, and others
for amateur dramatics, and so forth, every innocent leisure occupation
is catered for by organizations known to and ultimately controlled
by the Party; what is more, these organizations can provide the funds
for every leisure purpose, from chess to cheap summer holidays.
But let anyone try to start an independent, organized club or circle
and he will, unless the members are extremely discreet, soon find it
investigated by the KGB. It is remarkable that the 'Committee to

search for constructive ways of securing Human Rights', founded by Academician Sakharov and some of his colleagues, has apparently been allowed to continue its existence for at least a year at the time of writing. Its terms of reference, however, are carefully defined to make it an organization interested in collaborating with 'the organs of State power', and its sponsors are among the State's most valued servants. The students who protested against the invasion of Czechoslovakia were none such privileged persons: one hundred of them were sent down, immediately after their demonstration, from one Siberian university alone. (Being sent down meant that they were barred for ever from higher education anywhere in the Soviet Union.) As to the courageous few who protest in Red Square or other public places, calling for fairer political trials and for the observance of the rights which are guaranteed—on paper—in the Soviet Constitution, the whole world knows of the prison and labour camp sentences, the enforced confinement in mental hospitals, the exile, humiliations and persecutions which are suffered by such as General Grigorenko, Pavel Litvinov, Larissa Daniel, Bukovsky, Galanskov, Yakir, and the rest.

Comparatively few Party members are concerned with the ideological control of literature and the arts, of which we rightly but disproportionately hear so much in the Western press: it is the responsibility of one of the Party's central departments. The oversight and circumscribing of religious activities is carried out by the State Council for the Affairs of Religious Cults, which also has local representatives. There is an official Society of Atheists, whose members harass believers with propaganda or worse; some members of the Komsomol gather to jeer at religious services; places of worship are continually being closed down on various pretexts; and the general treatment of religion during the present period has become less liberal, in contrast to the attitude in so many other spheres.

One is bound to admit that the Communist type of organization is far more effective as a system of government than any Tsarist government ever was. If Peter the Great came to life again it would surely have his admiration; Stalin, he would judge, had solved the problem of how an autocrat was to govern. It must also be admitted that it is a system far more in touch with the people—both in the way it administers them and the way it caters for their needs. The information which it collects about popular opinion has been greatly improved during the last fifteen years or so: under pressure from scientists the leadership has permitted a great deal of sociological research, including opinion polls—something which would have been unthinkable in earlier days, when the state of mind of the workers was supposed to be definable in a few general concepts taken from the Marxist catechism. The leadership is naturally too nervous to allow some kinds of question to be asked, but there have been polls which revealed, for instance, that very few people read the boring front-page articles in *Izvestia*, that 18 per cent out of a sample of 26,000 readers thought the paper not altogether fair in its handling of international news, that only 40 per cent of manual workers in a group questioned found their work satisfying, that only 34 per cent in another group, all under thirty years of age, were satisfied with their wages, that nearly half of a sample of 1,000 senior schoolchildren did not know what to do with their spare time, and that 85 per cent of a sample of male university students admitted to having premarital sex relations.

During the same period the Party has also somewhat opened up the Soviet Union, allowing foreign ideas and information to permeate increasingly. This may seem a strange statement in view of the extraordinary difficulties which confront Soviet citizens who wish to visit Western countries or even to meet foreigners.* But thanks to sputniks and atomic missiles, and to the policy of peaceful coexistence initiated by Khrushchev, the Soviet Government nowadays feels a good deal more secure than it used to, and this feeling has filtered through to the people. In 1963, when there was a disastrously bad harvest, the Government had to spend three hundred million pounds of hard-earned foreign currency in buying North American wheat; they made no secret of the country's plight, whereas in 1947 news of an equally bad harvest was kept as close as possible, no foreign help was sought, and it was only later that the world learned that people had starved to death in the Ukraine. Because the leadership feels more secure, it has abandoned the pretence that material standards in the workers' state are higher than those in Western countries: it admits the opposite in many particulars, and by importing so many

---

* The last time I visited the Actors' Club in Moscow my host acknowledged the smile of a nervous elderly man as we went in. As soon as we were out of earshot he said: 'That's the man I told you of. We were both on the trip to Paris, and he was the one I found going through my suitcase.' Not, one need hardly add, that the elderly man was a thief: he had been assigned the duty of going through his room-mate's belongings to see whether he had acquired any political contraband—letters, perhaps, for someone in the USSR—and weak old survivor of the Stalin period that he was, he thought it safest to carry out the search instead of pretending, as my friend would have done in his place.

foreign clothes and shoes it has given the Soviet people a preference which will prove almost impossible to reverse: foreign goods will probably retain at least a snob value even if Soviet manufactures eventually catch up with them in quality. It is no longer alleged, as in Khrushchev's time, that the Soviet Union will catch up with and surpass the United States in 1980, or 1984, or at any other date.

The foreign language libraries have been allowed to acquire a huge collection of literature, some of it quite out of keeping with the narrow official outlook; and in the specialist libraries dealing, for example, with economics, we are told that there are 'dozens of Western magazines'—from some of which readers might discover that $2\frac{1}{2}$ per cent of the American population achieve a better agricultural yield per acre than the 22 per cent of the Soviet population who cultivate the collective and State farms. Soviet citizens go abroad in thousands, for short visits, where formerly they never went at all, and they bring back foreign books and foreign articles whose effect has spread far; foreign radio services are only sporadically jammed (since jamming is expensive), and even during the invasion of Czechoslovakia the BBC Russian Service could be heard as near as twenty-three miles outside Moscow, while the BBC General Overseas Service can be heard over a great part of the Soviet Union and is listened to avidly by many who understand English. The volume of foreign influences is slight in comparison with the indoctrination received in school, and the expounding of Party lines through the press and radio, but it has the irresistible charms of novelty and independence against the monotony of what issues from the Party; most Russians are extremely curious about the outside world.

However, all this opening up of communications indicates, in my opinion, not only the adaptability but also the great strength of the Party system. The leaders are quite wise enough to know that the country needs a flow of information from abroad, and not merely technical information: more than one book has been published about Britain which praises British good manners and mutual forbearance, and enviously admires the prevalence of trust which permits cheques and other forms of credit to be used. The leadership has also wanted a certain loosening of international contacts, for both internal and external reasons, so that the USSR can appear to be a little more like a member of the comity of nations. In spite of their quasi-religious attachment to the idea of a Marxist destiny, the leaders, like other Russians, are well aware of Russia's late appearance on the world scene, and they are probably a little nervous, as are a great many of their citizens, that they may not yet be rated as full members of the club, so to speak. But none of this foreshadows any general or indefinite loosening up, and it certainly does not point towards what the Western world would call democratization. It has been followed, in fact, by a sharp reaffirmation of Party primacy in all fundamental matters of doctrine and organization, as well as the well-known clamping down on criticism in works of literature or in the theatre.

The system has, however, produced such results, though creakingly and imperfectly, for the ordinary man and woman, that it is difficult to see, at least in the short term, any basic change in its nature. It will continue to suffer from three major defects: the overloading of the vertical channels of communication towards the top of the hierarchy; the overcentralized system of selecting personnel, which favours mediocre, conformist, directing types—masterly conservatives rather than innovators; and thirdly the myth that whatever about-turn of policy may take place, the Party has been right all the time and only individuals (including Stalin) have been wrong. (There is even a *Journal of Questions of Party History* to make sure that the Party face is always saved, whatever changes of interpretation there may be.) This myth would have to go if the Party leaders were to come thoroughly clean about the Terror: they would have to admit either that the whole Party had been mistaken, or that a faction had perverted the Party, and therefore some other faction was in the right. (It is not possible to lay all the blame at Stalin's door, as some of the best men outside Party circles have already pointed out.) At present it seems that the leadership will cling to the principle of infallibility as tenaciously as the *apparatchiks* cling to their jobs, which under democratic representation they would probably lose.

The Party prefers on the whole to recruit workers and technical specialists rather than intellectuals: it can offer a career to those who enjoy power, and it gives quite as good a chance as most Western countries to the boy from a modest home, without much education, in this respect. The Party will probably listen more and more to the intelligentsia as specialists, so long as they do not try to organize themselves into a faction nor meddle with government: but it is of prime significance that candidates from families of the intelligentsia are not admitted to the Higher Party Schools, whose three-year courses train men for key jobs in the system. The machine will continue to favour the production of *apparatchiks*, but it is always possible that some rogue elephant, some new Khrushchev who has been through all the Party mill, may arise: on the other hand it is difficult to believe that any democratically-inclined reformer could submit himself to the twenty years or so of toiling up the Party ladder in order eventually to have the chance of changing things from the top.

The general result of all this over-organization and supervision is that the country has completely run out of political steam—apart from the new impulse which arises from the brave but totally inadmissible protesters. But it has been clear for some time that the nation's main tasks are the improvement of administration, management, standards of work, standards of quality and of communication. No very stirring matter for slogans, compared with 1917, but they are what everyday Soviet lives need in the 1970s.

10. Society and the Individual—and the Future

I wanted a weekend out of Moscow. I was tired of the theatres—even the two hundred and ten different spectacles—theatre, opera and ballet—advertised in the poster that goes up every ten days. The other posters offered concerts which would have been over-subscribed long ago, films which I had seen, swimming lessons, a new turn by Himalayan bears at the Circus, a children's circle at the Museum of Eastern Art, adult courses in Renaissance and Spanish Art, and auditions for the National Theatre of Recitation (an art which Russians practise superbly). But I wanted to get out, and after the usual formalities which foreigners have to pass through, I arranged a weekend visit to where the better-off Muscovites often go—to Yaroslavl and Rostov, which are two of the oldest and most picturesque towns in Russia.

You start from the old station which is also the terminus of the Trans-Siberian and the lines to Kazakhstan. On your way to the platforms you pass through a series of great waiting-halls, their floors all but covered with passively squatting people in coarse clothes, caps and scarves, a few of them in eastern robes, and all of them guarding home-made bundles of every odd shape and size, some disguised in newspapers, some in great nets, some with poles sticking out of them, some with kettles slung on the corded bedding. It was not a waiting-room, it was a khan; somewhere among the waist-high throng I would not have been surprised to see a camel. To an English eye the crowd were all 'peasants'. Some of them had arrived laden with watermelons from Asia; now they had sold them and were going home with spoil from the Moscow shops; some of them had bought watermelons and were taking them back to Siberia, and a lot of them were workers from the Siberian cities, returning east after an expedition to furnish their homes. But all were passively squatting.

Then I came out on to a clean and well-ordered platform and the Yaroslavl train, with every seat numbered, and at every carriage a woman in a long dark uniform coat checking the tickets. Railway workers are rather alike all the world over: their responsibilities give some meaning for once to the phrase 'the dignity of labour', and they show it in their bearing. Soviet trains leave on time and nearly always arrive on time; this is one section at least, I thought, where Soviet administration seems to work perfectly; trains leaving the Moscow terminal to about forty destinations, and more trains starting from Yaroslavl, going regularly west to Rybinsk, and north to Vologda and Archangel, and east to Kineshma and Gorky and south-east to Ivanovo, and slow trains to old towns like Kostroma and Galich— and all this is but one small block of the huge Soviet network of railways.

A lot of the passengers were young and lively, some carrying easels for a painting weekend among the churches by the lake at Rostov. Across the aisle I saw a girl reading a French grammar; we made some French conversation, and as she belonged to Yaroslavl I decided to stick by her and her broad-shouldered young man when we arrived. We were discharged, as I expected, into the usual uncontrolled, unbearable Russian scrum for tramcars; there were no taxis, and the hotel was a mile and a half away. An English football crowd would hardly stomach this free-for-all, but somehow I was jammed into a tram at last, I dragged the kopecks out of my pocket and paid my fare and I got put down at the right stop. The hotel, for once, was not a brash new affair, and it bore the sign of a bear carrying an axe, the old civic arms which Yaroslavl, along with a few other old towns, is still allowed to use. (The train had been honoured with a bear too.) The stony-faced woman at the desk even broke into a smile when she had checked my reservation, but I wanted supper, and she said that was the affair of the restaurant, down the corridor. The glass doors were barred by a board thrust through the handles on the other side, and a straw-haired youth in a white coat, looking like a house serf in a play, waved his arms at me: 'We're closed! We're closed!' It was eleven p.m., when even Russian restaurants may be closed, and it would not be the first time I had gone to bed supperless in Russia. But suddenly the youth pulled out the board and said: 'What do you want? Supper? *Pozhaluista!* Come in!' He was only there to keep out the drunks, and so I got a good chicken supper, though the waitresses were almost dropping on their feet.

Next morning was Sunday, and people from the town came into the hotel buffet to linger blissfully over a late breakfast of things like cold mutton and cocoa. I saw the magnificent old walls and churches of the Yaroslavl Kremlin, the monastery where the manuscript of *The Lay of Prince Igor* was found, the eighteenth-century theatre, the fresco of a harvest scene reminiscent of Dufy. I looked at the market and marvelled at the high prices being asked by the peasants, and then I took a trolleybus for another mile and a half out from the centre, to the country bus station—a place with a huge booking-hall and the usual rows going on about luggage: should the old man be allowed on the bus with such a large picture frame? We all had to get not only tickets but reservations: I could go to Rostov on the two o'clock bus if I would accept a standing ticket. The old Russian smells, now almost vanished from Moscow, were rising ripely among these peasants, and I had no great hopes of the 'restaurant' for lunch. It was a choice of macaroni or soup, with tea, and there were no knives. A tall middle-aged man excused himself with a delightful Irish sort of charm so that he could sit next to his ten-year-old son; and then instead of making the boy use a spoon, he let him get his head down to the edge of the table and slurp his macaroni off the plate like an animal. I got to Rostov, standing, and there was a highly-cultivated lecturer for the tour of the churches in the rather decaying old Kremlin by the lake, and more peasants listlessly trailing in the sandy streets, and a café of modern design with a lot of glass, which sold only coffee and fruit cake, and a bookshop with plenty of stock, including Plato's Dialogues, just as in Moscow.

Back in Yaroslavl I thought I deserved a good dinner with some Armenian brandy, but the waitress, in a tone like a policeman, said *Niet*. Vodka also *niet*. 'A bottle of this Bulgarian wine then?'—'A *whole* bottle to yourself?' she objected sharply. Sunday night is apt to be a rough time in Russian restaurants, and she had clearly been recruited into the anti-alcoholic campaign, so we compromised by my offering to share the bottle with two medical students at my table. Not that they were gay company; by English standards they were something much more conventional than medical students, and I retired to the fringed lampshades and firmly stuffed armchairs of my room. Next morning I almost missed the train because I had forgotten that one must have a seat reservation. I felt sure there must be some spare seats, but the conductresses were quite unbiddable: I must dash up three flights of stairs in a building apart from the station, where I look despairingly at the queue, but there is another uniformed woman looking after such latecomers as me, and after all, three minutes later I am on board in a reserved seat. Then when I get to Moscow it has turned wet and cold and I am shivering, and several trains seem to have arrived from Siberia together; if I plunge down into the Metro

I shall have twelve minutes' walk at the other end, but can I bear to join this immense, this seventy-yard queue for taxis? I risk it: there is a huge policeman in a great cape regulating the queue, and the taxis come. They come fast, they come four abreast, and in about six minutes the policeman beckons me with his truncheon and I am on my way home.

Going around like this, one might get the impression that Russian society is hardly even a mixture of cultures, but something pretty well atomized; there can be so much of every-man-for-himself when officialdom is not working—so much crudity, and a coarseness which is not even a sort of low-grade 'culture' like barrackroom coarseness, but just one-man pushing coarseness. Or even one-woman pushing ... I was told of a queue in Riga, despairingly waiting for the best part of an hour, when an Uzbek woman arrives with a baby and puts herself right in front. The man who had been at the head of the queue protests: the Uzbek woman says nothing, turns round, takes her breast out of the baby's mouth, and sprays him from head to foot.

But get people away from the queues and the worst of the crowds and they are as different as can be, different from their crowd behaviour and different from each other—far more different than they used to seem thirty years ago.

The old, for a start—in spite of all that they have been through, how rarely are old people unpleasant in Russia! Possibly this is a survival of older manners—and I mean the manners of all classes, for old peasants can be beautifully, humanely courteous—but it is due much more, I think, to the fact that the old have a respected place both in society and in the family. They are listened to as individuals and often deferred to. And the young or middle-aged of either sex automatically give up their seats in trams and buses to anyone who looks more than about sixty. So the old make something of a stabilizing element in society, in a modest way, quite apart from what is imposed by authority.

Then there are young hooligans, some of whom in the outer suburbs carry knives; there are the snide young intellectuals flaunting English-type blazers, some young men with challenging smiles (which is new), gangs of girls full of genuine girlish feelings, and there are the really womanly women—women like the doctor Vera in Solzhenitsyn's *Cancer Ward* (though they may have such a solemn exterior that you could misjudge them entirely until they talk). There are, too, the nasty, narrow-eyed little men who may be pickpockets or black marketeers, and the cheerful, matey working men, idealistic young teachers, smug, well-fed bureaucrats whom nobody likes when they see them in the Metro, and the carnivorously-smiling types who deal in spare parts, or fix small repairs, or arrange to get your father buried or his grave surrounded by a low railing.

Perhaps Soviet Russia is simply becoming petty bourgeois, in a party official, partly black-market way? There are foreigners who, returning to the country after twenty years' absence, say this is how it strikes them now, and 'petty bourgeois' does express a good deal of the surface appearance. But I do not think it at all a good description for the state of Soviet society, because only a tiny proportion of the population, other than the peasants, are legitimately in business for themselves, and although a huge proportion are thought to be involved in making a little something on the side, it is usually only a very little something. And there is no one, except possibly one or two of the top criminal operators, who could possibly be classed as 'grands bourgeois'—and they, for obvious reasons, not for long.

It is true that most people over thirty tend to be self-indulgently overweight, though that might be because they find little to spend their money on other than food and drink. And it is true that some people's flats are becoming full of very poor knick-knacks, and some childless families are putting all their energies into accumulating possessions: *Krokodil* caricatured one couple who sat among their gaudy vases, bears' heads and storks made of horn, contentedly contemplating, parked on their garish carpet, their most treasured possession—their minicar. And in popular music, Palm Court tunes like *Moscow Nights* or pop taken down from the BBC have quite superseded manly and meaningful songs like *The Partisans*, or *Polyushka, Polye*, which people used to sing in the early days. But such signs as these are not, I think, the most deeply significant. One could hardly expect anything other than a rush for possessions, after fifty years of doing without, and having to entertain yourselves in a bare home, on vodka* and the slap of dominoes.

It is not just possessions, but jobs, for women as well as for men, which have been changing the Russian people—jobs which offer a thousand modes of individual life, technical, managerial, scientific,

---

* From the official figures of consumption, tens of millions of Soviet men must still be downing at least two or three pints of vodka a week, although it is much more expensive for Russians than whisky is for us. Dominoes are still one of the commonest recreations.

cultural, or in social service, which were not open to more than a tiny proportion of Russians before the Revolution. In the early days of the Plans there might well have been more convenience and more interest to be found in one's place of work than in one's home. And now, for the last twenty years there have begun to be homes fit to return to, and the class which Soviet Russians call the intelligentsia, meaning all white-collar workers and everyone with some specialized training, amounts to 30 per cent of the working population.

And the new flats, and the fact of so many mothers being out at work, and the new goods which parents now want to spend their money on, have brought a dramatic result—a drastic fall in the birth-rate. In the cities the average family now has one child or none, hardly ever more than two, and the city birthrate is insufficient for the population to reproduce itself. Between 1959 and 1970 the total population grew by only 16 per cent, and the figure would have been much lower if the Moslem Republics, who have different ideas, had not produced a growth of up to 50 per cent. The Government is uneasy about these figures, but there is very little it can do.

The basic bringing up of children is also changing. For some time past, it seems to me, there have been at least five different conventions in bringing up Soviet children: (1) in many of the villages, and in some of the 'workers' settlements', which are as isolated as villages, the children still run about together all the time and regard all the adults as their uncles and aunts, in the old-fashioned way which is probably still quite as strong an influence there as the rather inadequate schooling. (2) In some of the new flats, encouraged by their cosy isolation, there are over-anxious or over-indulgent mothers who keep their child at home as much as possible and lavish too much attention on it; they seem to be creating a number of delinquent adolescents. Among the privileged, such families often abuse their position to indulge their children at the expense of others, pulling strings for them outside the home. (3) In other new flats many families, especially among the intelligentsia (in the Russian sense of the word), are concentrating attention upon their children in a more responsible, didactic manner, some of them according to the strict but warm principles which they call 'Communist', others in a manner rather more reminiscent of the 'Western' way in which the pre-Revolutionary intelligentsia used to bring up their children. (4) A great number of families, one must assume from the discussions in the educational press, are uncertain how to bring up their children, preserving some of the old

14

communal feeling in which they were themselves brought up, thankful if they still have a granny at home, and leaning a lot on the infant teachers for advice. (5) About 10 per cent of children under two, and 20 per cent of children between three and six years, attend public nurseries all day, where they are trained in collective life and taught to play together, 'work together, help each other, and be responsible for disciplining each other'. They are grouped into large play-pens, about half a dozen in each, and the pens are raised on legs so that the adult helpers can talk to the children and deal with them on a face-to-face level. It is emphasized that as they grow older the children should be trained not only in self-discipline but in respect for their elders. For example, 'The children should know that in greeting someone they should not extend their hands: this may only be done when the adult himself offers his hand.' The teacher instructs the children to listen attentively to what an adult is saying; when answering him, to look him in the face; to carry out quickly and willingly requests or demands, to yield the right of way to an adult, and to stoop and pick things up for adults.*

These nurseries are expensive because of the high staff ratio, and one may wonder if they will ever be offered to the majority of pre-school Soviet children (i.e. the under-sevens). In Moscow, which is usually ahead of the rest of the country, only half the applicants can be accepted. It would be rash to conclude that the whole child population is eventually to be conditioned by this sort of system, and one ought to stress that it is nothing like as severe as it sounds, because severe in the handling of children is what all Russians are not. They are *serious*, in a way which we in England, at least, are not used to in dealing with children—but that is nothing new. Mme. Jarintsov, whom I quoted on political life under the last Tsar, wrote with delight about the seriousness of the 'real Russian peasant boy', so responsible, so capable with an axe, so manly. Western diplomats who have sent their young children to a Soviet school have found that though they enjoyed school and enjoyed the company of Russian children, they became affected by the atmosphere after a time: they became 'more reserved' than Western children are normally expected to be. But perhaps they were also learning to be more independent?

What nearly all Russian children seem to have from their upbring-

* Information and figures from *Soviet Preschool Education*, Vol. 1 (translated from the Russian), with an introduction by Urie Bronfenbrenner (Holt, Rinehart & Winston, 1969).

ing is a great but not usually aggressive self-confidence, which is exactly what one sees, of course, in most adult Russians; they may lack the superficial appearance of confidence, the exterior which passes conventionally for self-confidence among certain nations, but the depth is nearly always there. This is what has carried them through the worst days, and this is what accounts for the fact that among Russian women, however resigned and grey they may be, one almost never sees that chain-smoking, child-dragging, tensed-up-to-breaking-point exasperation which is so familiar among overloaded British housewives. Above the level of this confidence, however, there are great differences in people's social orientation, and these differences seem to me to be increasing. The majority of the population is under social pressures of one sort and another—not always very consciously felt—to break out of the centuries-old Russian communality, the *sobornost* or congregationality, into the individualism, the individualities, and the individualizing of the modern world. People are affected by individual responsibilities at work, by life in individual flats, by ideals of individual distinction and emulation in all kinds of sport, and ideals of individual culture and behaviour. In fact Russian society, like that of most countries today, is very much in a state of transition. The effects, I thought, were succinctly put by an elderly professor who was telling me about his Moscow students. They are students in Moscow but they come from all over the Soviet Union, and they fall, he said, into three types: the 'communal', who are only happy in a group and will probably go along with any group—which in effect means the groups arranged by authority; the newer, careerist, individualist types, who are after the best jobs and the best money; and finally, the newest type of all, who opt out as far as possible, and look for an easy job rather than a well-paid one: 'The Soviet equivalent of the hippy,' said the professor.

The first type belong to the old Russian tradition, still buried in *sobornost*. And certainly *sobornost* could be delightful. Foreigners were often captivated—I was and still am—at being so easily received into the communally-surrounding warmth and the direct person-to-person relations of a group of Russians. It is an upbringing in *sobornost* which makes so many a Russian look for a table where someone else is sitting when he enters a restaurant; he does not want to be by himself. It is due to *sobornost* that when someone's health is proposed in a Russian gathering he does not remain modestly seated as in England, but stands and drinks with the company, because by proposing his health they have not separated him, they have emphasized that he is received and embraced into their great family. *Sobornost* is delightful because the Russian 'congregation', like a good Christian congregation, accepts every sort of person: it does not judge them for their sins, and oddities or deformities are hardly noticed. It is the comfortableness of this congregationality which entices so many foreigners back to Russia. It is pleasant to be among people who are not asserting themselves all the time: when they argue or quarrel—and they argue a lot—they do it on a lower note than we are used to. A Russian rarely raises his voice and shouts 'WHAT!' If he is cross he says 'What-what-what!'

But after some time a Westerner usually begins to feel somewhat uneasy, because everyone in the congregation seems to have such an underdeveloped superego, compared with what he is used to at home: no one seems to want to take responsibility, so what happens when it becomes imperative for some one person to assert himself? You find to your surprise that these apparently natural people prefer that authority, if there must be authority, should be imposed from outside.* This is the old Russian way (though certainly not the way of many newer Russians), and it has, of course, been a fatal weakness all through Russian history. These were, and often still are, the people of whom Amalrik,† most radical and original of the protesters, bitterly writes: 'No oppression can be effective without those who are prepared to submit to it'—such people as the peasants on the Siberian farm to which he was exiled in 1965, who would not uproot a post

* An examination of 3,000 Russian defectors carried out by the Harvard Professor of Sociology, Alex Inkeles, with Eugenia Hanfmann and Helen Beier, found that most of them seemed to prefer 'control from without' to self-generated control of elements in themselves which they knew needed to be controlled. (*Human Relations*, Vol. XI, Feb. 1958.) The British psychiatrist Henry V. Dicks, examining a smaller group, came to similar conclusions about them: they seemed to want 'a moral corset' (*Human Relations*, Vol. V, 1952), and so did a Swiss investigation by Maria Pfister-Ammende, published in 1949. Professor Dicks concluded: 'I believe that the Soviet system works chiefly because of the obstinate persistence of unofficial, un-Communist, but uncommonly Russian patterns of "backsliding" into fraternal, affectionate, and easy-going human relations; because of the capacity of the Russians to tolerate and cope with bad objects in virtue of the undoubted deep optimism created by the good though fitful nurturance they receive as infants, and because any developing society gives some scope for constructiveness and the kind of achievement which raises morale.' These were all investigations of men and women who left Russia at the height of the Stalin period, however, and much as my own impressions would agree with the findings concerning the older generation, I believe the same investigators would find a remarkable growth of newer, more independent types today, and a little less of fraternal human relations.

† Author of *Will the USSR Survive Until 1984?*

which was in the way of the ploughing, or undertake anything, even to their own advantage, which they had not been specifically told to do by the collective farm authority.

But the new classes, the new intelligentsia, and a lot of the new technicians turn their backs on *sobornost*. One of my Moscow friends bitingly says: 'Stick to *sobornost* and you get Soviet tanks in Prague —because everyone leaves it to the few to take decisions. *Sobornost* is the past we want to get rid of!'

To deal with some of the newer, more individualized kinds of Russian can indeed be a relief. Not that all of them are pleasant: one can feel sympathy, in principle—when one is not being immediately inconvenienced—for some of the law-breakers, such as the young who steal the receivers from telephone boxes to make electric guitars; but there are a lot of mean, very small-scale traders (because it is impossible under the Soviet system to be anything but mean and small-scale),* and a lot of incompetent repair men who overcharge for their services. Inside the system there is a great deal of exploiting of its creaking joints, a lot of mean self-seeking and covering up at other people's expense. Which last is one of the favourite themes of Solzhenitsyn, as in *Cancer Ward* or *Matryona's House*.

However, it is fair to say that there is also, if only to a small degree, rather more individual courtesy and common sense in explaining the way, or in helping one out in minor *contretemps*, than there used to be: the example of good manners, as well as bad, seems to spread. And if the courtesies are welcome new individuations, I have to admit, once I am back in England, that the rough, pushing crowds are a case of new individuation too; they are out to get their rights instead of being ordered about, and one could well count this for a good, if primitive, sign. (The Uzbek woman with the baby would a generation ago have been wearing a horsehair veil, and too timid even to speak to a man.)

The private interests and hobbies of Russians can be surprising nowadays, yet the English word 'hobby' had to be borrowed into the Russian language, so little occasion had there been for such a concept until a comparatively few years ago. If one ever saw a dog during the Stalin period it was probably a police dog, whereas now there are

* It is permissible to sell anything one has made or grown oneself, or to hire out one's private services (with a few exceptions), but buying in order to sell again is 'speculation' and a serious crime; so is the private employment of others for gain. (Domestic servants—of whom there are few—can be hired at officially regulated rates.)

dogs of many breeds and sizes in the Moscow streets; a friend writes to me for an English book on clipping poodles; and in 1969 I saw a woman walking a St. Bernard and talking to it like a child, though how she fed it or even accommodated it in her flat I find hard to imagine. One may even, very rarely, come across a pet shop where one may buy perhaps a tortoise or a cage-bird; a little more frequently one may find a garden shop which, even in the depth of winter, attracts collectors of evergreen indoor plants and cacti. Anything exotic is always a draw. Some years ago I was told by the editor of the Indian Government magazine which sells in Russia that the subject about which he got most correspondents was something quite outside normal Russian concerns—yoga.

If you are quite well off you may be able to shoot or fish. I have on my wall a map of the Moscow province studded with the locations of a dozen kinds of beast, from the lynx and wild hunting-dog down-wards, and also showing a couple of dozen kinds of wildfowl, and fish in great variety. But it helps a great deal to be a member of a club —connected with your place of work, or trade union, or your unit if you are in the police: many clubs have shooting or fishing rights reserved for them over an area.

In Russia, as in other urbanizing and industrializing countries once they have risen out of poverty, there is more openness about sex and also a more civilized and sophisticated expression of it than before. Foreigners at first may notice only a prevailing puritanism, and certainly there is no flaunting of sex: Russian women remain modest in bearing, and if some girls adopt minis, they are far from being microminis. But the contrast with the Stalin period, once again, is remarkable. The less inhibited, better fed, gayer young couples of today have come quite a way from the time when a little holding of hands was all that was permissible in public. The first screen kiss was back in 1956, and at the theatre, which is always freer than the cinema, one can nowadays occasionally hear some frank real-life dialogue. In the play *A Film Is Being Made* the film director takes his infatuated young assistant to the Black Sea, where they find a room in a private house. 'Pretty girl you've got there,' says the proprietor *sotto voce*. The director brushes him off stiffly: 'My wife is called Anna.' 'Oh, we don't bother whether you're married or not here— it's like it was in the war.' This play was taken off because it had so many passages which made fun of the Party's control of film-making, but during my most recent visit I was glad to see that the repertoire still included other plays—fortunately unpolitical—which have some equally frank bits of dialogue.

All this new development, it might be objected, is no more than the small change of the new process of individuation, though at least it seems a good thing that there should be such a flood of small change in circulation to back up what one might call the more valuable 'pieces' —the intellectuals. Certainly it is the intellectuals and those who work in the arts who are the class most respected by Russians in general. They do also earn a certain amount of philistine contempt and even hatred from some of the simpler members of the public: it is from among such people that the KGB can always find a 'public' to fill the court and shout 'Parasite!' and 'Layabout!' at the trial of some outspoken writer whom the bureaucracy wish to humiliate. But the great majority of the public think differently; they want their children to go into educated jobs; they keep their contempt and hatred for the Party bureaucracy. In the industrial town of Ufa, for instance, out of 3,200 parents who were questioned, 78 per cent wanted their children to become doctors, graduate engineers, teachers, or scientists, or to take up other professions for which higher training or special gifts are required. Yet between 70 per cent and 80 per cent of school-leavers in Ufa every year necessarily go into modest jobs in industry. Similar preferences appeared when parents and children were questioned in other towns.

It is education, and something which Russians in a broad sense call 'culture' which, it seems to me, mainly determine social ranking in Soviet Russia. There are men in powerful positions, in receipt of very high salaries, with access to 'closed' shops and other privileges, whom one might expect to rank socially highest of all, but they excite cynical envy or contempt in most people, rather than respect: they are only admired by a small class who are the Soviet equivalent of parvenus, and those who are in the way to becoming parvenus, in a bourgeois society. Salaries are not the primary matter in establishing one's status, since rent, including lighting and heating, is calculated as a proportion of income—usually only 7 per cent or 8 per cent— and since, in view of the very high level of most retail prices, doubling one's salary comes nowhere near to doubling one's standard of living. Actually a large number of professionally trained men and women —doctors, teachers, and graduate engineers, for instance—usually earn only about 40 per cent above the average working-class wage. Managers, editors, and the more important Party secretaries may get from two and a half to four times the average wage, but so do a few of the heavy manual workers—some of the crane drivers and excavator men. Academics and people at the top of the artistic professions get still higher salaries, and white-collar workers in any of these higher grades may have other privileges, such as the right to a larger flat.

The Soviet Government is faced with two problems which can arise in any developing country: how to keep young people satisfied with manual work when education is so new and carries such prestige, and how to avoid too much inequality and privilege. On the first count the Soviet authorities are not having much success, although they have already spent hundreds of millions of roubles in raising the lowest wage rates, particularly those of the peasants. The fortunate ones who get some kind of higher education—say the 30 per cent of the labour force who in Soviet terminology form 'the intelligentsia'— generally despise manual work even in the shape of odd jobs in their own homes; it seems to be on the whole only a proportion of women from the higher intelligentsia who even take any great pleasure in cooking. However, there might be a spreading of Do-It-Yourself if more materials became available; Ulanova and some of the best-known artistes are said to enjoy servicing their own cars, and their example could spread downwards through society, so great is the prestige of the top intelligentsia and artistic circles. But it will be a long time before any such upgrading in social status affects the doing of manual work to earn one's living, however well that work may be rewarded in terms of money.

Privilege is of course an unavoidable result of shortages. In the early days there were so few bicycles that they were often given away as rewards to the best workers: nowadays it is easy to get hold of a bicycle, but how is the Government to distribute cars—even the 600,000 cars a year which are promised? If even $2\frac{1}{2}$ per cent of the population want cars and are prepared to save up for them, that makes 6 million people; how is the annual output to be allocated, at one car to ten persons? And cars are only an extreme example of the situation in consumer goods of nearly all kinds—small articles of daily use as well as heavy machines. The basic principle, ever since the early days of Stalin, has been rationing by the purse, combined with a general scale of incomes so that the highest rewards go to those who in the general scheme of Soviet society are thought to deserve them. In this kind of grading the Soviet organization has been fairly close to popular opinion—the peasants always excepted. Most of the high incomes are

13. Watching football, Irkutsk, Siberia (John Massey Stewart)

14. Central Market, Moscow (John Massey Stewart)

15. Bread counter in a Moscow suburb (John Massey Stewart)

16. Book week in Moscow's Gorky Park (John Massey Stewart)

17. Evening off for geologists in far Siberia (Novosti)

18. Moscow Metro (Novosti)

19. Dawn on Moscow's most modern avenue, Kalinin Prospekt
(Novosti)

not objected to as undeserved—except of course for the *apparatchiks*; what is resented is the existence of another kind of rationing which is insulting to the ordinary citizen—the system of 'closed' shops, foreign currency shops, 'closed' clinics and so on which gives a very small class, consisting mostly of officials and some top army men, a comfortable private life with large flats, no queues, the best choice of meat and imported foods, special medical attention, and priority in trains, holiday accommodation and the ownership of cars. There are even rumours of riotous orgies in these circles, but at least there are no glossy magazines nor society pages to blazon abroad the life which such people may lead: it is very much a thing apart.

The existence of this class is resented more, I think, than it might be in many Western countries. All the well-rewarded jobs are accessible, in principle, to one's children if not to oneself. Yet actually the children of peasants and even the children of manual workers form a rather small proportion of the students in higher education. And this disproportion appears even in the higher forms of schools. Compulsory schooling is from the age of seven to the age of fifteen; a Soviet researcher in 1964 showed that in the classes for sixteen and seventeen-year-olds in the Gorky Region 42·8 per cent of the pupils had fathers in 'specialist' occupations, while at the bottom of the school the percentage was only 25·8 per cent; the figures for workers' children were 24·6 per cent and 50·2 per cent respectively. In many village schools there is still no education to be had after the age of fifteen, and one hears of places where children escape even before that age. Education, including university education, is free, but student grants are very low; if students have no help from home they often have to make up their living expenses by doing odd jobs. As to the senior schoolchildren in the Gorky Region—or anywhere else—many of them leave at fifteen to start work in lowgrade jobs, or they take brief technical courses which can start them earning earlier than those who stay on for higher education. Thus although there is no 'eleven-plus' in Soviet schools, there is in practice a good deal of selection later, by parental income. At the university and polytechnic level there is fierce competition, since only about half a million places are available annually, and the average number of school-leavers is three million a year. Boys who go to the university (but not to a polytechnic) can postpone their military service and enter eventually as officers, and it is no wonder there are attempts to bribe university staff at the entrance examinations.

However, the dangers of creating a hereditary class system are not quite so great as might appear. Not all the university places are open to school-leavers, a proportion being reserved for those who have already been at work, and who enter through a different examination. Then there are correspondence and evening courses for university and polytechnic qualifications which are followed by more than two million students. Also, parents are obliged to send their children to the school in their own district; they are not supposed to shop around for a 'good' school, though probably a few people with 'pull' can get round this. Exception is made for the 'English' and other schools where most of the instruction is in a foreign language: there is competition to enter these, and I have heard of foreign-born Soviet citizens who coach children in a language for this purpose.

I think there is no doubt that the leadership, in principle, really want to spread all grades of education equitably through the country. As part of the current Five-Year Plan, for instance, they have promised to raise student grants. And they have succeeded, as much as any government could desire, in imbuing the nation with the idea of self-education. Reading is by far the most popular pastime, and every other book which one sees being read in a bus or tramcar is a text-book. When the bookshops announced the new edition of that (mostly) very respectable reference work, the Great Soviet Encyclopaedia, the advance orders totalled half a million sets, which is about 150,000 more than the sum of all the libraries and all the secondary schools in the Soviet Union. Allowing even for other institutional orders, it seems as if 100,000 private persons, at the very least, must have wanted to possess the Encyclopaedia. Politically speaking, the leadership must hope that education will make for a more technically-equipped nation, a soberer one, and even perhaps a nation corresponding to the Marxist ideal, where there shall be an assimilation of culture between town and country and between all grades of workers. The leadership might well be nervous of a minority which was too highly educated in comparison with the rest, just as they are nervous of the intelligentsia today. They put out a lot of propaganda to remind the favoured ones that they too are part of the nation and not a class apart, and they constantly recruit intellectuals to give courses of popular lectures.

But inside the Party, although there are fulminations against officials 'losing touch with the masses', it is unlikely that the leadership would ask the Party élite to give up their present privileges. Thus the Party élite will continue to be unacceptable to the public as a social élite. But the Party does not want its leading personnel to be leading social figures, nor well-known figures in the way that Western politicians are well known; they must stand somewhat aside, and be thought of as the more effective for being somewhat detached, like a doctor or a priest. This would seem to be one of the permanent disabilities of such a constipated, artificial, old-fashioned political system as the Communist system. But meanwhile the intellectuals play the part of a social élite, and some of them attract warm admiration from a considerable number of the people, especially the young, because they take on something of the responsibilities of the 'intelligentsia' in the old, pre-Revolutionary, socially-conscious sense of the term. They are able, in plays and novels and sometimes in films, to speak up, if only through satire, for the ordinary man and his problems.

The best and boldest, such as Solzhenitsyn, Tvardovsky or Rostropovitch, or scientists such as Sakharov, the Medvedev brothers, Kapitsa, and so many more, write letters to the authorities protesting against injustices both general and particular, warning the Government against a revival of Stalinism, and proposing programmes for a free Soviet Union. They use their influence to try to get political sentences reviewed; in this they occasionally have success, as they did in extracting the biologist Zhores Medvedev from the mental hospital where he was said to be showing signs of incipient insanity, on the grounds that he did not accept everything about the Soviet system. There are sometimes genuinely contested elections for the governing bodies of important organizations such as the Union of Soviet Writers, with a choice between 'liberal' and strictly Party-line candidates. The Party does its best, by rounding up yes-men or by other manipulations, to avoid such occasions, and of course the public only gets to hear about any conflict through information passed from hand to hand. But nowadays a great deal of this kind of information is passed from hand to hand; in the regular *Chronicle of Current Events*, which circulates in duplicated form, and in all the *samizdat* (i.e. privately circulated) literature. Some typists are said to make a good living out of reproducing copies of the novels of Solzhenitsyn, the programme of Academician Sakharov, and other documents, which reach a large audience in this way. In fact so much underground literature circulates that there is a strong rumour that, as in Tsarist times, there may be a few officials of the political police who are secretly working for the 'liberals'. This may well be true, but a further, very plausible theory is that the KGB prefer not to make many arrests, because if they did, an organization such as that behind the *Chronicle* would only become more hydra-headed; it is simpler for the KGB to keep a watch on the devils they know rather than have the job of uncovering dozens more. This policy would seem to reflect the current attitude of the régime, which wants no subversion, of course, but seems to want even more that there should be seen to be as little subversion as possible.

However, hopeful Westerners need to be warned against over-estimating the power and scope of any underground movement in Soviet Russia. The rare—indeed very rare—act of violence, such as the attempt on the life of Brezhnev by a Lieutenant Ilyin the day after Jan Palach set fire to himself in Prague, would seem to be as futile as any of the political assassinations in Tsarist times—in fact more so, since the machinery of Soviet control is much more effective than Tsarist machinery was. Similarly, we learn from a brief report in the *Chronicle* that a conspiracy including several military men,* which aimed at setting up a new régime, was unearthed not long since in Leningrad, but the leaders were executed, and the total effect must have been a good deal less than that of the one-day Decembrist rising in 1825. There are occasional riots, such as the 'great battle' between police and workers in Tula, which Amalrik tells of in his *Involuntary Journey to Siberia*. It arose because the police had been using their new weapons—their truncheons—for the first time, and all Soviet citizens had been brought up to despise the truncheon as a symbol of 'the American way of life'. Some years ago there was a more serious riot—over a rise in food prices—where a commanding officer is said to have shot himself rather than order his men to fire on fellow-Russians. But spontaneous riots and the very occasional organized strike are no real danger to the authorities, though news of them is suppressed; they are not the work of any movement.

No outsider can be well-informed enough about Soviet affairs to anticipate a possible *coup* at the top some time in the future; and for change to come about through such a *coup* would certainly be in line with old Russian tradition. But political changes are more likely to come, I think, in two other ways—through well-judged pressure

---

* The military have always been excluded from the Politburo, with the exception, for a few years only, of Marshal Zhukov. There is a small proportion of military men in the Central Committee, and the highest military appointments are made by the armed forces department of the Central Committee and the General Staff in consultation together.

on top Party circles by top scientists and specialists, or through a long process of diffusion.

Academician Sakharov, the historian Roy Medvedev, and the physicist Turshin have already addressed to Brezhnev, Kosygin and Podgorny, and to the Central Committee, a sober analysis of the state of the country, in which they conclude that the USSR is falling behind and will stay behind in the Second (i.e. electronic) Industrial Revolution, unless scientists, technologists and managers are allowed much more freedom of information, more contact with each other, and with foreign countries, and more liberty of research and organization without interference by unqualified persons. And Sakharov is one of the nation's most prized servants, one of the creators of the Soviet atomic bomb. There is no evidence yet that documents such as this—and there have been several—have had any effect on the political policies of the country's sixty-year-old leaders. And their successors, to judge from everyone I have ever been able to ask, are likely to be 'faceless men', 'unknown men', super-*apparatchiks*. However, circumstances will press harder still on these successors, and history has many examples of the talent and originality which ultimate responsibility can bring forth in men who had been previously unregarded: in the Soviet Union Khrushchev was the last outstanding example.

A clever leadership, giving a proper ear to complaints from men in the highest positions in industry and science, might decide, and be able, to oust the most reactionary *apparatchiks* from key jobs. This would have to be done by degrees, since a complete and sudden purge of such people would be thought to weaken the public image of the Party too severely, and it would probably lead to unbearable strains inside the Politburo itself, as various members saw their principal protégés dismissed. Another possibility would be the lifting of the ban on sons and daughters of the intelligentsia entering the Higher Party Schools. At present they are probably mistrusted because they and their parents are not directly engaged in production, and because —partly through this lack of experience—they are suspected of wanting to move 'too fast', and further because they tend to discuss principles in a theoretical way, outside Marxism, smacking of the long-winded pre-Revolutionary discussions. There is a real class distinction in these Schools which train people for the highest jobs, though I am told that, as with everything in Soviet life, the distinction is 'got round' sometimes. The abolition of the class distinction would hardly admit any very liberal-minded members of the intelligentsia to Party counsels, but it could by degrees contribute a leavening element of academic-politicals of a type which flourishes in other countries. Finally there may well be a slow growth of more democratic practices inside the Party itself.

Such possibilities as these may seem a minor affair, but personally —and here I differ from many observers—I think they are the most likely type of change in the near future. The Party is very heavily entrenched and likely to remain so, but because *some* of its policies are stupid, because its treatment of *some* individuals is inhuman, and because the whole thing is in theory totalitarian, I think outsiders can easily underestimate the capacity of its leaders for pragmatic common sense. All kinds of independent protests, any attempts to push the authorities, and particularly anything done in public—all these will continue to be suppressed; at the time of writing they are being suppressed, by post-Stalin standards, rather severely. The Party alone must be seen to decide. But that being securely established, there may well be a slow and cautious releasing and relaxing of some controls from the top; the Party may even take over as its own, as the Communist Party did in Hungary after the rebellion, some of the policies whose supporters are at present being sent to prison camps.

In any case, however, there seem to be good opportunities for another process—for a diffusion of ideas which might become so widespread, in the long run, that the Party would be unable to counteract it. This is what seems to be intended by partizans of the 'Democratic Movement' in Russia. This Movement has no organization, and no real leaders, though from time to time one or two of its bravest supporters become known because they make some public protest and are whisked away to a trial whose result is a foregone conclusion. But public protests, and still less demonstrations, are not felt to be the primary business of the Movement: what they are after is the irresistible spreading, by private contacts, by a sort of osmosis, of decent standards and justice among those who hold positions of even the smallest responsibility. 'We can wait twenty years', and they all say the last thing they want is revolution or an attempt at revolution, either of which would be disastrous. This osmosis is a very Russian way of proceeding, and in such a vast country it is impossible for 'the authorities' to know all that goes on, or to know whether some of those who exercise authority have not themselves been affected, or as hardline Party men would say, 'infected'. There are some local possibilities already: a book which might never see the light in Moscow may find an obscure but enlightened publishing house in Minsk or Alma-Ata. The Soviet Union, with all its defects and inefficiencies and corruptions, is a complicated modern State, and it is impracticable for those at the centre, so stupidly centralized is the system, to know of all the significant developments that may be taking place.

However, the possibilities of 'Democratic' diffusion are also only a matter for speculation, and it seems to me important to try to judge the political atmosphere against which, and among which, such movements have to operate. It is not easy, even after long acquaintance with the Soviet Union, to estimate how far the relaxation of Party control and the growth of little liberties since Stalin have had an effect on the political attitudes of the population; it is certainly a mistake to regard the political aspect of this relaxation as the major one, as Westerners are too easily apt to do. (The social, or what one might call the social-economic picture, is what has been most affected, as I have tried to show.) The question 'How much political effect?' has to be answered, I think, in two parts: (a) as regards the mass of the people one must say, 'only in a diffuse and limited way (with the exception of a minority of individuals)'; (b) as regards the intellectuals one can say, 'profoundly and widely', though again with a fair minority of exceptions—careerists and such conformists as the psychiatrists, for instance, who were willing to certify Medvedev.

The average rank-and-file worker, I feel, does not want to be bothered with government as such; on the other hand he has probably no ambition to break out of organized industry and become, say, a private repair man. He so often lacks any little qualification which he could exploit, unlike the *kulturny* ones who advertise private lessons in languages or music or typing; neither does he own a *dacha* or a car which he might hire out. The workers have their own solidarity, an unspoken solidarity which does not need to be organized, which shares out the little advantages they can milk from the system, and which expresses itself communally today in taking things easily, and indeed more than easily. One is hardly in the country an hour before one will see something of the slow, idle, even non-existent pace of work—or else, perhaps, because the quarterly target-day is approaching, there is a slapdash burst, with the paint splashed about and never properly wiped up, and the top coat left to run anyhow over the undercoat. There seems to be the same attitude, or so say many observers, in offices, where men and women are absent from their desks on no excuse, no one ever stands in for anyone else, no one reckons to know where anyone else is to be found.

This is the ground bass of Soviet life today: is it said to affect even the space programme, and although it is not often actually named, it is actually the biggest problem the Party has to face. It will not be cured, as the country's experts have been pointing out for many years, until the natural forces inside industry are given more of their head: but that would mean withdrawing a lot of Party control. I have no wish to cast a slur on the innate capacities of Soviet workers. The men who change a bogie in ten minutes at Brest, where the international train has the whole of its underpinnings exchanged to fit the Russian gauge; the young men who sort out priorities at airports; the radio operators who send and receive Morse at forty words a minute; most railway personnel, and many others who have responsible duties and a little independence—they are able to show what can be done with such freedom. But inside a factory petty checks and regulations, perhaps designed with the idea of defeating slackness, frequently make things worse, operating in a vicious circle.

The present state of many of the workers might be characterized as the new 'tacit conspiracy', like the 'tacit conspiracy against all authority', which was the phrase an English newspaper correspondent used to describe the state of the nation in the simmering pre-Revolutionary year of 1913. But although this national go-slow may well be considered 'political', to the extent that it is a reaction against petty discipline and the restrictions of Soviet life, it is not a political simmering of the 1913 kind. Ask any of these ca'canny workers and clerks, even on a suitably private occasion, what they think of some political act of their Government, such as the invasion of Czechoslovakia, or the imprisonment of protesting writers, and most of them will approve: whatever its faults, it is their Government and probably in the right.

The workmen take their liberties with the system, but it seems to be very much the old *sobornost*, the spirit of the *mir*, which makes the working life congenial for them. Most Russians are not very competitive people, and this suits the authorities who, after all, were mostly reared in an atmosphere of *sobornost* themselves. It is significant that the only 'political' activities where the people are to some extent trusted are the little group organizations which depend on a communal spirit for their successful operation—the house committee, the parents' committee, the 'greenery group' of a block of flats, or the 'comrades' courts' which can deal out small punishments for offences against neighbourliness. (Incidentally, if Russia is ever to have more responsible representative institutions, such activities as these are by no means to be despised for the experience, though modest, which they can provide.)

There have been a few workmen among the public protesters, and in the collection of *Letters to Pavel Litvinov*, and the letters written to Solzhenitsyn* after the publication of *One Day in the Life of Ivan Denisovitch*, there are some written by working men—a turner, a driver, a sailor—who show as much independence of spirit as any intellectual. A worker from Volgograd reflects: 'How did we come to let power slip through our hands?' and he quotes his factory mates, when they were asked to spy out 'internal enemies', as saying: 'It seems that the security bodies haven't been created so that we can work in peace, but rather it is we who have been created so as to provide them with work.' These letters contrast sharply with the abusive ones—from men of various social ranks—who considered that Solzhenitsyn and Litvinov were dragging their country in the dirt, Solzhenitsyn by daring to attack 'the camp system, soldiers and guards', and Litvinov by questioning the justice of the trial of Bukovsky and others for making a small public demonstration against the injustice of an earlier trial.

To return to the intellectuals—those who know loyalty to the historic international standards of science, of philosophy, of literature, those who just want free correspondence with foreign colleagues, and the right to receive copies of *Nature* unscissored by the censor, and even the right which Hungarians have, to take two trips abroad per year if you can raise the currency—perhaps the most important thing for Westerners to understand about them is that they are, almost without exception, intensely patriotic citizens. They stress continually that they are campaigning for the realization in practice of the rights which are guaranteed to the Soviet people on paper, in the Constitution of 1936. They are patriotic like Solzhenitsyn, who would not leave his country to receive the Nobel Prize in case he was not allowed to return, and who writes in order to force his fellow-Russians to realize the shame, the ignominy, that such a great country, such a potentially

* *Letters and Telegrams to Pavel Litvinov, December 1967–May 1968,* edited and annotated by Karel van het Reve (D. Reidel, Dordrecht). These were received after BBC broadcasts made known to millions of Russians Litvinov's protest about the trial of Bukovsky, and the way Litvinov himself was treated by the KGB. The letters to Solzhenitsyn are reproduced in *Solzhenitsyn: A Documentary Record,* edited by Leopold Labedz (Allen Lane: The Penguin Press, 1970).

15

greater country with such a fundamentally humane people, should be soiled by so much baseness, cowardice, self-seeking and inhumanity in the present. In 1969 visitors to Moscow found dozens of intellectuals eager to express their disgust and shame at their Government's actions in Czechoslovakia, but the same intellectuals were equally unanimous in their condemnation of the defecting writer Kuznetsov, who had just then reached Britain: 'He was a deserter. He should have stayed with us.' (The only man I met who thought Kuznetsov had a right to leave was an elderly pensioner, a retired fitter.)

Russian patriotism, in view of the country's almost unrelievedly sombre history, is a remarkable phenomenon. It is not a reflection of military or naval prowess, and not, primarily, a reflection of pride in cultural achievement, as in France. (Russians are sensitive about the fact that their great writers and composers only appeared in the last 180 years or so.) Russian patriotism is expressed through all those questionings in Russian novels—'What is Russia?'—'What is it to be a Russian?' The questions are still asked in a few contemporary works, such as those of Paustovsky. To be a Russian is felt to be something special; it used to mean pride in being a member of the one true Christian Church, but more recently, apart from sharing 'the broad Russian nature', there has been doubt as to its further meaning. It has been like a vast expansion of 'congregationality', which can bring together protesters and rank-and-file workers and intellectual rebels and acquiescent types just as in the past. To the old intelligentsia, however, patriotism always meant something more than mere devotion to one's home patch and fellow-citizens: it implied also a desire to do something for one's country. Living in America today, a Russian lady of aristocratic birth and liberal ideas, Mme. Avinova, recalls in her memoirs how in 1910 she first met the man who became her husband, and she wrote to a friend: 'He is not only an intelligent benevolent panther with the kindest eyes on earth and an adorable smile: *his love of country borders on the sublime.*'

Today, driven by their love of Russia, many of the young and very many of the intelligentsia plunge themselves greedily into the old, the 'genuine' Russia; they take great walking tours, as the writer Soloukhin does, to discover the 'real' peasant; they collect antique wooden objects and pots, desperately hard though these are to find; they collect ikons and even light the little red lamp in front of them, without being believers; out of love for literature they try to get hold of the Old Slavonic Bible; they go to church sometimes, out of intellectual curiosity, or patriotic curiosity, or 'as a form of protest', because the Church continues to be persecuted; and thousands of them are actually joining the Orthodox Church, in spite of the fact that in order to keep in with the authorities it has constantly to remind its members of their duty to be loyal Soviet citizens; some young men and women are joining the Baptists, a sect which is recruited mainly from the working class and which accepts the teachings of modern science; and others, if they are not joining a Church, are reading Dostoevsky or the great philosophers and looking for spiritual nourishment where they can, so that many whom I met declared warmly 'We are all believers!' Not, they explained, that they all went to church; they were not even Orthodox, but Christian or not, they all believed in something beyond mechanistic and material systems. (If they had been British, some of the non-Christians would have called themselves humanists.) And I was shown an article in the youth magazine, *Yunost*, complaining that man's 'innermost essence', his 'soul' (*dusha*), his conscience, his need to live by more than bread alone, were being catered for by religious teachers but were neglected by Soviet writers and teachers and those responsible for youth.

All these explorations would be reckoned by the explorers, I think, as being undertaken partly in a patriotic, a 'Russian' spirit, as attempts to make themselves more enlightened and better-rooted members of the great Russian community, rather than solely as searches for individual salvation. And here the explorers would join with the less inquiring, more conformist majority of their countrymen, for whom the symbols of patriotism are the first sputnik, and the first man in space, and all those Olympic medals, and a general feeling that, in spite of all frustrations, a Government that has done so much must be pretty well right—but for whom also the essential, obvious basis of being Russian is the old sense of brotherhood (even though, they would say, a lot of the jumped-up types are getting more than their fair share nowadays).

The Party is recruited mainly from this conformist majority, and it is a help towards understanding Russia today if one can think of the Party as also a Russian growth: it makes the relationship between Party and people somewhat more credible. So much of what is clumsy, what is anachronistic about the Party comes straight out of the old Russia, but it is not usually felt as old because the Party is so much more successful as a system of government than anything earlier in Russian history. But the hierarchy, and the manipulation of the masses, are not to be found in Marx; they are Russian, and that is why they still suit a good part of the population reasonably well, and another part feels the Party can be supported because of what it has done for Russia, while a minority which gets bigger every day is yearning for a system which will provide a lot more scope for the individual. The Party has brought the nation to a pitch where a great part of the nation no longer needs the Party, or certainly not the Party in anything like its present form.

They have all come such a long way in so short a time. For centuries the Russians seemed to be simply standing still, and now, out of the communal, the mediaeval, the partly-pagan-partly-primitive-Christian culture there has grown this rumbling, uncomfortable, over-organized, modern state. I think of Ivan, whom I met by chance, an opinionated old Party type, standing on his Russian dignity, a perfect example of the national-pride-national-inferiority syndrome. He recently retired from an agricultural profession (for which he was trained without having had normal secondary education), and he said: 'When I was a child in the steppe, near Taganrog, there were nine of us and we all dipped in the same bowl. We had nine spoons but only one bowl.' And now his three children are all in the professions and have all visited Western Europe. Ivan's generation went through more shocks than any detribalized Negroes; they went through more shocks than those generations of Englishmen and women whom we forget—the deracinated country people who fled from the bitterness of farm labour, or were forced out of the old family crafts, into the coarse, ugly proletarian world of the first industrial era, who made something of a culture of their own, and who became the ancestors of more than half the most distinguished and respected men and women in England today. We now have a comparatively stable society which can carry a great amount of divergence, protest, or eccentricity. But Soviet society is not stable; not only the Government but the average citizen will go on being nervous of divergencies for some time to come.

The rulers of the USSR will necessarily go on devoting most of their attention, as they do now, to the domestic problems of their huge country: their behaviour over international affairs, in fact, can often only be assessed as a reflection of their concern with home affairs. Soviet support for international Communism will of course never stop, but it will continue to be a secondary matter, never pursued to the point where it might endanger the interests of the Soviet Union itself. Though foreigners have often failed to realize the fact, this has been the policy for the last fifty years, ever since Stalin came to power, and the realistic rulers of today are certainly not going to make a change. They keep 'Communism' prominently in front of their people as an international force—a beacon for the oppressed, and so forth—but that is largely because 'Communism' has become such a spent ideology at home. The USSR will naturally continue to be involved in occasions of international friction, even serious friction, over other matters than the spread of Communism; but there are also likely to be more and more instances of a policy which doesn't often get an important place in the news, and that is—co-operation over practical matters, quietly pursued.

It would seem that the urgent international problems of the future are going to be much less matters of division of territory than a joint concern for survival, in a world where the pollution and destruction of the environment by which we all live are already beyond the bounds of containment by even the largest nations. At home the USSR already has some areas of serious pollution, in the Caspian and Black Seas and in some of the cities, and so far the Soviet Government has shown no more severity than the leading capitalist countries in dealing with this. But they are well aware of the international scale of the problem, and a leading technologist, son-in-law of Kosygin, has been nominated to the 'Club of Rome', the group of scientists and industrialists from many countries which is trying to initiate action throughout the world to conserve the global environment. The 'Club' has already had one meeting in Moscow, and it is not wishful thinking to anticipate that the Soviet Government will eventually share in controlling world pollution and wastage of resources, in the same way that they have given smooth-running co-operation for many years in, for example, the world meteorological service.

This book has been mainly a history of the Russian people, and I have tried to suggest in this last chapter that there are social forces in Russia which now have very much a life of their own. Russians have often been held back by the underdevelopment of their care for objects compared with their acute sensibility for persons, but although they have been acquiring so many techniques of all kinds, I think most of them will go on trusting human contacts rather than techniques. It would be reasonable to fear that their new-found individualism and their new-found egotism, bred by the Soviet system, might diminish what the young American whom I quoted in Chapter 3 calls 'the wonderful simplicity and sincerity of their relationships with one another'. However, I do not myself feel that any great harm has yet been suffered by more than a minority. That primary sensibility and understanding for the person, which the great Russian writers have communicated, and which draws so many of us back to Russia, is the most precious quality the Russian people have. With any reasonable luck, in spite of all barbarities and upheavals, and even in a world of increasing technology, they will continue delighting us with it in the future.

If the future of the world demands a stabilizing or diminishing of industrialization, then obviously the Soviet Union, for whom industrialization is so new and painfully won, will be one of the last countries to accept a new kind of restriction, and the Soviet people, who have suffered so much, will be among the last to acquiesce in any shrinking of living standards, or of the prospects of living standards, if that should become necessary. But the USSR is big enough to have more time in hand than other industrial countries; a majority of its citizens have already taken their own startling steps towards Zero Population Growth; and in time the necessary new policies may easily become acceptable, if their advantages are made sufficiently clear. As we all approach that new stabilizing or de-industrializing period—if we are fortunate enough to do so—the Russian people, who have preserved so much of a pre-industrial set of human relationships, may very well help to show us all the way to the kind of relationships which we shall need to make the new society viable. They will probably call it a 'Communist' way, but we shall probably call it simply Russian.

Some Important Dates

About 300   Armenia and Georgia became Christian.
onwards

  (432   Ireland and then Scotland became Christian.)
onwards

  (596   England became Christian—St. Augustine, etc.)
onwards

  860   First Varangian expedition against Constantinople.

  (870   King Alfred crowned.)

  882   The Scandinavian, *Oleg*, established in Kiev.

  988   *Vladimir* of Kiev and his people became Christian.

1025   Foundation of Yaroslavl.

1037?   Cathedral of St. Sophia, Kiev, begun.

1113–25 *Vladimir Monomakh*, grand prince of Kievan Russia.

1147   First written mention of Moscow.

 (1166   Growth of national system of law in England.)
onwards

1185   Prince Igor's expedition against the Polovtsy.

1230   Kiev sacked by Mongols.

1237–42 Mongol conquest of Russia.

1252–63 *Alexander Nevsky*, grand prince of Vladimir.

 (1265   First English Parliaments.)
onwards

1325–41 *Ivan I of Moscow* ('Kalita' or 'Moneybags').

1367–81 Moscow Kremlin first fortified in stone.

1380   Battle of Kulikovo: Tatars defeated by Dmitri Donskoi.

 (1381   Peasants' Revolt in England; serfdom fades away.)

1439   Council of Florence: reunion of Eastern and Western Churches.

1441   Russian Metropolitan deposed for accepting Council of Florence.

1453   Turks capture Constantinople.

1462–1505 *Ivan III, the Great*—the first Tsar.

1480	Mongol rule ended.
(1534 onwards	Church of England breaks away from Rome.)
About 1550	Military service established on basis of land tenure.
1552	Kazan (Tatar capital) captured: St. Basil's Cathedral built in celebration.
1553	Richard Chancellor opens White Sea route from England to Russia.
1564	First book printed in Moscow.
1571	Crimean Tatars burn Moscow.
1570–1600	Cossack settlements begin on the 'frontier'.
1581	Yermak leads conquest of Siberia.
1598–1605	*Boris Godunov.*
1610–12	Poles in Moscow.
1613–45	*Michael Romanov* (elected Tsar by Assembly of the Land).
1640	Russians reach the Pacific.
1649	Last vestige of escape for serfs removed in Code.
(1649	Charles I of England executed.)
1653	Last full Assembly of the Land.)
1654 onwards	Great Schism in the Russian Church.
1654	Ukraine united with Russia.
1670–1	Peasant revolt led by Stenka Razin.
1682–1725	*Peter the Great.*
1697–8	Peter visits Western countries.
1703	St. Petersburg (Leningrad) founded.
1709	Peter defeats Swedes at Poltava.
1721	Treaty of Nystad confirms Peter's conquests from Sweden. Peter adopts title of 'Emperor'.
1725	Academy of Sciences founded.
1755	Moscow University founded.
1756–63	Seven Years' War.
1762–96	*Catherine the Great.*
1772	First Partition of Poland.
1774	Black Sea steppes conquered from Turkey.
1773–5	Peasant revolt under Pugachov.
1781–6	Ukraine brought fully under Russian rule.
1783	Crimea incorporated in Russia.
(1789	French Revolution.)

1793	Second Partition of Poland.
1795	Third and complete Partition of Poland.
1796	*Paul I*—the 'mad Tsar'—murdered 1801.
1801–25	*Alexander I.*
1801–29	Transcaucasia conquered.
1812	Great Fatherland War against Napoleon.
1823–31	Pushkin (1799–1837) wrote *Eugene Onegin.*
1825–55	*Nicholas I* ('the Gendarme').
1825	Decembrist rising.
1830–1	Polish rebellion suppressed.
1836	Glinka's opera *A Life for the Tsar* (*Ivan Susanin*).
1847–52	*A Sportsman's Sketches* written by Turgenev (1818–93).
1848	The Communist Manifesto published by Marx (1818–83).
1853–56	Crimean War.
1855–81	*Alexander II* (the Liberator).
1855–60	Far Eastern provinces acquired from China.
1861	Emancipation of the serfs.
1863	Polish rebellion suppressed.
1863–4	Independent courts established, with trial by jury; some state schools founded; local councils (*zemstva*) began.
1864–5	Central Asian provinces conquered.
1866	*Crime and Punishment* published by Dostoevsky (1822–81).
1867	Alaska sold to the United States.
1873–7	*Anna Karenina* written by Tolstoy (1828–1910).
1881–94	*Alexander III.*
1885–87	Famine.
1891	Trans-Siberian railway begun.
1892–1903	Witte minister of finance, etc.
1894–1917	*Nicholas II.*
1898	Moscow Art Theatre founded by Stanislavsky and Nemirovitch-Danchenko.
1900	Manchuria occupied.
1901	First performance of *Three Sisters* by Chekhov (1860–1904).
1902	*The Lower Depths* by Gorky (1868–1936).
1903	Lenin divided Bolsheviks from Mensheviks at London Congress of Russian Social Democratic Party.
1904–5	Russo-Japanese War.
1905	'The First Revolution'.
1906	The first Duma.

1906–11	Land reforms of Prime Minister Stolypin.
1914	First World War begins.
1917	March Revolution.
	November (Bolshevik) Revolution.
1918	Treaty of Brest-Litovsk with Germany.
1918–20	Civil War and War of Intervention.
1921–2	Famine.
1921–8	New Economic Policy—NEP.
1924	Lenin died.
1927	Trotsky expelled. Stalin in power.
1928–32	First Five-Year Plan: agriculture collectivized.
1933–37	Second Five-Year Plan.
(1933	Nazi Revolution in Germany.)
1934	USSR admitted to League of Nations.
1935	Soviet–French alliance signed.
1935–8	The Terror and the Purges.
1936	The 'Stalin' Constitution adopted (still in force).
(1936–9	Spanish Civil War.)
(1938	Czechoslovakia handed over to Germany at Munich.)
1939	August: Soviet–German alliance signed.
	September: Second World War began. USSR occupied Eastern Poland, Estonia, Latvia, Lithuania.
1939–40	Soviet–Finnish War. USSR expelled from League of Nations.
1941	Germany invaded USSR.
1945	End of World War.
1946–51	Fourth Five-Year Plan.
1953	Stalin died.
1953–7	Most prison camps closed and political prisoners rehabilitated.
1956	Twentieth Party Congress: Khrushchev attacks Stalin.
1964	Khrushchev succeeded by Brezhnev and Kosygin and others.
1968	Soviet invasion of Czechoslovakia.

Index